W9-COS-571

ECONOMIC SYSTEMS IN ACTION

The United States, the Soviet Union, and France

4.50
X

ECONOMIC SYSTEMS IN *ACTION*

THIRD EDITION

The United States
The Soviet Union
and France

Alfred R. Oxenfeldt
Columbia University

Vsevolod Holubnychy
Hunter College of the City University of New York

HOLT, RINEHART AND WINSTON, INC.

New York   Chicago   San Francisco   Toronto   London

LIBRARY
FLORIDA STATE UNIVERSITY
TALLAHASSEE, FLORIDA

Soc
HC
54
O9
1965

April, 1966

Copyright © 1965 by Holt, Rinehart and Winston, Inc.
Copyright 1952, © 1957 by Alfred R. Oxenfeldt

All rights reserved

Library of Congress Catalogue Card Number: 65–14872

26799–0315

Printed in the United States of America

PREFACE

Although the third edition of *Economic Systems in Action* is very different from its predecessors, its objective is the same—to make thoroughly understandable to intelligent laymen three very different approaches to a nation's economic problems. The book is definitely not intended for specialists, but should be able to pass their scrutiny on grounds of accuracy, objectivity, and timeliness. Each economy is discussed in sufficient depth to convey general understanding of both the rationale and the weaknesses of three quite different systems. To achieve brevity, some topics were omitted or only sketched, but the core mechanisms of each economy were scrutinized very closely. This book emphatically is not a "once-over lightly."

Many factors explain the great changes made in this edition, which is marked by the participation of Vsevolod Holubnychy, a long-time specialist in Soviet-type economies and a multilinguist. The authors often started from quite different positions, argued out major disagreements (sometimes interminably), and—by further research and deliberation—reached a mutually acceptable position. Although this extended greatly the time required to complete the book, the resulting manuscript is all the stronger for it.

The biggest changes made in the book are obvious. It has gained an unseemly girth. Also, several sections of the previous edition are missing. Specifically, the sections on the United Kingdom, China, and the east European economies have disappeared altogether—and it was painful to let them go. They had to be given up and many pages added, moreover, to make room for a substantial deepening in the treatment of the United States and USSR and, mainly, for the large section on French planning.

The chief similarity between this and the previous editions is the basic framework. Much of the discussion of each economy revolves around the same five questions that provided the structure for the first two editions. Other features of the earlier editions that have been retained include an attempt to see each economy whole—taking account of the nation's values, traditions, political system, history, and the like; objectivity, especially when it hurt; and emphasis on actual method and performance rather than theory and rationalization.

This edition has been strengthened markedly—and the confidence of the authors in its basic validity has been greatly enhanced—by conversations that the authors held with high-level Soviet and French officials. Professor Oxenfeldt met with some planners and academicians in Moscow during September 1964 and others in the United States during December 1964. In addition, he had the benefit of conversations with experts on French planning in France—including one high-level member of the Commissariat du Plan. Vsevolod Holubnychy had several long conferences with Soviet planners and factory managers who were members of a Soviet delegation to the United States in December 1964.

The authors received help from many people in preparing this edition. We are particularly indebted to Professor Leo Kaplan, who gave the entire manuscript a searching reading and made many helpful suggestions, and to Dr. Ivan S. Koropeckyj who read the Soviet section. We are also grateful for the help we received on the French section to Messrs. A. Nowicki, R. Demonts, J. Dessau and F. Perroux of the Institut de Science Économique Appliquée; L. Charvet and F. Légéndre, both of the Conseil Économique et Social; B. Cazes and P. Bernard, both of the Commissariat du Plan; J. C. Antoine of the CETEC, Paris, and Dr. Hackett, who is himself a coauthor of an excellent American study of French planning.

Among those whom we talked to about the USSR were Victor M. Lisitsyn, deputy chairman of the Gosplan of the RSFSR, Ivan S. Malyshev, first deputy chief of the Central Statistical Administration of the USSR, Dr. V. M. Shamberg and Dr. S. Menshikov of the Institute of World Economics of the USSR Academy of Sciences, Professor P. Mstislavskiy of Moscow University, and others. These men provided little new information, but helped us to put together what we already knew in a more accurate manner. Also, they were good enough to disabuse us of some false impressions we held. It need hardly be recorded that they disagree with much said here.

Those to whom we spoke and the sources we consulted presented highly dissimilar viewpoints and would not agree with us on many points. Nevertheless, we did go to great lengths to obtain critical reactions to the manuscript from persons in the USSR and in France. The book is all the more accurate for these laborious efforts. Although we cannot guarantee that everything said here is accurate and properly interpreted and the most current information available, we can state that we tried hard to make it so. But, only by such efforts can one keep the errors and misinterpretations to modest proportions when dealing with the kinds of subjects treated here. The reader must not assume that this little book offers him the golden truth about some of the most controversial and complex problems of our times. Unfortunately, we know of no place he might go to find it—no matter how much he would be willing to read and how deeply to ponder.

Chief responsibility for the section on the United States was Professor Oxenfeldt's; Vsevolod Holubnychy was responsible for the chapter on the USSR. The section on France was a more evenly divided effort. As suggested, however, each of us wrote sections in every chapter and worried over every sentence in the entire book.

A. O.
V. H.

February 1965

CONTENTS

CHAPTER 1

THE STUDY OF ALTERNATIVE ECONOMIC SYSTEMS

Some in the United States regard the study of foreign economic systems as either superfluous or dangerous—superfluous, because the United States has nothing to learn from other nations; dangerous, because others, if persuaded that another economic system is better, might become disloyal. The first conclusion requires a comparative study to establish its defense; the second confuses patriotism with unquestioning loyalty to particular economic institutions—a common, but mistaken, notion. A socialist in the United States can be as patriotic and as dedicated to public service as a person who believes in capitalism.

To propose that the United States retain its economic system without considering alternatives is peculiarly out of step with most other American views. As a people, Americans have traditionally opposed the static. They pride themselves on the number and rapidity of changes in methods of production and in the kinds of goods produced. They call these changes improvements and see them as signs of progress—and indeed, most of them are. One might suppose that they would also be eager to try new economic arrangements if these appeared superior to existing ones.

EXISTING ECONOMIES VERSUS THEORETICAL SYSTEMS

For the purpose of this study we could analyze and compare economic systems that have been proposed by various writers. These proposed systems generally single out the major principles around which an economy might be organized, but they admittedly do not describe a "total" economy. We can speak of such proposals as "theoretical" or "pure" systems.

1

Everyone will admit that "pure" capitalism, "pure" socialism, and "pure" communism do not now exist anywhere. Most economists will agree that they never have existed and that they never will. There is considerable disagreement about how closely our economy resembles "pure" capitalism and how closely the Soviet economy resembles "pure" socialism. Analyses of abstract economic systems have real value, but conclusions about the nature and merits of existing systems based upon such analyses must be used with caution. If one wishes to compare "pure" capitalism with alternative economic systems, he is obliged to compare it with "pure" socialism, and the conclusions would scarcely be applicable to actual economies. *That one type of economy might be better "theoretically" than another does not necessarily imply that functioning examples of that type are "superior."*

It is no accident that real economies do not exactly follow theoretical patterns. Theories do not always take into account such factors as the need for those in power to make concessions for political expediency; the limitation of human intelligence, integrity, knowledge, and interest in economic and political circumstances; different goals of individuals, enterprises, and whole economic systems; the influence of technological change and of such unforeseen circumstances as wars, natural catastrophes, and accidents. That an actual economy will depart from the theoretical model is certain, though the degree of that departure cannot be predicted.

When seeking to understand a real economy and the measures required to remedy its particular defects, therefore, one is wise to study the *actual* economy in its full complexity rather than a theoretical abstraction. It is logical to try meritorious theoretical measures; it is also logical to expect that they may fail in practice. Arrangements that have already been tested, however, should present no great shocks or surprises when tried elsewhere, even though they will not everywhere have exactly the same consequences.

PROBLEMS IN STUDYING ALTERNATIVE SYSTEMS

A few cautions should be made explicit before examining the economies of the United States, the Soviet Union, and France. First, the following discussion is fairly general, since an economic system could not be described in total detail without confusing rather than illuminating issues. The generalizations offered are believed to summarize accurately most specific cases, even though exceptions can be found to most of them. On some matters, however, we lack sufficient information to generalize with confidence. Readers should therefore note the basis upon which the generalizations rest and the degree of validity attributed to each by the authors. Some represent little more than the authors' impressions; these can be distinguished from and given far less weight than those based on a large body of reliable evidence.

Second, the study of alternative economic systems is highly controversial. Few impartial and competent analyses exist, and the average layman has had access to none of them. The majority of the sources available to the general public advocate a particular point of view.

Most readers will find statements here that differ from anything they have read before, points of view that have been rejected out of hand and even ridiculed in their usual media of information. This divergence of opinion, however, does not prove absolute objectivity on the part of the authors. Everyone feels the pressures of the times. The writers have tried to make a careful and honest study and, if challenged, would sincerely and vehemently proclaim their complete impartiality. Nevertheless, let the reader examine critically whatever he reads. This study, dealing with matters unusually susceptible to emotional coloration, cannot be completely immune from environmental influences.

Third, the greatest difficulty faced in a study of alternative economic systems is to be found in the reader's own prejudice. Many people are afraid to make a dispassionate study of alternative economic systems, for if they depart far from prevailing opinion, they may endanger their sense of ease and identity with their neighbors, and sometimes even their very livelihood. It takes great effort to study foreign systems with impartiality; few persons will succeed fully in doing so. The effort is nevertheless worthwhile, for the greater the impartiality achieved, the closer will one approach full understanding.

Fourth, economic systems are dynamic; they are constantly being modified. Conclusions valid only a short time ago may be invalidated by some more recent legal enactment, technological change, or an improved understanding of how the economy works.

BASES OF COMPARISON

This book compares a capitalist, a socialist or Communist, and an "intermediate" economy. What meaning can be attached to such a comparison? Are not these economic systems so different in basic goals that comparisons are pointless? It is our contention that they are not, for if only by contrast these systems illuminate each other.

All contemporary economic systems have more or less the same economic objectives, although their political, social, national goals may differ. They seek to attain their goals with as little cost and as quickly as possible. All economic systems perform similar activities in pursuing this end. They produce, store, and distribute goods and services; they employ individuals, and make use of natural resources. If we consider them as economic, rather than ethical, systems, specific capitalistic, communistic, and socialistic nations can be compared on the basis of how closely they attain their general purpose and how efficiently they perform the five specific major functions discussed below.

1. Every economy seeks, first of all, to provide at least the minimum of goods and services that its population desires. A nation wants and requires many things. In all "developed" countries prosperous persons have unfilled desires for material possessions, and even the rich want more. Similarly, even the richest nations in the world suffer from a shortage of goods and services ordinarily provided collectively by government, including hospitals, schools, art museums, parks, and roads; they also provide less than they would like for foreign aid, defense capabilities, scientific research, and space exploration. Barring an unforeseen change in personal attitudes—of the kind that might be brought about only by the general adoption of some new religion or new moral code—we can anticipate a continuation of the present situation in which appetites for different goods and services are mostly insatiable.[1] The affluent society remains far from realization for a vast majority in the United States and for an even larger proportion of the population in other nations.

When one cannot have everything he wishes, he must select among alternatives. To obtain a car, he may be forced to forego other things that could have been acquired in its place. Hence, one major function of an economic system is to select the most needed things to produce from among all the things that might be made. We shall therefore examine various economies to see if the particular goods produced provide a high level of satisfaction for the population and the nation.

2. Every nation will want to use the most efficient methods of production and distribution. An economy might produce the most desirable combination of products in the best proportions and still get low total output because its production methods yield far less than could be produced by using equal amounts of labor, capital, and raw materials. Efficient use of resources, moreover, requires that involuntary idleness and "underemployment" of productive factors be minimized. Comparisons of economies must therefore consider production methods as contributing to full employment.

3. Every economy should direct individuals and all other factors of production into the occupations in which they are most productive. In addition

---

[1] J. K. Galbraith in *The Affluent Society* (Boston: Houghton Mifflin Company, 1959) contests this view. In his opinion, appetites for goods and services are rapidly being sated in our affluent society and new goals are being sought.

to the production of the "right" goods and services by the most efficient methods, a nation's level of living depends upon whether people work at the jobs they can perform most efficiently. Output will be low if square pegs are put in round holes, no matter what methods of production are used. Consequently, to evaluate an economy requires a consideration of the manner in which resources are allocated among the segments of that system.

4. If income is distributed in a manner that affords a few people enormous luxury and all others only squalor, the economic system can hardly be adjudged efficient. An efficient economic system distributes income on some ethical or rational basis, shares output in a manner that affords a high level of satisfaction for the population as a whole, and encourages individuals to make the maximum productive contribution consistent with health and a happy social and psychological adjustment. Since these objectives of income distribution appear to be potentially inconsistent with one another, the only thing we can do is compare this aspect of different economic systems and let the reader judge for himself.

5. Every economy should create new methods of production, new techniques, and new products. An economy that efficiently exploits existing technological knowledge will still be left far behind unless it also develops new products that satisfy unfilled wants or finds increasingly efficient methods of production. In short, an efficient economy moves forward toward higher living standards through "progress" in technological innovations and "growth" in output of new products. Consequently, one criterion by which an economy should be appraised is its rate of development.

In judging an economic system, one must not only study efficiency but also evaluate its effects in the political, social, moral, and psychological spheres. *Economic arrangements must meet more than the test of economic efficiency.* An economic system that produces a large output of material things but fails to satisfy many basic desires of its population, or increases personal insecurity, suppresses natural impulses, restricts movement or expression, violates personal, moral, and ethical codes, or perpetuates and increases inequalities in opportunities and wealth cannot be considered good—unless all alternative arrangements are even worse.

The pivotal questions around which the analysis of the American, Soviet, and French economic systems is organized in this book are therefore these: How, and by whom, are the decisions made to produce and sell certain goods and services at a certain time and place? Are the "right" goods produced and delivered, rather than "wrong" ones, and why? Who decides how resources should be allocated, on what grounds, and by which methods? How are people's incomes created and distributed, and why that way and not another? How are progress and growth achieved, new goods and new methods of production invented? The answers to these questions basically define an economic system, while different answers define the differences among these systems.

The following chapters also appraise three economic systems—those of the United States, the Soviet Union, and France—from the standpoint of economic efficiency and of their noneconomic consequences. For the most part, each economy will be examined separately so that the essential unity of each will be clear. The reader must always keep in mind that every economy is an organic whole in which the consequences of every arrangement depend largely upon the character of all other arrangements. Every economic system is part of a particular culture and arises out of peculiar historical circumstances. It is not simply the creation of brilliant social engineers, who can order people to be industrious, objective, and intelligent, and to behave rationally, ignore tradition and national honor. In every country, the heavy hand of the past shapes the economy very strongly even after long and bitter revolutions and violent changes in government structure, policy, and personnel.

CHAPTER 2

CAPITALISM IN THE UNITED STATES

Most readers of the following pages will be far better informed about the American economy than about any other. Our description will therefore be brief and the system's merits and accomplishments will be stated without elaboration. The main purpose of the discussion will be to set forth standards by which an economy's performance may be judged and to measure the American economy against these standards.

Since the American economy is the first to be discussed, it is impractical to compare it directly with the Soviet and French economies. Later chapters, however, will compare the three systems. In judging the American economic system in this chapter, then, we must use *absolute standards,* that is, we must compare it with the best performance we can reasonably expect. Even though other economic systems may be inferior to it, by using this standard we can discover ways in which its performance might be improved. *Superiority over other systems does not excuse remediable defects.* Nevertheless, it should be stressed that the American economy is charged here with defects that also exist in the Soviet Union and France, sometimes to an even greater degree.

A GENERAL VIEW OF THE AMERICAN ECONOMY

The economic system of the United States was not originally fashioned after any particular model. It just "grew," undergoing change as individuals altered their methods of doing business and as local and federal legislatures enacted or abolished regulations. Despite the lack of planning in the American economy, it has an underlying rationale that leads many people to believe that it operates efficiently. That rationale, however, must not be mistaken for reality; at many points the resemblance is not at all close.

In one important sense, the American economy does represent a system. The pronouncements of its public officials and the views expressed by the nation's economists and most enlightened citizens make clear that the economy possesses—or should possess—four chief elements: (1) vigorous competition, (2) free enterprise, (3) profit motive, and (4) a freely operating price system. Let us look at what these terms mean and consider how they fit together to form a system.

Chief Elements of the American Economy

Vigorous Competition

Competition means striving to gain an advantage over rivals; in business, it means making strenuous efforts to gain customers at the expense of others, to grow while they decline. Competition has two sides—to gain for oneself and to injure others. The average American businessman is probably more extreme in both aspects than his counterparts in other industrialized nations. Success, the demonstration of superiority, and the pleasure of winning probably means more to him than to businessmen in, say, Western Europe—and he devotes himself more wholeheartedly to business success than they do. He also shows less reluctance to defeat or injure his rivals.

The competitiveness of a nation or even of individuals is difficult to measure; doubtless it does vary from industry to industry and from individual to individual and has probably changed in past decades. Although the foregoing generalizations about the average American businessman would therefore be difficult to prove, few who have considered the matter will disagree with what has been said here.

Competition takes place both within and among businesses. From senior executives on down, individuals strive both to defeat competitive firms and to win promotions for themselves within the firm over their colleagues. Clearly, the achievement of either one of these goals could jeopardize the other. An executive, for example, might need to sacrifice personal glory to gain market success for the firm; similarly, he may be compelled to damage his fellow employee, or even the firm to prove his own superiority. On the other hand, the internal rivalry among members of a firm, if contained, can represent a powerful force working for efficiency.

Vigorous competition, however, does not always spring into being naturally. The notions that competition is natural and that "everyone wants to get ahead of the next fellow" are only partially true. Moreover, they are far more true of certain countries than of others. The culture of the United States places extreme stress on the achievement of economic success—without great regard to the means employed; and the rewards of success are great, relative to conditions in other countries. In almost no other nation is emphasis on success so great, though as we have indicated, one cannot really establish these conclusions on a statistical basis. Yet even within the United States, one finds marked variations in stress on economic success among regions and among certain religious and ethnic groups.

To achieve and preserve vigorous competition and free enterprise government measures are necessary. Thus, we have an apparent paradox. Government measures are required to establish and police arrangements to create competition so that we will need no *direct* government control over individual businesses. Accordingly, the United States has a body of legislation—the antitrust laws—designed to encourage competition and to combat monopoly.

Free enterprise

Free enterprise describes an economy offering the individual the right to engage in any business activity, with no fields reserved either to government or to selected individuals. If anyone who wishes can enter a business, free enterprise obtains in that line of business. If one requires a license to enter it and licenses are difficult to obtain, free enterprise does not. Similarly, if the activity requires a huge investment of capital to establish a firm that has any chance to succeed, enterprise must be considered limited.

The Profit Motive

The profit motive describes the key goal of business (not necessarily the only one) as the making of money gains on private investment. It matters a great deal in understanding the operation of an economic system whether its members seek immediate or long-run monetary gain. In the cluster of ideas surrounding the U.S. economy, it is not clear whether individuals "should" pursue long- or short-run gain. It is helpful to identify the types of goals, other than profit, that firms might pursue. Among the more important are: personal advancement for individuals, public service, security, compliance with the law, higher salary, philanthropy, and patriotism.[1]

The Price System

The notion of a price system is the most complex of the four chief elements that typify the U.S. economy; it is also the most fundamental. The basic rationale for an economy based upon competition, free enterprise, and the profit motive is found in the logic of a price system.

---

[1] A. A. Berle, Jr. in *The 20th Century Capitalist Revolution* (New York: Harcourt, Brace & World, Inc., 1954) holds that the very great profit-making power of the large U.S. corporation has compelled it to adopt many of these more altruistic goals in order to justify and preserve its existence in the face of public fears and suspicions over the unbridled use of such vast economic power.

The Rationale Underlying the American Economy

A free enterprise profit system characterized by vigorous rivalry allows individuals and businesses almost complete freedom to produce what they want, to employ any productive methods they desire, and to price their output and services as they wish. This condition is expected to result in an efficient economic system primarily because it generates a potent force—an "invisible hand"—called competition. In brief, the system is expected to achieve the results desired because of the strenuous efforts that most competing individuals make in order to gain something they desire.

But a price and profit system does more than build on the principle of competition, allow freedom to individuals, and decentralize decisions. It incorporates a delicately calibrated system of penalties and rewards; this system records the preferences of individuals and creates pressures to honor those preferences. Specifically, a price system allows individuals to express fine shades of preference for alternative products; they do so by the price they will pay to acquire them. The greater their desire for the product, the more they are willing to pay. Prices can vary by tiny amounts and thus express precisely varying degrees of desire. Similarly, individuals seeking employment (and owners of property or liquid funds) indicate how much they dislike alternative employments and unemployment by the amount of compensation they demand. When heavy price penalties are attached to the purchase of particular products, consumers are given a strong incentive to seek out alternatives that offer them greater satisfaction per dollar. Businessmen are likewise under pressure to find productive arrangements that keep their penalties (money costs) to a minimum. Ideally, a price system fixes penalties on the use of products and factors of production that will create just the desired relative pressure on potential users to economize in their use.

In a price system resources flow quickly to occupations where profits are highest. In this way the output of products in relatively short supply is expanded promptly and high profits prevail only briefly. Thus, in a price system, a high rate of profits performs the vital function of attracting resources to places where output is deficient.

In sum, it is argued that a system based upon individual freedom in productive activities will yield the following results: Sellers cannot charge much more than the minimum costs at which a product or service can be provided. Goods will be produced with maximum efficiency, and the factors of production will be employed where they are most productive and incur minimum sacrifice. Because remuneration will be based on productive contribution, everyone will exert himself to the utmost. Buyers will use their incomes in ways that give them the greatest satisfaction. Producers and consumers will use plentiful products and raw materials rather than equally useful products that are scarce, for the former will be less costly.

The foregoing explains why the American economic system—a price and profit system—might be expected to achieve excellent results in performing the functions common to all economic systems. The discussion represents an enlightened general rationale for the American economy; it is not, however, offered as an accurate description. So brief a description would be incomplete and misleading, even if one were describing the most simple and consistent economy. The U.S. economy is neither simple nor consistent. Individual sectors, regions, and industries differ very substantially; each sector changes—often markedly—with the passage of time. All who have studied it agree that the U.S. economy is "mixed" and that it has always been so. Government ownership and control—the opposite of free enterprise—have been significant features from the earliest days of the republic.

To understand why the U.S. economy is considered "mixed," it is useful to divide all economic activities into two segments: the first conforms more or less closely to a free enterprise economy, as its rationale was described; all other activities we can call non-free enterprise. Both segments exist and are substantial, but even those parts of the economy that are closest to pure free enterprise contain elements of non-free enterprise. The food industry, for instance, exemplifies free enterprise, on the whole; it is highly competitive in the main and is governed by the profit motive and price relationships. However, government controls influence the supplies and prices of many important foods through acreage controls, government purchases, and sales out of surplus, and the school lunch program; also, most states have laws that affect, directly or indirectly, the price of milk. The pure food and drug laws of the federal and state governments also exert a significant influence over the industry. Conversely, within the non-free enterprise sector one finds important elements of free enterprise. Government makes many of its purchases on the basis of competitive bidding; the raw materials and supplies used by government operated activities (military installations, TVA, the Post Office) are purchased on competitive markets. The government does not own and control any activity "from top to bottom."

Although few will deny that the U.S. economy is "mixed," many will argue about its true essence. Conservatives consider it a "welfare state"—if not actually socialistic. Left-wing liberals describe it as one of the most right-wing capitalist economies in the world. Obviously, both cannot be correct, though both groups are probably quite sincere.

Subsystems of the American Economy

Presenting a single picture of U.S. economic institutions is like trying to describe a bowl of fruit in one word. Consequently, we shall examine closely the main ingredients—we shall call them subsystems of the economy of the United States. Later, we shall consider how well they fit together. One central institution that goes far to determine the nature of the U.S. economy is the very large industrial and mercantile corporation, employing tens of thousands of persons, composed of dozens and even hundreds of separate divisions or stores that are scattered over the nation and possibly, over the world. In this subsystem a very substantial proportion (approximately 21 percent) of gainfully employed Americans earn their livelihood. At the opposite extreme is the individualistic subsystem of the U.S. economy, which include small family businesses with few or no employees. Although still numerically significant—and representing the overwhelming majority of all businesses in the nation—these firms are concentrated in retailing and service and constitute a steadily shrinking proportion of the economy. A third subsystem is the "professional" who operates a small economic enterprise based upon special skills rather than commerce; included in this category are doctors, lawyers, dentists, engineers, business consultants of various kinds, and the like.

Other subsystems are: Large-scale agriculture, which accounts for most agricultural output and employment. Family farms, another declining ingredient of the U.S. economy. The public utility sector, which includes mainly telephone, electric, gas, and transportation companies; it is subject to government control over rates (prices) and quality of service. The federal government sector, which includes the military establishment, the Tennessee Valley Authority, the postal system, and such things as the space program and technical and medical research. The state and local government sector.

The foregoing classification is employed mainly to highlight the fact that the economy is truly mixed and is neither "free enterprise" nor non-free enterprise—even though it is the most free economy in the world today. Three subsystems have been singled out for special treatment because they illuminate the enormous contrasts within the American economy. The reader must remember that the subsystems discussed below do not by any means include the entire economy: notably lacking are those businesses and farms that are "in the middle." These are neither giants nor small enterprises, but medium-sized. They do, however, account for a large part of business activity, though far less than the giants.

The Large Corporation

We shall consider the giant corporation only as an economic institution whose purpose is to assemble, mobilize, motivate, and direct economic resources so that they are put to effective use. We want to know *how* it works and *how well* it carries out these functions. This is no small assignment, for the giant corporation is highly complex; moreover, the information available on the subject is both slight and suspect. It is even difficult to identify the crucial questions that should be asked about the giant corporation. But difficult or not, we must cope with the subject, for it is essential to an understanding of the U.S. economy.

Corporations are organizations (they are "legal persons" in the eyes of the law) that are sanctioned by the government, which charters their existence and defines their legal powers and obligations. They pool the investments of many persons, thus permitting much larger businesses than any one individual could create, and limit the liability of those who invest in them. The corporation may be regarded as one of the major economic inventions of man. The large corporation is the foremost and a dominant institution in the U.S. economy. Measured by employment, funds invested, sales, value added, and the like, the large corporation is the largest single subsystem in the U.S. economy. (Some members of the other subsystems—and in particular public utility companies—are also large corporations.)

The large corporation is attacked on many scores, primarily that it is a monopoly. This criticism is refined further to charge it with demanding excessive prices, "administering" prices, and maintaining fixed prices, in other words, of failing to allow prices to reflect promptly changes in cost and demand conditions. Also, it is charged with collusion to divide markets or to obtain excessive prices. It is impossible and unnecessary here to evaluate these criticisms, some of which doubtless are valid for some large corporations. However, many people confuse business size with monopoly. Although there is some connection, often it is not close. To take an extreme example, one of the nation's largest firms is the A&P—the largest national chain of food stores and supermarkets. It, however, faces extremely intense competition, as almost everyone in the United States knows from personal experience, and its returns on sales and capital are modest. Most giant corporations vie against other giants. Although in many cases that rivalry is well mannered and shows a desire to avoid intense competition, in other cases it is intense. Similarly, generalizations about the pricing policies of large corporations apply only to some, certainly not to an overwhelming majority of large firms.

The large corporation has also been charged with violating the rights of the stockholders by placing control and decision-making power in the hands of management and depriving stockholders (the owners) of their rightful power. (The evidence is clear, however, that stockholders as a group have neither the interest nor the skill to exercise control over so complex a phenomenon as the large corporation.) Second, it is charged that top corporate executives serve the interests of management (survival of the firm, avoidance of risk, steady and moderate rate of profit) rather than strive to make a maximum profit. Of course, no one knows what the consensus of all stockholders' desires would be. Moreover, large firms as a whole have prospered and yielded attractive returns to stockholders.

Some readers may be surprised by the statement that the large corporation is such a mystery and so controversial. They have a clear picture of the nature of the large corporation. Moreover, most strongly favor this symbol of free enterprise and capitalism. Those who criticize it, like those who criticize advertising, are attacking the chief symbols of capitalism. In a sense this is quite a paradox; in many ways the large corporation resembles a socialist state far more than the type of firm ordinarily believed to compose a free enterprise economy.

One fact on which all students of the large corporation agree is that it is special and different. It is not simply larger than other firms; it is *qualitatively* different. It is different because it tries to do a most difficult job—to coordinate and manage a huge number of individuals' activities and an enormous fund of property. No handful of individuals can hope to keep informed about what is going on and to determine what should be done by simple diligence and personal observations. They must use some system for managing through others. As we have suggested, their problem is similar to that of a socialist state, and interestingly, large U.S. firms employ essentially the same methods as socialist states. The large firm does *not* rely mainly upon the price and profit system *within its borders* but, like the socialist state, depends upon the determinations of individuals—upon what one might call "arbitrary decisions." In other words, top managements of businesses simply make decisions on the basis of the information available to them. Their ability to crystallize alternative courses of action, their logical talents, their diligence, and their objectives determine the course they select. Their decisions do *not* represent simple and clear choices dictated by a comparison of cost and revenues. They possess great latitude to exercise discretion and the problems they face do not have simple, demonstrably correct solutions.

In an attempt to broaden our description to include all aspects of the large corporation that are germane to an understanding of its place in the American economy, the following section discusses some of the controversial issues surrounding the industrial giant.

One charge against the large corporation is that it is very inefficient—not compared with small firms particularly but with what it could be. (Many laymen probably assume that large corporations are models of "scientific management" and of efficiency.) The strongest criticisms of the efficiency of large corporations come from members of those firms and are made off the record. It is almost universal that those who associate with the senior and subsenior executives of large firms invariably hear sharp attacks on the competence of those who run the firm. Criticisms are usually phrased in terms of top management's lack of objectivity in making decisions, undue emphasis upon its own "pet" ideas, lack of economic intelligence, lack of information, inaccessibility, playing favorites, chaotic organization, politicking, and so forth.

The "politics" of the large corporation plays an important part in determining the behavior of those who make decisions; it is charged with causing both waste and personal insecurity. Top executives must keep their political fences in order with members of the board of directors—who may pay little attention to the grubby facts of running a large firm, but will intervene when it suits their fancy. Senior executives sometimes find that a project on which they were working is suddenly abandoned or arbitrarily sent off on a new course, because of a call from the chairman or a member of the board of directors who has some personal conviction or vested interest that is antagonistic to the project.

Large corporations are basically dictatorial organizations. (Many of the dictatorships are quite benign, but far from all. The power of top executives over their subordinates is extreme. It is, interestingly, far less over workers who are members of labor unions.) The executives can, and it is widely charged that they often do, make promotions, select suppliers including their advertising agencies, marketing research companies, banks and law firms, on the basis of personal friendships. As occasionally comes to light, a few even receive direct compensation as a result of favoring certain suppliers over others. One of the consequences of this situation is that individual executives have little personal security: often they are robbed of their self-respect by a domineering executive who criticizes and insults under conditions where a retort would surely cost a subordinate his job. The upper levels of management of many large corporations may be likened to the court of a strong monarch. There are the king's favorites; those who actively seek to become favorites of the king; the jester; and those who are seeking to depose the king.

Finally, large corporations are also attacked by some because of the great social power they possess—and could exercise for good or evil. For example, in employment policies some firms have indulged the preferences of their owners and top management to exclude or employ only token numbers of persons belonging to minority groups. Many of them use their "house organs" (corporation newspapers, distributed without charge) to disseminate propaganda favorable to top management's political philosophy. Also, by various means large corporations frequently lend assistance to particular political parties. As large employers and buyers, they are able to do favors on a grand scale and exert a substantial effect wherever they choose to lend their support, especially in local elections.

The foregoing discussion of the large corporation directs attention to some issues that are often ignored and are not easily studied. Hopefully, it is an antidote for the widespread assumption that the large corporation is an efficient, scientifically run example of capitalism at its best. A few giant firms may fit the description well, but others emphatically do not. A large corporation is, basically, a huge aggregate of economic resources that to gain some of the technological and market advantages of bigness, must devise ways of coordinating the efforts of thousands of persons who have no ownership stake in the organization.

To do so, it employs similar techniques of planning and coercion employed by many socialist states. Indeed, large firms have learned some things from the socialist nations—as well as their own capitalist government—about planning; similarly, socialist planners learn from the techniques employed by large firms.

On the other hand, the large firm clearly has contributed mightily to increased efficiency in production and has helped to speed technological improvement, both in improved methods of production and product innovations. In many industries, only the giant corporation (as here defined) can achieve the production economies required to exploit existing technology. Small firms have no chance to succeed in these industries. This fact suggests that the giants are relatively more efficient than the small firms and pass on at least part of their benefits to their customers.

The Individualist Sector

The small businessman has become a steadily less important member of the U.S. economy, though he remains a significant factor both economically and socially. Since most readers have had many personal experiences with small firms, only a few points will be mentioned about them here:

1. Small firms are concentrated in particular industries—service and retailing.
2. Small firms are being forced out of many industries, but are finding opportunities in others. In particular, the service trades—especially the servicing of durable goods and the provision of professional services—are growing.
3. The opportunity to start a small firm is a valued freedom by many people in this country, though a declining proportion avail themselves of the opportunity.
4. Small firms enjoy little security; they usually depend upon the health and diligence of one person and reflect changes in that person's condition. Also, they exist under the constant threat that some large firm, by virtue of superior resources, will win over the field.
5. Small firms do, in some respects, enjoy advantages over large; some owners of smaller businesses speak disparagingly of the giants in their industry. The small firm's flexibility, ability to know what is happening in all phases of the business, and ability to maneuver rapidly, are valuable advantages in many lines of business.

The Government Sector

Several layers of government are involved in the U.S. economic activity. Their activities all are significant parts of the economy. School districts and counties are important spenders for education and road building. The states are also involved in these activities; in addition, they are concerned with social security, police and fire protection, and conservation of natural resources. By far the largest single factor in the economy is the federal government, and this section is concerned primarily with its nature and activities. Measured by direct employment provided, the relative importance of local, state, and federal government is indicated in the following table, which shows that the latter provided about 2.5 million persons with direct employment. State workers number about 1.7 million and the approximately 90,000 local government units employ about 5.2 million persons. (Of these local employees almost 70 percent work in the field of education.) Combined civilian employment by all levels of government now account for approximately 13.5 percent of total employment—up from 9.5 percent in 1947 and 11.0 percent in 1955.

One obtains a very different picture of the relative importance of the various levels of government if one employs expenditures rather than employment as his yardstick. As Table 1 indicates, the various levels of government spent over $120 billion in 1962, about 20 percent of GNP in that year. It also shows that the federal government spends more than state and

Table 1. Employment in and Purchases by Various Levels of Government, 1962

	Employment	Purchases of goods and services
Federal government	2.5 million	$66.0 billion
State government	1.7	57.4
Local government	5.2	

SOURCE: U.S. Department of Labor.

local governments combined. The disparity of spending and employment results from the fact that the federal government primarily *purchases products* (military items), whereas the other governments actually *provide services* directly—for example, road maintenance and education. Accordingly, we shall consider the federal government first as a customer and then as an owner and operator of some vital economic activities.

The federal government buys many things; in many cases, it is the only customer of its suppliers. Consequently, it can and actually does determine the fundamental nature of such industries. Among the items purchased are many types of military equipment, including those that are secret. Also, items needed for the national space program have no direct civilian use and are produced exclusively for the federal government. Beyond these activities, the federal government is by far the largest sponsor of technical research. More than two of every three dollars spent for technical research comes from the federal government and goes to private firms and universities; only a small amount of such research is conducted in government-owned laboratories. In addition, the federal government is the major source of support for medical research.

How does government exert its effect as a customer? In what ways does that sector that sells mainly to the federal government differ from other sectors of the economy? In general, one must expect the timing, size, and incidence of government orders and spending to exert a direct and immediate effect on its suppliers. Also, purchases by the government are not dictated by the usual considerations that operate in private commercial markets. The government must consider the location of output on strategic grounds (ordinarily seeking dispersion, despite the higher costs it entails). In addition, the government rightly places great emphasis upon the superiority of the weapons offered by one firm over those offered by others. It may as a consequence shift its purchases of some military item entirely away from one supplier to another. The effect is to create great insecurity and instability of employment among persons who are employed in industries serving the federal government almost exclusively. Finally, the great importance of government orders entails the danger that political influence will be brought to bear upon the selection among suppliers. In particular, one finds congressmen pressing hard to get orders for their constituents—and not without effect.

The government sector differs from the private sector on other grounds. Prices are determined on most government purchases in ways that are markedly different from those found in ordinary commerce. In small part, the government buys on the basis of closed competitive bids, and this procedure ordinarily gives it low prices. One finds considerable allegation, often substantiated, of collusive bidding in sales to government, however.

On major military items prices are "negotiated." This is an elaborate and complex procedure, as it must be because the items involved generally are quite new and neither the buyer nor the seller knows what the costs will be—or even the capabilities of the item when it is actually produced. The federal government devotes great effort to the task of learning the costs incurred by suppliers and keeping prices in line with them. It is not always successful, by any means. Sometimes suppliers to the government incur enormous losses whereas their profits are extremely high in other instances. In both cases the process by which prices are determined and the degree of pressure exerted on the producers' costs in industries selling primarily to the federal government vary substantially from those found in private industries.

Beyond its influence as a customer, the government is an actual owner and operator. Among others, it owns and operates the following enterprises: the Post Office, the military establishment, a large number of hospitals under the control of the Veterans Administration, the Tennessee Valley Authority, the Atomic Energy Commission research facilities, uranium plants, land banks and several credit establishments, agricultural surplus commodities, housing projects, canals, and various recreational facilities, such as the many national parks. In these activities the federal government functions as a combination owner and manager subject to the policy-making powers of the board of directors—the Congress.

The chief difference between government-owned and privately owned activities warrants brief examination. In the first place, they differ mainly in objective: government enterprises pursue, at least partly, the goal of serving the public interest, even at the expense of incurring higher costs or suffering "losses." Second, employees are usually limited in their "rights." Specifically, their right to strike is curbed and, in some cases, actually forbidden by law. Third, these activities usually are free from direct competition; private firms understandably do not want to compete with government enterprises that are not under any compulsion to cover their costs.

Economic Determinations in the American Economy

Great illumination can be cast on an economic system by describing the main types of economic determinations, how they are made, and by whom. It is not suggested that each economic determination is neatly identified, classified, and assigned to specific individuals or groups—far from it. On the other hand, one way or another, vital matters about the economy are determined—perhaps by the collective actions and decisions of persons who are not conscious that they are doing so. To understand an economy one should understand the importance of each of these various determinations and how they are made.

The following classification of major economic determinations is not the only one possible; however, it is fairly straightforward and familiar. It divides these decisions on the basis of "level" and breadth of scope. Some economic determinations are *economy-wide*. They include such matters as: the proportion of total resources to devote to military uses; to public uses—like roads, parks, health uses, police protection, and the like; to private consumption—goods for individuals and families to buy and consume; and to private investment—plant and equipment for the production of other goods. How are these proportions determined in the United States? (Later, we shall explore how they are made in the USSR and in France.)

Other economic determinations are of somewhat smaller, though still broad, scope and might be considered *industry-wide*. These determinations are of such questions as: Should steel output be expanded? If so, by how much? What should be the rate of growth of each individual industry?

Regional economic determinations are about as broad as those that are industry wide, and concern the location of various economic activities. Included under this head are such matters as: Where should new facilities be established? In what areas should production be curtailed? At what rate should the various areas of the nation be expanded?

Some economic determinations deal only with *individual firms*. They concern such matters as: How much should this firm produce? In which of its plants should it produce a particular item? By what methods of production should it make its output? What kinds of models and how many versions of its products should it offer? Through what kinds of resellers should it distribute its output? How should it recruit, train, motivate and pay its employees?

Still other economic determinations are *individual*. They deal with such items as: How should this individual be trained? Where should each individual work? What items should each individual purchase and where?

All such determinations are somehow made in the United States. But how and by whom? The efficiency of the economy depends heavily upon the validity with which they are made. An economy that makes products in faulty proportions by inefficient methods, employing persons in occupations for which they have little skill or liking, is an inefficient economic system. One should not expect perfection always and on all levels; still, one must not accept whatever happens anywhere as necessarily the best and beyond improvement. And, improvement aside, the understanding of an economy requires analysis of all these different levels of economic decision.

The rationale of a price system, as described earlier, places emphasis upon decisions made by individual consumers, workers, and businessmen— that is, on the lowest level. Each individual, working within a narrow sphere about which he is extremely well informed, is to make decisions that, collectively, determine the behavior of firms, industries, and the economy as a whole. Indeed, many persons in capitalistic economies are opposed to having "some people make decisions for others"—partly on principle and partly because it is believed that they would to a poor job of it. We must therefore raise two basic questions: Who makes the decisions at each level? How well does this kind of decision making work out?

The earlier discussion of the subsystems composing the U.S. economy suggested that the answers were different for the subsystem composed of the giant corporations than, say, for the public utility or individual sectors. Clearly, the answer is very different for the government sector than for most of the others.

Let us consider two specific questions that relate to matters that will be discussed in later chapters. First, who decides what proportion of output will consist of consumers goods and what proportion of producers goods? Second, who determines the level of productive capacity in each industry and the methods of production employed?

The first question is exceedingly complicated in relation to the U.S. economy; we shall not be able to discuss it in detail. However, a few general statements will suggest the level at which this decision is made in the United States and the parties to the decision. In large part, the decision is the outcome of the individual decisions by the nation's chief financial institutions —commercial and savings banks, investment bankers, insurance companies, managers of pension funds, and other large lenders. In addition, the nation's monetary authorities, who are able to influence interest rates and the supply of loanable funds, exert substantial influence. Almost as important are the decisions of business executives and owners about the amount they wish to borrow. Finally, decisions of individuals and private firms about the amount to spend on current consumption and how much to save will affect the supply of funds available for investment in producers goods. Their combined decisions about consumption, of course, are the main factors that determine the amount of resources devoted to the consumer sector. *Thus, no single force and no central authority exerts a dominant voice in the division of output between producers and consumers goods in the United States. The division that comes to pass is the resultant of a very large number of factors that partly offset and partly reinforce one another.*

The second question, who determines the level of productive capacity in each industry, is also complex. In the United States, the individual firm determines the amount of productive facilities it will acquire, without consultation with competitors. Each one is guided by its forecasts of future markets for its wares, and estimates of the share of the total market that it will capture. The total supply of productive facilities in an industry is the outgrowth of the combined decisions of all managements in the industry. Presumably, each firm's management takes into account the supply of facilities already available in the industry and forecasts the behavior of its present and potential rivals. Determinations made under these circumstances are very likely to be mistaken—sometimes, very badly so. Specifically, even if each firm's management could accurately estimate the total market for its products, it could easily err in its decisions about the amount of facilities it would require. *Indeed, as one examines the major industries in the United States, he is likely to conclude that there is a persistent tendency to overexpand facilities. From the standpoint of most economic planners, this method of arriving at decisions about the supply of productive facilities is highly inefficient.* They believe that the decision should be made at a higher level than the individual plant or firm—it should be made for the entire industry. In that way, the major uncertainty about the actions of individual competitors would not introduce great opportunity for error.

Great stress has been placed here upon the locus and level of economic decisions because, as will be explained, this is perhaps the most crucial difference between the U.S., USSR and French economies. The price system, as already sketched, tends to push economic decisions far down the line—to the point of the individual consumer and businessmen. In the

USSR the chief economic decisions are made at or near the very top, by powerful individuals who set down basic economic objectives and prepare detailed plans to carry them out. In France an intermediate position is taken, with far more freedom and influence permitted for individual decisions, but with very active participation, guidance, and some control from the very top.

General Characteristics of the American Economy

We have examined the key features of the American economy and its underlying rationale; in addition, we have looked at the chief subsystems that compose it. These different ways of looking at the same thing each add illumination to the others. We shall take still another and very quick look at the American economy by presenting a summary list of its major characteristics. Numerous exceptions can be found to these general characteristics. In the discussion that follows, the significance of the more important exceptions to these generalizations will become clear.

1. There is private ownership of the means of production and distribution; that is, individuals own most of the nation's factories, machinery, shops, railroads, natural resource deposits, and the like.

2. In their economic activities, individuals strive primarily to obtain maximum money income. People ordinarily use their productive equipment, money savings, and labor skills in ways that give them the highest money return. Private capital is invested specifically to make profit.

3. The U.S. government does what might perhaps be termed tentative planning. It has a special organization (the Council of Economic Advisors to the President) which studies economic developments closely and forecasts levels of business activity. It provides information to government officials and to the business community on what is happening and on what can be expected. In addition, it examines how the various parts of the economy are meshing together to detect trouble-spots. Further, government agencies —especially the Federal Reserve System—can take actions in an effort to avoid such difficulties, and there is always the possibility that special legislation will be enacted to correct or forestall them. However, in the United States no individual business or labor union is compelled to take or forego actions in order to improve economic conditions. Nonetheless, even these meager "planning" measures that we have in the U.S. economy are strongly opposed by a very large majority.

4. Most individuals are compelled to take outside employment in order to provide for even their minimum needs. Only a small proportion of the population finds support by working with self-owned means of production. The majority can earn a livelihood only by taking employment with persons who own means of production.

5. The basic economic decisions about what shall be produced, in what quantities, by what methods, and for whom, are made by buyers and sellers, consumers and producers themselves through a price system. No central group of planners decides what goods shall be produced and specifies techniques of production and the like. These decisions are decentralized in individual firms. However, some firms are huge and their top managements make decisions that have far-reaching influence on output, prices, methods of production, and income distribution.

6. Production and sale of most goods and personal services occur under conditions of rivalry among buyers and sellers each of whom is pursuing his own self-interest.

7. Employed individuals are compensated in accordance with their productivity, their rewards depending primarily upon their ability to produce the kinds of things that other people desire, their own diligence, and the scarcity of the skills they possess.

8. Compared to governments of most other industrialized countries the U.S. government does not intervene to any large extent in business activity; businessmen are relatively free to pursue any course of action they wish.

9. A comparatively very modest proportion of the total U.S. output takes the form of welfare services or socially provided goods and services. These are generally distributed on the basis of need rather than ability to pay.

10. By direct and indirect taxes the various governmental units take a substantial proportion of the national income. Consequently, the economic incentives of the wealthiest individuals and of corporations may be dampened; at least, the economic gains obtainable by most persons who are already earning large incomes are strongly diluted by very heavy income-tax rates.

11. A sizable proportion (about 12 percent) of total U.S. output is siphoned off by defense preparedness, space exploration and foreign aid.

No listing of general characteristics can give a full understanding of anything so complex as an economic system. The essence of an economic system is to be found in the interrelation of its many separate parts. Accordingly, a more complete and realistic—but still quite general—description of the American economy will be attempted along other lines. We shall try to explain how basic economic problems are "solved" in the United States today.

SOLVING BASIC ECONOMIC PROBLEMS

In the United States consumers are free to purchase whatever they choose within limits set by their incomes and the minor restriction imposed by the government. The purchase of a very small number of products is either proscribed or limited by the government. The most important among them are harmful drugs and narcotics, sulfurous matches, and in some states, intoxicating liquors. In addition, the government discourages consumption of some goods and services by putting taxes on them. (Although not all these taxes were imposed for the purpose of limiting consumption, they do have that effect.) For example, taxes on cigarettes, gasoline, liquor, luxuries, theaters, movies, and night clubs discourage the consumption of these goods and services. Conversely, the government encourages consumption of some goods and services subsidizing them in whole or in part. Examples include education, public housing, agriculture, railroads and aviation. On the whole, government limitation and encouragement of consumption is small in scale. Businessmen are essentially free to offer whatever goods they wish, and consumers are at liberty to buy or reject them.

The original decision about what shall be produced and in what amount is made by producers; their decision, in turn, is based on what they expect to sell to consumers.

That consumers are free to purchase whatever they choose does not mean, however, that they make their selections in all cases on the basis of their own judgment. Moreover, free consumer choice cannot in itself be taken as proof that consumers buy the products that give them the greatest satisfaction obtainable from their expenditures. We shall explore the influences that dictate consumers' choices and in that way try to discover how efficient the altercation of resources in our economy is.

Are the "Right" Goods Produced?

The overriding objective of all economic activity is the satisfaction of material wants. An economic system should therefore produce such goods and services that satisfy consumers better than any other that could have been made *with the same amount of effort and inputs.*

Observe that this objective has been stated in terms of "satisfying the consumer." To speak of satisfying consumers implies that they have basic desires whose satisfaction contributes to good health or good spirits, and whose denial results in unhappiness, frustration, or political discontent. Conversely, it implies that they are free from superstition and are informed about what is available and how well different things will meet their desires and needs. Moreover, it implies that they should be free to purchase whatever they wish. It seems obvious that you can satisfy people best by giving them what they want.

It is on these grounds that most American and West European economists favor "consumer sovereignty"—buyers dictate to producers what shall be produced. Since in the United States today consumers are at liberty to choose whatever they please, they appear to be sovereign. Unless they wish to do so, they need not buy any particular item. Producers who make things that few persons will buy feel the lash of the consumer's disfavor in the form of financial loss or even business failure.

However, the problem of deciding who determines what shall be produced is not settled by a discussion of consumer sovereignty. We must determine why certain products are selected for purchase. Consumers may simply be induced, by subtle means, to do what others want them to do. Almost everyone in the United States has heard of the "hidden persuaders" who allegedly are able to manipulate consumers to an unbelievable degree.

Why Do Consumers Purchase What They Do?

Advertising is the most obvious "outside" factor in consumers' choices, since everyone knows that it is designed specifically to influence consumer behavior. Although it is impossible to measure exactly its effects in any specific case, all the evidence taken together seems to show that advertising often strongly influences consumers' choices, is moderately effective in most cases, and only rarely seems to have no influence upon consumers.

Many forces other than advertising influence consumers' choices. By far the most important is the desire and pressure to "conform." Individuals tend to imitate the people around them both from conscious desire to be like others and because their notions of what is right and wrong, good and bad, beautiful and ugly depend upon what others do and think.

Another circumstance in which consumer choice may represent a poor indication of consumer desire and consumer welfare is that of limited choice. At some times and in many places, there may be a scarcity of products of a particular type. Given limited choice, the consumer will settle for the best of the alternatives offered him. His purchase is therefore not really an accurate reflection of his desires—except that he prefers even that poor version of the product to other products and services available to him.

Consumer selection of goods sometimes directly reflects basic needs as adjudged by consumers themselves. When persons are cold, they will purchase something to keep them warm. A girl who has not eaten for several days will buy food rather than reducing pills—no matter how fashionable it is to be slim. However, if we wish to estimate accurately the comparative effect of "outside influences" and the recognition of their own basic needs upon consumers, we should have to find out what consumers would buy if they were entirely free from outside influences.

We realize that this is scarcely possible. No individuals have been, nor could they be, free from environmental influences. These vary widely in nature and power from place to place. We know, for example, of societies in which people have a far smaller appetite for goods than in our own.[2] Yet even in these societies, and certainly in the Soviet Union and France, outside pressures strongly influence consumers' choices. Differences in economic systems can be expected to create—as well as respond to—differences in such influences. Indeed, one of the more important bases on which to evaluate an economy is the nature of the desires it creates.

Is it possible to determine how intelligent is the selection of goods produced in the United States? Specifically, is it possible to compare what is produced with what "should be" produced? Can one accept consumers' choices as valid in any sense? Would we "trust" their choices between present and future income? Between social needs and private desires?

Do Consumers Buy the Best Products Available?

It is impossible to know what consumers should buy, apart from goods that satisfy their most basic needs. For example, one might specify the number of calories and vitamins needed for health at minimum cost, but it does not follow from anything yet said that consumers "should" purchase food on the basis of cost or "science" alone. We prefer a standard by which to evaluate the validity or efficiency of consumers' choices that does not require a decision about what their basic preferences should be. One possible standard is the degree to which they purchase the best available brand of a specific product. That is, we will not question the validity of their decision to buy, say, shoes; we will only try to discover whether they purchase the particular brand of shoes that gives them what they themselves want from shoes at minimum cost. To the extent that consumers purchase goods inferior to others available at equal cost, we can conclude that they choose badly. Such a finding would suggest strongly that free consumer choice does not lead to the production of the best variety of goods, even as it does not result in the production of only the best brands of any product.[3]

The standard of evaluation stated above does not measure exactly the efficiency of free consumer choice in the United States today. It is however the only one that can be applied on a factual basis at the present time.

A comparison of various brands of the same product according to their ability to satisfy the wants of discerning consumers reached the following conclusion: ". . . consumers of the products studied averaged about two thirds of the satisfaction per dollar of expenditure they might have obtained.

---

[2] The best current examples are to be found in the developing countries of Asia and Africa, where it frequently is difficult to persuade people to work, once their most elementary material need have been met. In the United States, Hutterite and Mennonite communities are examples of consumer groups having very modest desires for material goods.

[3] Distinguish carefully between products—like hats, autos, radios—and brands of a product—like Ford, Chevrolet, Plymouth.

Put another way, the results suggest that the average consumer of these products could have increased his satisfaction by 50 per cent if he had bought the product rated best by Consumers' Union." [4]

A comparison of the prices charged for brands of similar quality confirmed the foregoing results. It showed that the average consumer spent at least 56 percent more than he needed to spend.[5] This study also showed that the relationship between price and quality was relatively weak. ". . . while more expensive brands are higher in quality than cheaper brands for most of the products studied, the reverse was frequently true. For 9 of 35 products, the cheaper brands typically were of higher quality than more expensive ones." [6]

These results show clearly that consumers are not able to guard fully their own welfare, even judging by tests that they could be expected to meet fairly well. Consumer performance in selecting among alternative brands of particular products should be superior to their performance in choosing which products to purchase, since they could make brand comparisons themselves as well as study the results of research done by testing organizations, such as the Consumers' Union. There is no method, however, for assessing the amount of satisfaction to be obtained from different patterns of expenditure among alternative products.

The results of the study also indicate that competition does not ensure the survival of the "best" brands from the consumer's standpoint. Superior salesmanship and a strong marketing organization may enable an inferior product to displace one that is far better for consumers.

How great, then, is the error of the average consumer in his selection of products? Is he a wise sovereign? The results reported show that he can scarcely be considered very wise; the extent of his intelligence and knowledge can only be conjectured. We lack sufficient information to say whether consumers in the United States select goods more or less intelligently than consumers in the Soviet Union or France.

How Are Methods of Production Selected?

Businessmen are free to use almost any productive techniques they desire. Restrictions are placed on the methods they select primarily by the patent laws, which restrict the use of certain techniques and the production of certain items to those who hold a patent, and by the refusal of organized labor in some cases to permit the use of productive devices that may endanger employee health or decrease employment.

Some businessmen complain that they are "no longer the boss," and that

---

[4] A. R. Oxenfeldt, "Consumer Knowledge: Its Measurement and Extent," *Review of Economics and Statistics,* November 1950, p. 306.

[5] Oxenfeldt, p. 309.

[6] Oxenfeldt, p. 310.

they "must run the factory the way the union tells them to." For the most part, however, American unions prefer to leave the choice of productive methods to the employer.[7]

Generally speaking, production methods in the United States are selected by businessmen after an examination of alternatives.[8] Usually they will select the least costly method of production, since, the lower the cost, the greater the profit, and also the smaller the likelihood that competitors will force one out of business.

Does this method of selecting production methods result in an efficient economy? To answer this question, we must first decide what is meant by efficiency in production. Certainly it does not necessarily mean the use of the most modern and complicated type of machinery, for sometimes such methods require more workers, some of them more highly skilled than would be needed with less complex machinery.

Is efficiency to be judged by the number of labor hours used to produce a given output? Surely the answer must be negative, for a method that uses fewer man-hours than another, but which requires the most skilled workmen, would not be efficient. In addition to the number of man-hours worked, we must also take into account the labor skills used. But how can skills of different workmen be compared and valued accurately?

What then do we mean by productive efficiency and how might it be measured accurately? Ideally, efficiency means that we "give up as little as possible." But of what must we give up as little as possible? We must give up as little as possible of other things that might be produced from the given resources in place of the product in question.

There generally are many ways of producing the same thing. *The most efficient method is the one that requires the smallest sacrifice of other things.* An example might make this tricky notion clear. Assume that 1000 units of X product could be produced either by using 100 men of relatively low skill or by using 50 men of high skill. We can tell which method is more efficient only if we know what these men could have produced in other occupations. For the sake of simplicity, assume that the men could be used only in two occupations, in the X industry and to raise wheat. Assume further that the 100 men could raise 11,000 bushels of wheat per year, and that the 50 skilled men could raise 15,000 bushels. The method of

---

[7] In Europe, notably in West Germany, a movement that has gained considerable headway admits labor representatives to great participation (approximately 40 percent) in the top decision-making body of some large industrial corporations. This condition is termed codetermination.

[8] All factors of production affect productive techniques by requiring payment; the greater the payments they command, the greater the obstacle to their use. If all productive factors were free or received the same compensation, methods of production would be very different from what they are.

producing X involving the 100 workers would entail the smaller cost. Their use to make product X would involve a smaller decline in wheat output than would occur by using the fifty skilled men. Specifically using the 100 unskilled men to make X, we end up with 4000 bushels more of wheat as well as the same amount of X.

In actual practice, workers' output of all alternate products cannot be measured. Consequently, no available yardstick permits accurate comparisons of the efficiency of different arrangements. One is driven to the use of yardsticks that are only rough approximations.

It has already been stated that businessmen base their decisions upon the yardstick of money costs. Unfortunately, this standard is frequently defective as a measure of real costs—that is, sacrifices in all forms that we must make in order to produce something else. In as much as this standard is widely used, some of its limitations will be listed.

The reason for disparity between money costs and real costs are many. Certain groups of relatively unskilled workers are able to command high incomes because they use concerted action and even force to support their wage demands. While the output of these workers in alternative occupations is low, their money cost is high. In such a case, there is no close parallel between real cost and money cost. Similarly, some firms possess strong market power and the prices they charge for their products are far out of line with the real costs of producing them. Also some real costs involved in production are not borne by the producer of the end product, and accordingly are not included in his money costs. Examples of such real costs include: injury to health and inconvenience resulting from dirt, smells, noise, and traffic congestion that attend the production of some things. Persons in the neighborhood who suffer from these conditions are not always paid for their inconvenience or suffering. On the other hand, some producers incur money costs that are disproportionately high in relation to real costs. The most common excessive costs found in industry include: exorbitant managerial compensation where a firm is under control of nonowning managers; the preferential hiring of friends or relatives, even though more efficient employees are available at the same salary; failure to seek out or adopt improved production techniques; purchase of products from friends or relatives at higher prices or of lower quality than merchandise available elsewhere.

Further disparity between money and real costs results from inadequate opportunities for education and training for the poor, with a resultant overcrowding of the market for unskilled labor. The low pay commanded by unskilled labor therefore tends to understate substantially the real cost of that labor to society. By failing to train these workers, at very modest cost, the nation is deprived of the much larger output they could have contributed.

Even though money costs have grievous defects as measures of real costs, they generally are the best measure available. Frequently, we must use them for want of something better, knowing that we may err. As far as possible, we must consider real rather than money costs in evaluating productive efficiency.

If we take money costs to be an accurate measure of productive efficiency, to what extent are businessmen efficient? Do they keep their costs at a minimum? Do they know the cost of alternative production methods? How hard do they try to keep money costs to a minimum?

Businessmen insist that they constantly make strong efforts to reduce costs of production. In some cases, the stress laid on saving pennies on items that sell for hundreds of dollars (as in television and automobile manufacturing) is striking. On the other hand, business executives are notoriously unconcerned about economy when traveling on expense accounts.

Few achievements bring promotion, special bonuses, and distinction as quickly as being credited with reducing costs. Apparently that fact does not lead executives to pursue productive efficiency with the utmost zeal at all times. It has been well established that when the pressure on them to reduce cost is intensified—as when the firm becomes unprofitable—they generally find ways of reducing costs significantly.[9]

Some find the explanation for management's failure to press constantly for minimum costs of production in the fact that many top executives in large corporations do not personally bear the cost, or share in the added profits, resulting from changes in costs of production. Many own virtually no stock in the companies they manage. Another possible reason is that to attain increased efficiency would almost always require greater effort on their part. Sometimes their recommendations would entail risks of failure and in extreme cases might endanger their own position or reduce the scope of their authority (as where they might be wiser to purchase "on the outside" what they had been making for themselves).

Up to this point we have assumed that the businessman himself determines what productive methods to use, subject only to minor limitations by government and labor unions. Actually, a businessman's methods are strongly conditioned by the activities of his competitors. A businessman who knows the most efficient method of conducting his business may be unable to employ that method because of circumstances beyond his control. For example, consider a retailer who sets up his shop to serve an assumed number of customers most efficienctly, but finds that due to the advent of many new competitors his store never operates at full efficiency. The additional stores have caused his productive facilities to be excessive. Or, on the

---

[9] For examples see A. R. Oxenfeldt, *Industrial Pricing and Market Practices* (New York: Prentice-Hall, Inc., 1951), pp. 117, 120-121.

other hand, the competition might lower prices and force a businessman to produce more efficiently in order to survive.

Furthermore, businessmen are also limited in the productive methods they use by the size of their capital resources. Often they must forego the use of more efficient methods because they cannot pay for the new facilities required. Labor unions also influence productive methods, sometimes obstructing the use of new techniques, sometimes pressing for greater efficiency.

In assessing current productive efficiency in the United States, it is helpful to examine separately raw material extraction, agriculture, manufacturing, and distribution. We will find uneven levels of productive efficiency in these various fields.

Degree of Productive Efficiency in Raw Material Industries

Efficient raw material industries must meet four major conditions: First, raw materials must be extracted from the ground by use of minimum productive resources. Second, the rate at which raw materials are used up must be such that later generations are not deprived of valuable resources for the sake of a trivial gain to the present generation. Third, the resources provided by nature must be "used to the full," and no economically removable portion of the resource should be left in the ground unless it can be recaptured later. Fourth, materials should be reused as far as economically feasible.

Each of these criteria must be applied in an economic rather than a physical sense. It would be foolhardy to use methods of extraction that leave absolutely no raw materials in the ground. Even if such methods existed, they would almost invariably be enormously costly. To use all reusable raw materials would also involve very heavy costs; one would choose to reclaim only those materials that were readily accessible and of high value. The best possible use of a resource over a period of time poses special problems. It requires an estimate of future need as well as of available future supplies.

Since the criteria of productive efficiency in raw material industries are difficult to apply, we must content ourselves with a superficial discussion of this problem. As in other cases where information is not available or where the subject is highly controversial, conflicting arguments of recognized validity will be summarized.

Claims for the raw material industries:

1. The raw material industries have been extremely diligent in prospecting for new raw material deposits.
2. Raw material industries in the United States are very highly mechanized.

3. Raw material industries have made improvements in technology by virtue of extensive research efforts.

Charges against the raw material industry:

1. Raw materials are extracted with reference to immediate profitability alone. As a result, there is little regard for wastes in extraction. Raw materials are extracted in ways that aim to minimize money costs, and in so doing a substantial quantity of raw materials has been either unnecessarily destroyed or rendered unrecoverable. The petroleum, coal, and lumber industries have been the chief offenders.[10]
2. The industries producing raw materials have erred on the side of using up our natural resources at too rapid a rate.
3. Prospecting for new deposits of raw materials has been highly inefficient. Too many persons, many using primitive methods, are engaged in the search for raw materials; prospecting could be organized and made systematic and more efficient.[11]

Productive Efficiency in Agriculture

In 1963, less than 4.8 million people were employed in agriculture, out of about 66 million who were employed in all lines of activity in the United States. American agriculture has achieved very great increases in productive efficiency. It has released very large numbers of employees for work in other branches of industry—even while providing food for a steadily rising population. Whereas in 1940, 17 percent of the civilian labor force was employed mainly in agriculture, in 1963, the proportion was about 7.3 percent.[12] This dramatic achievement resulted mainly from a reduction in underemployment on the farms as farmers took advantage of the growth in employment opportunities in urban communities. Judged by absolute standards, however, American agriculture is still characterized by relatively low productive efficiency. On the other hand, compared to most other countries American agriculture is extraordinarily efficient.

American agriculture still ties up more people, machinery, and land than are needed to produce the desired output; in large part, this is the result of

---

[10] For a discussion of the manner in which resources were wasted, see "A National Plan for American Forestry," Senate Document no. 12, 73d Cong., 1st sess., 1933. See also G. T. Renner and W. H. Hartley, *Conservation & Citizenship* (Boston: D.C. Heath & Company, 1940), pp. 80-89, 230-232.

[11] For an illuminating and factual discussion of prospecting and extraction in the oil industry, see "Hearings of the Temporary National Economic Committee," pt. 14, pp. 7379-7404.

[12] For a discussion of these changes in employment and their causes, see John D. Black, "Agriculture in the Nation's Economy," *American Economic Review,* March 1956, p. 2ff.

government subsidies that make it possible for the small-scale family farm to survive and for the large-scale farms to overproduce.[13] A very extensive survey of agricultural methods reached the following conclusions:

> If the workers in . . . rural families could be employed at jobs where they would produce as much as the average worker on the medium-sized commercial family farm or the average rural nonfarm worker, the production and output of rural people would be increased 20-25%. This is the equivalent of adding 2,500,000 workers to the total labor force.[14]

Note that the standard of comparison used is not highest but only average productivity. Accordingly, the estimates of losses in output or manpower due to use of inefficient production methods and the unnecessarily large amount of labor tied up in agriculture are extremely conservative. It is inevitable that farmers sometimes will have little work to do and at other times will be extraordinarily busy. The estimate of a possible increase of 20 to 25 percent in output accepts as necessary and inevitable the average loss of working time sustained on the average medium-sized commercial family farm. Of course, some differences in productivity must be anticipated in agriculture due to variations in soil fertility and the beneficence of the elements.

Another indictment of American agriculture is that it wantonly wastes soil fertility. Reliable studies have disclosed that agricultural methods in the United States have permitted the loss of precious top soil and the exhaustion of soil minerals needed to raise crops.[15] Huge areas of the United States were farmed without regard to the social value of arable land. Cotton and tobacco farmers were compelled to move westward from the eastern seaboard as they depleted the soil fertility by exploitative agricultural methods. Dust storms, more serious once but still not confined to the past, result from farming methods and deforestation that literally allow a vital natural resource to blow away.

Although most American farms are highly mechanized,[16] and many farms are now operated by methods that restore soil fertility, agriculture in the United States is still relatively inefficient. Important strides have been made,

---

[13] Many people in the United States support the preservation of the small family farm via subsidization for noneconomic reasons. They believe that the small farmer is an important democratic force and helps to maintain the spirit of independence and dedication to democracy which Americans extol.

[14] Joint Committee on the Economic Report, *Underemployment of Rural Families,* 82d Cong., 1st sess., 1951, pp. 4, 5.

[15] See Fairfield Osborn, *Our Plundered Planet* (Boston: Little, Brown & Co., 1948); see also Renner and Hartley, pp. 107-137.

[16] Mechanical and electrical power per agricultural worker and/or unit of arable land in the United States is by far the highest in the world, although a good part of it is excess capacity that lies idle.

primarily under government auspices, to teach the best farming methods and to encourage farmers to give up low-quality farmland. However, much progress must be made before American agriculture approaches the optimum level of productivity.

Efficiency in Manufacturing Industries

In assessing the efficiency of manufacturing, we want to know about the amount of facilities available and the degree of skill and efficiency with which they are put to use. Studies of manufacturing capacity show two conflicting situations. Some industries seem able to produce far more goods than could be sold *even if the economy were fully employed,* that is, far more than they could reasonably hope to sell. Such industries attract new producers for a variety of reasons and end up with excessive facilities. Measurement of excess capacity is crude at best,[17] but there is undivided agreement that many industries have excessive manufacturing facilities,[18] though often these consist largely of technically obsolete equipment.

Other industries have fewer productive facilities than seem necessary to meet the nation's peak demands. Businessmen in those industries, either independently, by agreement, or out of mutual awareness of their common interests, refrain from expanding facilities. Industries that limit productive facilities cannot be charged with the wastes of excessive capacity. They may be guilty of the perhaps graver waste of underproduction.

With what skill and efficiency are manufacturing facilities put to use in the United States? Two types of evidence bear on this question. First, we could compare American methods with those of other countries. *By this standard, American manufacturing industries, in general, are unquestionably the most efficient in the world.* America's manufacturing processes have received more praise, sometimes in the form of imitation, than any other branch of American industry. This is not to say, by any means, that all manufacturing industries in the United States are more efficient than industry anywhere else in the world. Indeed, many nations now possess some firms and even whole industries that far surpass the United States in technological efficiency.

Second, we can compare our productive methods with the most efficient

---

[17] Some of the difficulties in measuring excess capacity can be listed; some idle capacity is warranted by uncertainty of the size of markets and danger that facilities might break down. More important, it is impossible to build new facilities at the same rate that consumption expands, for generally facilities must be added in big lumps— that is, a whole new plant must be built or a new deposit must be mined. Accordingly, there would ordinarily be, even under the best circumstances, some idle facilities until demand caught up with the expansion.

[18] An outstanding example is the whiskey distilling industry with productive capacity more than five times the annual output of whiskey. See Oxenfeldt, *Industrial Pricing and Market Practices,* p. 451.

that might be used. This second test is complex and will take a little explaining. Consider the case of a businessman who has been producing inefficiently, but who is not aware of his competitors' superior methods. Assume that he is at liberty to use the superior methods. If this man had been diligent—if he had kept abreast of technical developments or had hired engineering consultants—he would have learned of these methods. We would consider this man inefficient.

The wide variation in the apparent efficiency of individual firms in the same industry suggests that some firms use relatively inefficient techniques. Differences in efficiency, however, are not proof of inefficiency. It would be wasteful from the individual businessman's point of view and for society as a whole to discard existing equipment every time an improvement in productive methods is made. The economies made possible by improvements must be set against the losses of scrapping equipment. The losses may exceed the gains, in which event the firm should continue to use the old techniques. However, despite the difficulty of interpreting differences in techniques in the same industry, business and labor union officials agree that the efficiency of firms in any industry, however measured, varies widely.

Another reason for suspecting that productive methods are not as efficient as they might be has already been suggested. American firms characteristically make substantial improvements in productive methods under pressure—during depression and price wars. Presumably, efficient managements would have made these improvements in the absence of strong pressure.

Productive Efficiency in Retailing

Although envied and admired by most of the world, distribution arrangements in the United States are much criticized at home. The high proportion of each retail sales dollar that goes for distribution has been a source of considerable concern in this country. Some industries—especially gasoline retailing—have become almost public jokes. Gas stations on several corners of an intersection are commonplace. Many other lines of retailing—such as liquor, shoe, hat and drug stores—seem to have visibly excessive facilities in most communities. Duplication of retail facilities apparently is the general rule.[19]

In assessing the efficiency of retailing, difficulties are faced in obtaining desired information and in devising reliable criteria. Can we be certain that there are too many gas stations? If so, what standards are we applying? Even if we grant that gas station facilities are excessive, how large is the excess? No demonstrably correct answers to these questions are possible.

---

[19] In 1957, for example, 40 percent of all retail stores had an average daily sales volume of $57. *Statistical Abstract of the United States,* 1959, p. 830.

There is little we can do here but again rely on observation and "common sense." Both are treacherous, but we have no choice. Common observation, common sense, and the views of specialists indicate that retailing in the United States is characterized by excessive facilities and manpower.

Productive Efficiency and the Full Utilization of Resources

The ability of an economic system to use all resources available is an essential test of its productive efficiency. To use *employed* resources efficiently but to leave a substantial proportion of all resources unemployed saves with one hand what is wasted with the other. *Mass unemployment has been a feature of the U.S. economy over much of its history; when it did not exist in fact, it nevertheless represented an ever-present fear to a large proportion of the population. Social critics and reformers have attacked capitalism mainly because of its demonstrated inability to afford employees economic security.*

It is possible to estimate, albeit very roughly, the waste of resources through unemployment. This is done by placing a money value on the goods that would have been produced if there had been no unemployment. The over-all unemployment rate over recent years has averaged between 5.5 percent and 6 percent. Since the unemployed have included a disproportionate number of unskilled and semiskilled workers and persons with limited work experience (though this fact is partly offset by the fact that a substantial number of the employed have been limited to only part-time work), one might place the loss of output at about 4 percent or 5 percent of present total output. That would mean a loss of between $25 billion and $35 billion every year.[20] Even if that estimate is quite far from the mark, it does suggest that unemployment is extremely costly in economic terms. The human costs—psychic pain, loss of self-confidence and self-respect, disruption of lives—would seem to be far greater, but these cannot be measured.

Unemployment results from different causes. In the past, unemployment in the United States was essentially "cyclical." That is, it resulted from *temporary* declines in sales (which were due to other factors, which in turn, had causes of their own, and so on back) that led employers to lay off some of their workers. These declines in sales were followed, in time, by revivals in demand and rehirings—though not evenly—distributed over the nation, rather than concentrated in single areas, industries, or classes of employees.

Since about the mid-1950s, the nature of unemployment apparently has changed. Even during periods of *general* full employment, many persons in the United States suffer material privation because of unemployment. In June 1964, during one of the most prosperous periods in U.S. history, 37

---

[20] J. K. Galbraith would interpret these facts differently, arguing that the extra $25 billion to $35 billion, when the nation already has a GNP of over $600 billion would be of slight consequence. He finds the greatest damage done by recessions in the loss of personal incomes to individuals, rather than to the nation as a whole.

major labor market areas out of 150 in the United States were afflicted by "substantial unemployment" according to the classifications employed by the Bureau of Employment Security.[21] (That designation means that 6 percent or more of the total labor force in the area was unemployed and that this level of unemployment was expected to continue over the following four months.) Although some cyclical unemployment arises from time to time, there seems to be a "hard core" of unemployment that does not disappear even when general business conditions are extremely prosperous. This permanent unemployment is "secular" as opposed to cyclical. It apparently results from the following causes: (1) Automation—the substitution of labor-saving equipment for manpower to effect savings. Such unemployment has hit a variety of industries, the foremost among them being radio-electronics, food processing, and electric appliances. (2) Long-run decline in demand—the product has lost favor with consumers or has been superseded by superior products. Among the industries in this category are bituminous coal, men's hats, and cotton fabrics. (3) Industrial relocations—businesses have moved out of an area because of the depletion of natural resources, unfavorable labor conditions, and the like. Industries thus afflicted and the areas involved are e.g., Gary, Indiana (automobile), and almost all of coal-mining Pennsylvania. A central feature of secular unemployment is the inability or unwillingness of many laborers to change their occupation or relocate. The human costs involved in shifts of this kind are very great, and many individuals who are otherwise diligent and responsible cannot make the necessary transition. Consequently, they remain linked to an area and an industry that offers progressively less job opportunity.

One can readily understand that the measures employed to cure unemployment must vary according to its causes. Moreover, we obviously cannot discuss here the many different measures developed to combat this problem. It may be helpful, however, to mention the main approaches that can be taken and then to indicate how the most powerful methods work. There are two broad types of measures available: the first is general, and the second is specific—to particular areas, industries or work skills. Each of these types can be subdivided according to whether they are preventive, corrective, or simply seeking to relieve the suffering of those who are unemployed. It should be noted parenthetically that we have not demonstrated much ability to anticipate unemployment and prevent it; at best, the need for action can be recognized soon after it arises and before difficulties snowball.

The most powerful approach to curing widespread (cyclical) unemployment is termed fiscal policy. The rationale underlying its use is fairly

---

[21] See U. S. Dept. of Labor, Bureau of Employment Security, *Area Labor Market Trends,* June 1964, p. 4. One year earlier, thirty-nine markets had substantial unemployment.

simple. The U.S. government, like most others, raises huge sums via taxes and borrowing; it also spends very large amounts. (The federal government alone collects taxes each year equal to approximately 22 percent of all personal income received—about 16 percent of the gross national product; it spends an equal or larger amount, as a rule.) Because of its massive taxing and spending activities, the federal government *necessarily* exerts a major effect upon the level of employment. It can try to use its influence in as neutral a manner as possible, or it can consciously attempt to combat unfavorable movements in the economy. In the Employment Act of 1946, the federal government assumed the commitment—in principle—to use its fiscal and other powers in ways that would alleviate unemployment. How might the government do this?

Mainly the government can use its taxing and spending powers to combat unemployment by raising total demand for goods when business has begun to slip and by directing its expenditures into areas and industries most afflicted by unemployment. That is, it could (1) reduce taxes, thereby leaving consumers with more to spend; (2) take the same amount in taxes but spend more than before—and in areas where unemployment is greatest; and (3) take less in taxes and spend more than before. All three usually mean incurring a government budget deficit.

Fiscal countercyclical measures, especially deficit spending and personal income tax cuts, are the most powerful means at the U.S. government's disposal to combat recessions and to prevent depressions. Furthermore, in case of need, Congress can pass legislation, such as that increasing unemployment relief and public works spending, youth training, accelerated capital depreciation write-offs which reduce corporation taxes, and so forth. Congressional action is usually very sluggish, however.

In addition to these direct antidepression measures, the U.S. government constantly uses indirect monetary means to influence the business cycles. The Federal Reserve System has great, though far from complete, powers over the total volume of banking credit and over its cost (interest rate). By making credit easier and cheaper, it supplies more investment funds to the economy; by making credit tight, it curtails investments. It appears, however, that these monetary measures are much more effective for curbing the expansion of business than for stimulating it when needed. Compared to fiscal measures, monetary measures are relatively weak in their effects.

One of the great "discoveries" of recent times is that governmental deficits need cause no harm, and can actually serve a very useful purpose when the demand for goods from nongovernment sources is inadequate. Although this conclusion is accepted by virtually every respected economist, it is still contested by many persons whose "common sense tells them otherwise." Consequently, we possess remedies for unemployment that public opinion and political leadership may not be willing to employ.

To deal specifically with unemployment in the United States—and it is a serious problem even now (early 1965, a period of truly great prosperity) —secular unemployment has proved to be highly intractable. It does not cure easily, and the problem is likely to become more serious before it is resolved. At bottom is the need to ensure that the work force, especially young persons seeking work for the first time, obtain the skills for which there is a market. In this period of rapidly changing technology and wide-spread substitution of machinery and electronic devices for human beings, unskilled persons will find it increasingly difficult to obtain employment. For such unemployment, fiscal policy alone will not provide a solution.

The Allocation of Productive Agents among Occupations

Who Decides Where to Employ Productive Agents

In the United States each worker and each owner of property and funds is at liberty to use his services and property as he wishes. The government places only slight obstacles in his way. These obstacles may take the form of zoning restrictions, which limit the uses to which land and property may be put; or the government may outlaw certain occupations, such as gambling, the production of liquor and dangerous products, and prostitution. Restrictions on free occupational choice have been erected by some organizations of laborers and professional workers. Ordinarily, these restrictions set unnecessarily high requirements for entrance into a union or for certification as a member of a profession. Moreover, some positions, often the most renumerative and socially important, are preempted by persons with personal and political influence. In addition to these limits on occupational choice, some positions are closed to workers on grounds of sex, race, or religion. Possibly the greatest limitation on free occupational choice results from a lack of jobs during depression. How do workers and owners of other productive agents decide what employment to accept—when they have a choice?

The following discussion is phrased in terms of only one factor of production—labor—because labor, measured by any index, is by far the most important productive factor. What is said here about labor is substantially but not exactly valid for the other factors. Put differently, land, liquid funds, and natural resources probably are divided among alternative employments more efficiently than is labor.

What Employments Will Workers Favor?

One would expect individuals to select the employments giving them the greatest "net advantages," that is, the employments in which the combined money income and nonmonetary aspects of the job give the greatest return. A hypothetical illustration will clarify what is meant by "net advantages."

Consider a worker who could earn $100 and $90 a week in the two highest paying positions he can obtain. We will assume, realistically, that he does not like both jobs equally well. Assume also for illustrative purposes that the worker likes the higher paying employment less than the other, and prefers the employment paying $90 a week to the point of being willing to give up $10 a week to work there rather than to work in the higher paying job. He may prefer the second job because he finds the activities more pleasant, because he likes his associates on that job more, or because the position is more secure or offers greater opportunity for advancement; the particular source of his preference need not concern us. Under these conditions, his net advantages are greater in occupation 2 than in occupation 1 by roughly 10 percent. We can assume that if the worker knew about the two positions and could accurately predict his reactions to working in them, he would select occupation 2, for it would make him "better off" than the other.

While logic leads us to expect each factor of production to enter the occupation offering the greatest net advantages, we must inquire into how productive factors actually select the occupations they enter. The answer to this question will shed considerable light on both the personal happiness of individuals and the productivity of the economy, for the ability of individuals to make a productive contribution varies widely from job to job.

Where Should Workers Be Employed?

The suitability of an occupation for a productive factor can be judged by two standards: the personal point of view—which, as indicated, would afford each individual maximum net advantages—and that of the nation as a whole—what is termed the social viewpoint. What difference, if any, exists between the personal and social viewpoints concerning where a factor of production should be employed? Are they likely to conflict?

It is not difficult to imagine a situation in which the net advantages of occupations are highest in occupations where physical output is low. That is, the jobs which involve the smallest production of material goods and services might be extremely pleasant otherwise, so that—all things taken together—individuals might prefer to work in those occupations rather than in others where their productive contribution would be far greater. Under such circumstances, if individuals selected employments yielding the highest net advantages, national output would be lower than could have been obtained by a different distribution of labor. Of course, a flow of labor into such occupations would then reduce many wages and tend to reverse the trend at some point.

In a society that places the individual's interests above those of "the state," there would be no conflict. In ordinary times, a nation has no right, nor should it have the desire, to require individuals to work in employments without regard to their personal preferences. The disagreeableness of a job paying a high income to a worker might not nearly compensate the pleasure of being able to buy more goods. Consequently, there need be no conflict between the choice of occupations by individuals on the basis of net advantages and what is best from the social viewpoint. (Exception should be made for considerations of national defense, for national output might well be a rough measure of a nation's ability to withstand attack. And of course, during wartime itself, all nations recognize a conflict between the personal and social viewpoint and invoke the draft and sometimes forced "direction" of labor.)

Do Workers Enter the Occupations They Should?

It is well recognized that workers prefer high-paying jobs to those that pay poorly. Consequently, many workers try to enter employments that pay high incomes, and those occupations have the pick of the best workers. We must inquire whether it is desirable that the best workers go into occupations that pay best. Does the importance of a job to society vary with the rate of pay offered?

Pay and Social Importance. Rates of pay in any occupation are determined by a variety of factors, only a few of which are related to social importance. Pay rates depend primarily upon the scarcity of the skill that is required, the intensity of competition among productive factors for available jobs, the costs of training, the relative market power of workers and employers, and the amount that buyers are willing to pay for the thing produced. Of these factors, the relative market power of employer and worker often is the most important influence upon wage rates, although there is no necessary connection between market power and the importance of a job to society. The other determinants of wage rates—particularly the amount that buyers are willing to pay for the product—clearly reflect the value of the job to society.

Scarce factors of production generally command a high price. For example, the high pay of the best prizefighters results from the scarcity of men with the necessary qualifications and the desire to be in the fight game. Their relatively high incomes may also be taken as evidence of social contribution. It can be argued that a successful prizefighter's pay is high because a large number of people are so interested in fighting that they will pay substantial sums to see him perform. Whether one likes to watch fights or not, he is forced to concede that the skilled professional fighter serves the large number of people who do. In almost all cases, the payment of large incomes to productive factors is accompanied by large consumer payments for what those factors produce.

The pay of public school teachers and college instructors helps to illuminate the relationship between compensation and the social importance of an occupation. The quality of teachers as an influence on the value of education has never been recognized more than today. Moreover, largely because of the low salaries paid to teachers and the relatively heavy birth rates of recent years, the shortage of teachers is acute—and widely recognized. Nevertheless, the rise in teachers' salaries has been very slow for a variety of reasons. Among them are the ability to increase the size of classes without suffering a readily demonstrable drop in the quality of education; the difficulty that unions face in bargaining with governmental units, which employ teachers; the reluctance of teachers to engage in union activity; the ability to use teachers of low ability and training—because the product (education) cannot be measured precisely and a poor quality of output can go unrecognized for a long time. Educators are almost universally agreed that in public school teaching, pay is an extremely poor indicator of the social importance of the productive contribution made by teachers.

If the rate of pay obtainable in an occupation does not always measure its value to society, what other criterion could be used? No alternative has been advanced, a fact which is not surprising in view of the large number and complexity of factors that must influence the measurement of a job's social importance. However, the absence of a better measure is no justification for regarding the one available as fully accurate. We must recognize that rates of pay in individual occupations are determined to a large extent by factors that are irrelevant to social contribution—particularly market power. Most people pick jobs primarily on the basis of rates of pay from among available jobs for which they have the requisite skills. As a result, they may enter occupations where their contributions to total output will be lower then they would be in some other occupation.

Knowing Alternative Employments. If workers are to take the jobs among those open to them that offer the highest net advantages, they must know their job opportunities. Do workers have the time necessary to canvass carefully the job opportunities in their own communities? Do they make an effort to learn and follow up opportunities in distant communities? For many persons, the answer seems to be a decided negative. People seem to learn about jobs mostly in accidental ways; systematic job seeking seems to be the exception rather than the rule, especially among fairly skilled persons, who feel they lose status by looking for a job.

The growth and the improved operation of employment agencies—especially under government auspices—provide workers with a much better knowledge of their job opportunities. However, employment agencies are not used, either by employers or workers, for many types of job. In particular, professional and executive positions are heard about and personnel sought out mainly through informal and unsystematic channels. Employment agencies are used mostly for unskilled jobs, and for those like typing and stenography for which there is a heavy demand and supply.

To explore carefully all job opportunities in even a small community takes considerable time and effort. If a worker applied that time and effort to a job about which he had already heard, he would obtain immediate income. Workers who are under pressure to obtain steady income probably do not canvass the job market carefully. Although they may use an employment service to obtain jobs, they rarely take the time to search out employment that the placement services do not tell them about.

Developing Productive Capacities. This question raises the issue of "equality of opportunity"—an ideal held by an overwhelming majority of persons in the United States and in the world generally. This ideal is expressed in the statement, *"free* education for all." It has not, however, led to *equal* education for all, even at the grade and high school levels—especially for some minority groups. In addition, large regional differences exist in the quality of primary and secondary education in the United States. Inequality of educational opportunity is greater at the college and postgraduate level. Except for those high school graduates who get scholarships (about 1.5 million each year) [22] of some kind and those who have access to heavily subsidized colleges,[23] education is purchased privately, much as any other service. Those who can afford higher education are relatively free to buy it. They must be able to gain admission, but even below average students can attend some accredited university—though not always the one of their choice. Those who cannot pay for education, or who cannot afford to forego the income they might produce if they entered the work force, must go without its benefits—they have no choice.

Equality of opportunity is a subtle notion. The greatest inequalities of opportunity among individuals are perpetrated at birth. Some inherit greater talents, better health, physical attractiveness, energy, and emotional balance than others. Greater differences than these probably exist in the nature of the homes and in the caliber of parents as teachers, guides, personal examples, and providers of opportunities that depend upon income

---

[22] See Edmund D. West, *Financial Aid to the Undergraduate* (New York: American Council on Education, 1963), pp. 50-51.

[23] A surprisingly large number of colleges in the United States charge extremely low fees, even while the so-called Ivy League schools are approaching tuition charges of almost $2000 annually. For example, in 1961-1962, about 90 percent of the public institutions charged $300 or less and about 25 percent charged under $100 for tuition and required fees. Of course, for students who do not have a college in their community, it is necessary to add the cost of room and board—which would cost far more (perhaps three times the tuition charge of $300 made at most public colleges). West, *op. cit.*, pp. 65ff. Another study found the median cost of tuition, fees, and books during the freshman year of college to be above $450 while the median cost of living expenses during the same period was about $510. About 26 percent of the students received some grants of scholarships. See *Project Talent,* Final report for cooperative research project no. 635. U. S. Office of Education, Pittsburg, 1964, p. 10-60.

and inherited wealth. Given these great inequalities at birth, even with wholly equal opportunities for all thereafter, some individuals will develop their productive capacities far more than others. It would appear that the least favored at birth deserve the greatest opportunities to offset these inequalities. That certainly is not the usual situation; opportunity is so distributed that it generally reenforces and magnifies hereditary inequalities.

What opportunities do individuals in the United States receive to develop their productive capacities? Clearly, the kind and amount of training and experience required to develop latent capabilities vary by employment. For the professions, government, executive and managerial posts, the arts, journalism, and education, academic training is a prerequisite for success. Other types of training are required for skilled manual work. Because each major type of employment cannot be considered separately here, our discussion is confined to those employments that require formal education.[24]

Can everyone who possesses superior talents complete his formal education? If not, what groups lack the opportunity to do so and in what numbers? What proportion of *untalented* students do enjoy this opportunity?

One method of obtaining relevant information on this point is to study what happens to talented students, especially to those who show talent at a fairly early stage in their career. A particularly crucial group are high school students who are close to graduation. One would want to know what proportion of such students do not even finish high school and for what reasons. One would also want to know what proportion of talented high school graduates are unable to attend college. Surely, the answers to these questions depend upon the way one defines "talented." If one applies the term only to the top 1 or 3 percent of students, just about everyone can continue his academic studies. If one considers as talented everyone above the average (about half of all students) or the top quarter, then the answer is very different. Both definitions are pertinent. *A nation or economy that ensures higher education only to its very best students is highly inefficient.* An economic system gains from the productive contributions of *all* its members. It depends upon and must serve all—not just the most talented or capable.

Talent consists of many different attributes. Brainpower (I.Q.) can be measured only very imperfectly and is only one possible basis for high productivity and success. Diligence, the ability to work well with and to inspire others, good working habits, imagination, ambition, reliability, integrity and the like, account for achievement in certain fields far more than does intelligence. And these qualities are, if anything, more difficult to measure than brainpower. No doubt many young people of great native talent pass

---

[24] Implicit in this discussion is the assumption that those who attend college do develop thier productive capacity *fully*. That assumption surely is false, as a result of which this discussion understates the waste of talent.

unrecognized because of poor home training, low motivation, and mediocre schooling during their early years.

Our interpretation of the term "talented" is dictated by the data available. Fortunately, comprehensive and thorough nationwide survey, launched in 1960, has provided a great deal of valuable information on this subject, and will yield more in the years to come. The survey results are based upon a detailed examination of 440,000 students, a 5 percent sample of all students in grades 9 through 12 and 1353 schools throughout the country. These students took tests that required two days to complete and provided additional information covering their background, plans, interests, and preferences. The results of this investigation that are already available are not in themselves an accurate and full measure of the equality of opportunity to develop productive capacities; they do, however, greatly illuminate the subject. Consequently, we shall summarize briefly the impact of this study.

Perhaps the key finding of this investigation is that among the students who were graduated from high school in 1960 and 1961, about 43 percent had entered college within one year after graduation. Ninety percent of the students who ranked in the top 10 percent in aptitude for academic work entered college the first year after being graduated from high school. Twenty percent of the students in the top quarter failed to enter college, while 18 percent of those in the lowest quarter of academic aptitude did enter.[25] Of those who continued their education somewhere other than at college (which in this study included both four-year colleges and universities and two-year colleges) some attended technical institutes, schools of nursing, trade schools, or schools conducted by the armed forces.

Among those who were graduated from high school and did not attend college, approximately 58.5 percent did not want to go to college. Their reasons were:[26]

1. I wanted to earn money	23.5%
2. I wanted to get married	9.7
3. I wanted military service	4.6
4. I wanted other schooling	13.7
5. Some other reason	7.0
	58.5%

The balance wanted to go to college. The reasons they gave for not attending were:

---

25 John C. Flanagan, "Project Talent," *National Educational Association Journal,* January 1964.

26 The table does not add up to exactly 100 percent. See *Project Talent,* U. S. Office of Education, pp. 10-6 and 10-7.

1. Could not afford it	19.9%
2. Family emergency prevented	1.4
3. I was married	2.8
4. I hadn't taken the right courses	3.8
5. My grades were too low	4.3
6. I was not accepted	1.2
7. Some other reason prevented	8.2
	41.6%

One aspect of these findings should not be overlooked: they describe only what happened to high school graduates and therefore ignore the large proportion of students who fail to finish high school.

It thus appears that many extremely able persons in the United States do not have the opportunity to attain the highest positions for which their native talents fit them. Inability to obtain the required training compels many of these people to take relatively unskilled positions. *The result is a twofold loss: They never realize their potential, and society is deprived of the benefit of their capabilities.*

Up to this point, we have considered only the degree of opportunity in the United States to acquire the formal education required to develop one's productive capacities. In order to make use of their abilities, persons with the necessary training must be given an opportunity to obtain job experience. Of course, their full productive capabilities will be utilized only if they can obtain positions requiring their special skills.

Unequal and limited job opportunity characterizes important sectors of the U.S. economy. Equally qualified persons do not possess equal chances of obtaining the position for which they apply. Nepotism is commonplace. Many fathers are spurred on in their business efforts to "make a business for their children to take over." Those who "choose the right father" typically occupy better positions and obtain higher incomes than many more talented persons. Given a choice, especially in those occupations requiring considerable education and training, employers favor persons who belong to their own social group, share their political and religious convictions, are "friends of friends" or of the family, and attended the same schools.

Furthermore, as already noted, some lines of work are virtually closed to persons on the basis of considerations other than their potential economic contribution. Members of minority groups, for example, are often relegated to occupations requiring less skill than those for which they may be best suited. Members of the majority group often occupy posts for which a member of a minority group might be better equipped. As a result, society is denied output that would be produced if the best person filled each job.

No reliable quantitative estimate can possibly be made of the output lost due to insufficient and unequal opportunity in the United States. *In many respects, however, opportunities to develop one's productive capacities and to obtain suitable employment are being equalized.* The GI Bill of Rights, which permitted many servicemen to obtain academic training they would not otherwise have been able to afford, probably gave talented persons a unique opportunity to acquire the training for the more skilled jobs of which they were capable. Prejudice against minority groups seems on the decline, though it is still apparent. One factor partly offsetting these developments is that the time and cost required to become highly skilled in a trade or professions has been increasing substantially. *On the whole, it appears that the output lost because of insufficient and unequal opportunity for individuals to develop and to use their productive talents is still substantial.*

The Distribution of Personal Income

The distribution of personal income in the United States is quite unequal. Several factors determine the income that any individual receives. They are (1) his productivity—that is, his ability to produce goods that buyers want; (2) personal property holdings—that is, income in the form of profits, interest, rent, and dividends; (3) market power—the ability to raise the price one obtains by exerting economic or physical force; (4) social services obtained from the government, such as social insurance, pensions, bonuses; (5) personal and political influence—including "pull" and "contacts" that permit a person to obtain a desirable job even though there are superior candidates for it; and (6) the opportunity one has to develop his productive capabilities to the full.

The most important question about the distribution of income is this: Do we distribute income in a manner that affords maximum net satisfaction to the population as a whole? That is, after taking into account the effects of income distribution on incentive—and therefore upon total output—is income so distributed that the nation as a whole is better satisfied than it could be with any other distribution of income? As with the other questions we have raised, no statistically exact answer can be given. We can, however, examine the current situation and the changes that have taken place and perhaps draw some fairly valid conclusions.

Present-day Income Distribution

The distribution of money income among individuals and families in the United States has been measured annually in recent years with considerable accuracy.[27] Data on income distribution are among the most difficult to in-

---

[27] On the other hand, the distribution of wealth among individuals has not yet been measured or studied in this country to any satisfactory extent, although from the viewpoint of welfare and incentives the accumulation of property is undoubtedly not less important than the flow of current income.

terpret, however, and any brief summary may mislead rather than inform. In particular, we must recognize the important differences between farm and nonfarm families in their "needs for money"; the fact that many of the lowest income recipients receive funds (including gifts, charity, scholarships, special grants, and the like) that are not income from productive activities in the strict sense but which give them resources to meet their requirements; that some of the lowest income recipients are persons who are temporarily ill or out of work but virtually reassured of reemployment at a high salary; and that some persons are just starting businesses and professional practices that have great prospects of success but are still showing money losses. In addition, it is essential to distinguish between data describing income distribution before and after taxes.

To take the last point first, federal income taxes redistribute personal income to the degree indicated in Table 2. It shows, for example, that in 1962 the most prosperous 5 percent of all income recipients (with an average income of $28,482 before taxes and $23,000 after taxes) had their share of total money income of the nation reduced from 19.6 percent to 17.7 percent by the federal income tax.

Table 2. Distribution of Personal Income before and after Federal Individual Income Taxes, 1962

Family Incomes	Proportion of total personal income received	
	Before tax	After tax
Lowest fifth	4.6	4.9
Second fifth	10.9	11.5
Third fifth	16.3	16.8
Fourth fifth	22.7	23.1
Highest fifth	45.5	43.7
Of which: Top 5%	19.6	17.7

SOURCE: Jeannette M. Fitzwilliams, "Size Distribution of Income in 1963," *Survey of Current Business,* April 1964, p. 8, Table 10.

Changes in Income Distribution

Income equality in the United States has increased substantially since 1929 (see Table 3). Most of the increase took place after 1939; income distribution had stayed within a rather narrow range during the preceding twenty years.[28] Nevertheless, income remains quite unequally distributed, and a sizable proportion of the nation's families receive an extremely low income and must be considered poor. The sharpest change in income distri-

---

[28] Simon Kuznets, *Shares of Upper Income Groups in Income and Savings* (New York: National Bureau of Economic Research, 1953), p. xxxvii.

bution has taken place among the relatively small groups receiving the highest incomes. For example, whereas the richest 1 percent of the population received 12 percent of total personal income (after federal income taxes) in 1939, they received 8 percent in 1959.[29] During the same period, the top 5 percent's share of total personal income dropped from 23.7 percent to 18 percent. (As shown in Table 2, that share declined further to 17.7 percent in 1962.) It would be erroneous, however, to draw general conclusions about income distribution from data about only the very richest few in the nation.

The changes in income distribution that have taken place over the last three decades are shown more fully in Table 3, which indicates the proportion of total income received by each fifth of the population in selected years. This table shows three things: First, the top fifth of all income recipients suffered a relative decline in their share of the total national income even before income taxes were taken into account. (The decline would be even greater if the figures showed income after federal income taxes had been deducted.) Second, the proportion of total income received by the poorest members of the population has not shown a pronounced change. Third, since 1955, whatever change took place seems to be toward greater rather than less inequality.

Table 3. Distribution of Personal Income before Income Taxes in the United States, 1935-1936, 1941, 1948, 1955, 1962

Spending units arranged by size of income	Percentage of income accounted for by each fifth of the population				
	1935-1936	1941	1948	1955	1962
Lowest fifth	4	3	4	4.8	4.6
Second fifth	9	9	11	11.3	10.9
Third fifth	14	16	16	16.4	16.3
Fourth fifth	20	22	22	22.3	22.7
Highest fifth	53	50	47	45.2	45.5
All groups	100	100	100	100.0	100.0

NOTE: These data report incomes of "spending units," including as separate units both families and individuals who do not pool their incomes with their families, even though living with them, and single persons living alone.
SOURCE: Council of Economic Advisers, *Annual Economic Review,* January 1950, p. 144 and January 1951, p. 229. For 1955 and 1962, J.M. Fitzwilliams, "Size Distribution of Income in 1963," *Survey of Current Business,* April 1964, p. 8, Table 10.

We can see one of the sources of general increase in income equality by examining changes in incomes of persons in different occupations. If one

---

[29] For 1959, see H. P. Miller, *Rich Man Poor Man,* Table I-2, p. 5.

divided men into four occupational groups—professional and managerial workers, craftsmen, semiskilled factory workers, service workers and non-farm laborers—and studied the changes in their incomes between 1939 and 1961, one would find that the gaps in their incomes declined substantially. The first group, which was the highest paid in 1939, was also the highest paid in 1961; its average income increased 343 percent from over $1900 to almost $7000 a year. At the opposite extreme, service workers and non-farm laborers' incomes went from $730 in 1939 to over $3000 in 1961—an increase of 414 percent. (See Table 4.) Interestingly, as Table 5 shows, the closing of the gap took place primarily between 1939 and 1950. Since then, the highest paid group enjoyed the greatest increase in income, and the lowest paid obtained the smallest increase.

Table 4. Changes in Earnings by Occupational Groupings, 1939-1961

Year	Professional and managerial workers	Craftsmen	Semiskilled factory workers	Service workers and nonfarm laborers
1939	$1,986	$1,309	$1,007	$730
1950	3,890	3,405	2,736	2,041
1961	6,821	5,527	4,344	3,019

SOURCE: H. P. Miller, *Rich Man Poor Man* (New York: T. Y. Crowell, 1964), pp. 44-45.

Table 5. Changes in Men's Income, by Occupation, 1939-1961

(figures represent % increment during the period)

Period	Professional and managerial workers	Craftsmen	Semiskilled factory workers	Service workers and nonfarm laborers
1939-1961	243%	322%	331%	314%
1939-1950	96	160	172	180
1950-1961	75	62	59	48

SOURCE: H. P. Miller, *Rich Man Poor Man*, p. 45, Table IV-2b.

Position of Lowest Income Recipients

The information describing general income distribution reveals one disconcerting fact: The poorest members of the community did not improve their *relative* position, while the richest members lost ground. Put differently, the problem of *relative* poverty has not been alleviated by the income redistribution that has taken place. (However, their *level* of income did improve, as shall be explained, by the general rise in total income.) Despite the general improvement in absolute income levels, there remains a large number of families and persons in the United States who are truly poor and suffering great privations because of low money income. For example, in 1962, approximately 12 percent of all families and unattached individuals received incomes of under $2000. Although some of these families may have had sources of funds other than current income, included among these nearly 7 million families were a great number who were poor by any standard. Although some strides have thus been made in reducing extreme riches, the problem of income inequality remains. More important, the nation continues to face a serious problem of extreme poverty.

Table 6.   Average Income of Families in Constant Dollars, 1929-1962

(after federal income taxes)

1929	$4,200	1952	5,200
1935	3,700	1955	5,700
1941	4,400	1960	6,200
1946	5,200	1961	6,300
1947	4,900	1962	6,400

SOURCE: H. P. Miller, *Rich Man Poor Man,* p. 26.

Social Services and Welfare Expenditures

One factor to be considered in estimating a family's income, as already indicated, is the amount of social services obtained from the government. In every country, all individuals receive some valuable services without paying for them directly. These are generally called social services and are provided collectively through government action. The distribution of social services varies according to individuals' needs and incomes. Even the very rich receive social services, without specific payment. Included in this category are: police protection, military defense, public education, roads, parks, fire protection, use of waterways, and city sanitation and improvement. Of course, the very poor will ordinarily receive more social services than the rich. They may obtain unemployment insurance, free medical care in city-owned hospitals, low-cost public housing (this is not free but subsidized, so it might be considered partly free), some free food (under the stamp plan), and the like.

In some nations, the amount and proportion of personal income in the form of social services is very substantial. As we shall explain, social services represent an estimated 31.5 percent of total personal income in the Soviet Union. They take the form of heavily subsidized housing, free medi-

Social Welfare Expenditures under Public Programs, Fiscal Years 1940, 1950 and 1961

Millions of Dollars

Program	Total Expenditures			From Federal Funds			From State and Local Funds		
	1961	1950	1940	1961	1950	1940	1961	1950	1940
Total	57,862.4	23,201.1	8,702.2	27,112.1	10,028.4	3,291.2	30,750.3	13,172.7	5,190.6
As per cent of gross national product	*11.1%*	*8.2%*	*8.7%*	*5.2%*	*3.5%*	*3.3%*	*5.9%*	*4.6%*	*5.2%*
Social insurance	22,357.2	4,911.2	1,216.4	15,992.6	2,059.6	350.2	6,364.6	2,851.6	866.2
Old-age, survivors and disability insurance	12,160.7	784.1	28.1	12,160.7	784.1	28.1			
Railroad retirement	991.8	304.4	115.7	991.8	304.4	115.7			
Public employee retirement	2,870.2	743.4	254.5	1,701.2	433.4	107.5	1,169.0	310.0	147.0
Unemployment insurance and employment service	4,310.3	2,230.1	551.7	801.9	361.9	65.8	3,508.4	1,868.2	485.9
Railroad unemployment insurance	213.4	119.6	18.9	213.4	119.6	18.9			
Railroad temporary disability insurance	58.0	31.1		58.0	31.1				
State temporary disability insurance, total	382.1	72.3					382.1	72.3	
Hospital and medical benefits[1]	43.5	2.2					43.5	2.2	
Workmen's compensation, total	1,370.7	626.2	247.5	65.6	25.1	14.2	1,305.1	601.1	233.3
Hospitalization and medical benefits[1]	440.0	193.0	90.0	8.7	5.2	5.2	431.3	187.8	84.8
Public aid	4,441.0	2,496.2	3,598.7	2,333.9	1,103.2	2,245.9	2,107.0	1,393.0	1,352.8
Public assistance[2]	4,301.0	2,490.2	1,124.3	2,193.9	1,097.2	281.1	2,107.0	1,393.0	843.2
Other[3]	140.0	6.0	2,474.4	140.0	6.0	1,964.8			509.6
Health and medical programs[4]	4,757.0	2,344.3	697.3	1,788.0	661.2	99.3	2,969.0	1,683.1	598.0
Hospital and medical care	3,093.0	1,506.0	460.0	880.0	383.0	50.0	2,205.0	1,123.0	410.0
Civilian programs	2,314.9	1,174.0	415.0	109.9	51.0	5.0	2,205.0	1,123.0	410.0
Defense Department and Medicare	778.1	332.0	45.0	778.1	332.0	45.0			
Maternal and child health services	152.4	29.8	13.8	39.4	20.1	7.8	113.0	9.7	6.0
Medical research[5]	565.2	51.3	3.0	539.2	51.3	3.0	26.0		
Other public health activities[6]	445.1	328.4	179.5	88.1	80.0	37.5	357.0	248.4	142.0
Medical facilities construction	501.3	428.8	41.0	233.3	126.8	1.0	268.0	302.0	40.0
Defense Department	28.2	a	a	28.2	a	a		a	a
Other	473.1	428.8	41.0	205.1	126.8	1.0	268.0	302.0	40.0
Other welfare services	1,248.1	401.6	114.1	435.9	166.7	9.7	812.1	234.9	104.4
Vocational rehabilitation, total	112.8	30.0	4.1	73.0	21.0	2.0	39.8	9.0	2.1
Medical rehabilitation[1]	20.4	7.4	.4	12.9	3.7	.2	7.5	3.7	.2
Institutional and other care[7]	506.9	107.9	65.0	39.9	21.7	6.1	467.0	86.2	58.9
School lunch	403.9	158.8	n.a.	308.9	119.7	n.a.	94.9	39.0	n.a.
Child welfare[8]	224.5	104.9	45.0	14.1	4.2	1.6	210.4	100.7	43.4
Veterans' programs[9]	5,278.1	6,380.8	535.0	5,193.1	5,918.8	535.0	84.3	462.0	
Pensions and compensation	3,690.1	2,092.8	447.8	3,690.1	2,092.8	447.8			
Health and medical services	1,007.3	745.8	86.3	1,007.3	745.8	86.3			
Hospital and medical care	932.5	585.9	72.1	932.5	585.9	72.1			
Hospital construction	53.7	156.2	14.1	53.7	156.2	14.1			
Medical research	21.1	3.7	.1	21.1	3.7	.1			
Education	252.9	2,689.1		252.9	2,689.1				
Welfare and other	327.8	853.1	1.0	243.4	391.1	1.0	84.3	462.0	

Education.........................	19,585.3	6,655.0	2,536.6	1,208.9	106.9	47.0	18,376.4	6,458.1	2,489.6
Elementary and secondary, total........	16,888.5	5,745.7	2,323.4	512.1	63.9	32.5	16,376.4	5,681.8	2,290.9
Construction¹..................	3,107.8	1,018.7	258.0	71.6	5.2	n.a.	3,036.2	1,013.5	258.0
Higher education and other, total........	2,696.7	909.3	213.2	696.7	43.0	14.5	2,000.0	866.3	198.7
Construction¹..................	352.9	310.5	20.6	26.9	5.9	n.a.	326.0	304.6	20.6
Public housing...................	196.0	12.0	4.2	159.1	12.0	4.2	36.9	..	..

Note: Data represent expenditures from public funds (general and special) and trust accounts, and other expenditures under public law; exclude transfers to such accounts and loans; include capital outlay for hospitals, public elementary and secondary schools, and publicly controlled higher education; include administrative expenditures. Fiscal years ended June 30 for Federal Government, most states, and some localities; for other states and localities fiscal years cover various 12-month periods ended in the specified year. The annual statistical series on social welfare expenditures in the United States, together with a review and analysis of the data, appear each year in the October or November issue of the *Social Security Bulletin*

1 Included in total shown directly above; excludes administrative expenditures, not separately available but included for entire program in preceding line

2 Old-age assistance, aid to dependent children, aid to the blind, aid to the permanently and totally disabled, and, from state and local funds, general assistance. Public assistance total in 1940 includes $1 million administrative costs and FERA funds for which distribution by source of funds is not available. Public assistance total in 1961 includes $588.9 million of vendor medical payments, $253.5 million from federal funds and $335.4 million from state and local funds

3 Value of surplus food distribution to needy persons, work program earnings, and other emergency aid programs

4 Excludes expenditures for domiciliary care (in institutions other than mental or tuberculosis) included under institutional care; excludes health and medical services provided in connection with veterans' programs, public education, public assistance, workmen's compensation, state temporary disability insurance and vocational rehabilitation (included in total expenditures shown for those programs); also excludes direct expenditures for international health activities and certain subordinate medical program expenditures such as those of the Federal Aviation Agency, Bureau of Narcotics, Bureau of Mines, National Park Service, U. S. Civil Service Commission, etc.

5 Medical research expenditures of the Public Health Service, Food and Drug Administration, Atomic Energy Commission and the Department of Defense

6 Excludes expenditures for water supply, sanitation services and sewage disposal but includes regulatory and administrative expenditures in connection with these activities. Also includes expenditures for medical equipment and supplies in civil defense

7 Includes expenditures for homes for adults (not including amounts shown under *veterans'* programs) and for dependent or neglected children, and value of surplus foods for nonprofit institutions

8 Excludes expenditures of courts and public institutions serving children, public day care centers and appropriations made directly by legislatures to voluntary agencies or institutions

9 Excludes federal bonus payments, appropriations to government life insurance trust fund and accounts of several small revolving funds. State and local data represent state expenditures for bonus and other payments and services for veterans; local data not available. Burial awards included with pensions and compensation. Vocational rehabilitation, specially adapted homes and automobiles for disabled veterans, counseling, beneficiaries' travel, loan guarantees and domiciliary care classified as welfare and other readjustment allowances not included here but classified under *Social Insurance* as *unemployment insurance and employment service*

a—Included in total shown directly above   n.a.—Not available   Source: Social Security Administration

529

From National Industrial Conference Board, *Economic Almanac, 1964.*

cal care, and education through the Ph.D. level. Some governments—such as the French—provide bonuses to those who have large families, support the aged, the sick, and the injured, and provide "protection from the cradle to the grave." Nations that provide many social services in large amounts are sometimes described as welfare states—a term of opprobrium in the United States. Let us take a brief look at the amount and form of social services currently available in the United States through the federal government and examine the trends in such services.[30]

One essential aspect of social services will be omitted entirely in the following discussion—that is, the conditions under which they are made available. We shall ignore the important and complex question of "eligibility" to receive social services and consider only the sums expended to provide them. One possibility that should not be overlooked is that some persons who receive social services actually are not entitled to receive them.

It is difficult to identify expenditures that are purely "welfare." One can find a welfare aspect in almost every government outlay; indeed one would expect that to be the case. If one confines his attention to expenditures explicitly providing services to help the needy, he can make substantial progress—even though he cannot obtain a precise measure.

The Social Security Administration has prepared an illuminating, though not exact, tabulation of social welfare expenditures under public programs for the years 1940, 1950, and 1961. It shows (see Table 7) that in 1961 the combined expenditures of federal, state, and local governments for social welfare amounted to 11.1 percent of the gross national product. The biggest items were social insurance (over $22 billion) and education (over $19.5 billion). These two items represented almost three quarters of the total expenditures of $57.8 billion. State and local expenditures accounted for somewhat more than those of the federal government.

Social welfare expenditures have been increasing in recent years. They more than doubled in dollar amounts between 1950 and 1961 and rose from 8.2 to 11.1 percent of gross national product over that period. Federal welfare expenditures have become a steadily larger source of social welfare expenditure over the years covered by this study.

Missing from this tabulation are such items as police and fire protection, the provision of recreational facilities, and assistance to farmers. These omissions, while notable, are not serious. (Many persons would not even regard them as social welfare expenditures.)

---

[30] John K. Galbraith in his very interesting, though possibly premature, book entitled *The Affluent Society,* describes social services as social consumption, and calls for a very substantial increase in such consumption since, as he sees it, the nation is already affluent.

Table 8. Average Annual Rates of Growth of GNP, Seven Major Countries, 1950-1960

(percent)

Country	1950-1955	1955-1960	1950-1960
United States	4.3	2.3	3.3
Soviet Union[a]	7.0	6.5	6.8
France	4.5	4.2	4.3
West Germany	9.0	6.0	7.5
England	2.6	2.7	2.6
Japan	7.1	9.4	8.8
Italy	6.0	5.9	5.9

NOTE: [a] unofficial estimate.
SOURCES: Organization for European Economic Cooperation, *General Statistics,* July-September 1961; Bank of Japan, *Economic Statistics of Japan, 1961;* U. S. Department of Commerce, Business and Defense Service Administration, *The Gross National Product in the Soviet Union: Comparative Growth Rates* (Washington, D.C.: Government Printing Office, 1963).

Progressiveness of the American Economy

Progressiveness and growth (related but different things) have received heavy emphasis during the last decade or so. It might be said that a major issue of the 1960 presidential election was "economic growth." One also sees many detailed comparisons of the rate at which different nations have expanded output in current publications. *These comparisons show the United States in a very unfavorable light;* its total production is rising more slowly than almost every major nation in the world. (See Table 8.)

To assess an economic system, one should consider whether it provides the highest living standards possible *under existing circumstances* and whether its output grows more or less steadily. An economy could provide a high standard of living *for a while* by wasteful use of natural resources, failure to develop labor skills, neglect of technological development and abstention from investment in plant and equipment. These policies would, in time, make future output far lower, however, than it might have been.

The simple arithmetic of economic growth is most illuminating. One might not be impressed with the difference between, say, an annual increase in output of 2.0 and 2.5 percent. From one year to the next, this increase would be nominal. However, a 2 percent increase in output *per person* will double total output in about thirty years; a rate of 2.5 percent increase will do so in about twenty-five years. These figures reveal the importance of modest increases in output when one thinks in terms of twenty- or thirty-year periods. Economies that fail to grow will, in a relatively short time, fall far behind those that do. For example, if we estimate the 1964 per capita income in the USSR to be approximately one half what it is in the United States and if we take the annual *per capita* rate of growth in the United States to be 2 percent (which is about what it has been between 1950 and 1963) and that in the USSR to be 5 percent (which is about what it has been during the same period), then the United States will be overtaken in *per capita* output by the USSR by 1975.

This arithmetic contains some significant implications. Mainly, it suggests that a country would be unwise to jeopardize its chances to improve productivity in order, say, to make income distribution somewhat more equitable. In time, if the economy were made less progressive, the condition of *even the poorest* members of the community would have been worsened in comparison with their condition in a more progressive economy with a less equal income distribution. One must not misuse this argument to depreciate the importance of *all* efforts to equalize incomes; greater equality of income may not reduce the rate of economic growth. On the contrary, if increased income equality permits—as it might—the fuller utilization of the latent skills and ingenuity of the underprivileged members of the community, it would speed, rather than impede, economic growth.

The Perverse Effects of Competition

Early in this chapter, we sketched the rationale of a free enterprise economy. Mainly, we showed how rivalry among competitors and freedom of entrepreneurs to pursue profit opportunities lead to speedy satisfaction of customers' demands, a rapid erosion of high profits, and pressures to produce at minimum cost. Now that some of the features of the U.S. economy have been explored, it is possible to deal quite directly with the effects of competition and free enterprise *in practice*.

Granted that many sectors of the U.S. economy are not intensely competitive, let us concern ourselves with those sectors that are admittedly highly competitive. Foremost among these are: agriculture—especially grain and cotton farming; the cotton textile industry; most industries that produce apparel; most divisions of the food processing industry; and most retailing trades. Does one find, upon close inspection, that the competitive industries substantially achieve the advantages claimed for competition and free enterprise? Or, does one find that *under realistic circumstances* they have important adverse effects?

One cannot evaluate even a single industry thoroughly in the confines of a book of this size, let alone in a few paragraphs. Consequently, we must be content with broad and oversweeping generalizations. *By and large, the most competitive industries in the United States have been the least progressive;* that is, they have developed new products, new techniques, new marketing approaches more slowly and later than much less competitive industries characterized by large firms. In addition, they have developed chronic overcapacity and, in general, have not been models for the rest of the economy. This conclusion should not be interpreted to mean that monopoly is superior to competition; extreme monopoly is also wasteful and unprogressive—though relatively few examples are to be found of persistent monopoly in the United States that has not been regulated by the government.

But, to return to the point, competition turns out to be far less appealing in practice than in theory. One way of explaining this is to identify some of the perverse effects of competition—that is, ways in which competition works toward waste, high prices, inefficiency, and other undesirable consequences. The following is intended as a partial list:

1. Competition, when extreme, often leads sellers to depreciate the quality of products in ways that consumers cannot recognize. In that way, they can lower cost and offer lower prices than their competitors. Consumers, however, obtain products of inferior quality, not worth the lower price they pay.

2. Extreme competition leads to overcapacity, for when profitable opportunities arise and are widely recognized, many more firms may enter the industry than the demand can support at prices that would cover costs.

3. Competition leads to secrecy in many ways. Firms do not announce new products until they are ready to be introduced. Consequently, some customers will buy products just before they become outmoded or technically obsolete.

4. Competition leads to extremely frequent product changes in an effort to persuade customers that important product improvements have been made when that is not the case at all. These changes often involve substantial but unnecessary costs.

5. Competition sometimes takes the form of manufacturers' offering resellers of their products higher margins of profit in order to "push" their brands over competitive brands also carried by the same resellers. In this way, competition serves to push prices up, rather than down.

6. By constantly putting the inefficient or obsolete firms out of business, competition produces at least temporary unemployment of those workers and facilities that work in such firms or trades.

7. Competition frequently leads to manifold duplication of research efforts and expenditures.

Research and Development

Progressiveness and economic growth call primarily for new production techniques and new products. The conscious production of new ideas is termed "research," and it is generally agreed that most worthwhile new ideas are no longer discovered by accident or by sheer inspiration.[31] At the base of almost all important recent developments is painstaking and expensive research. Consequently, we must expect a fairly close connection between research effort and progressiveness. How is the volume of research effort determined in the United States? How do our expenditures for research compare with those of other countries?

Before discussing these questions, we should clear up one common source of misunderstanding. Nations with the most "modern" methods of production are not necessarily the most progressive. Modern methods may result from the possession of large financial resources rather than from the generation of new ideas. Prosperous nations often can purchase and carry out developments made by other nations better than those nations themselves. Also, highly efficient methods of production that give large output per person may be very uneconomical. That is, they may involve much higher costs (economic and money costs) than more primitive methods. Many poor countries waste their resources because they simply imitate the production methods employed in prosperous countries.

Research effort in the United States has undergone an almost incredible increase since World War II. Whereas prior to 1941 annual expenditures for research and development amounted to about $570 million—far less than 1 percent of the gross national product (even this represented a substantial increase in government expenditures inspired by the threat of war) —by 1961 they had shot up to almost $15 billion—2.8 percent of GNP.[32] Even if one allows for the increase in population, the growth in national income, and rising prices, research activity has expanded faster than just about any other facet of the U.S. economy. Despite this rapid growth, one must nevertheless ask whether the research efforts made in the United States are sufficient and whether they are devoted to the uses most likely to increase output and growth.

A distinguished group of scientists and government administrators made a study of this subject in 1947. Their conclusions, which follow, describe

---

31 Dr. Alfred N. Whitehead considered the discovery of the "art of invention" the greatest invention of the nineteenth century. He was referring to the fact that modern inventions most commonly arise from a routine and systematic application of elaborate mathematical formulas. See A. N. Whitehead, *Science and the Modern World* (New York: The Macmillan Company, 1925).

32 See *Economic Almanac,* National Industrial Conference Board, New York, 1964, p. 98.

the history of research efforts in the U.S., before the great transformation took place following World War II.

1. In the past our country has made less than its proportionate contribution to the progress of basic science. Instead, we have imported our theory from abroad and concentrated on its application to concrete and immediate problems. This was true even in the case of the atomic bomb.
2. The Soviet Union's 1947 budget, for example, is reported to provide $1.2 billion for research and development. The Soviet national income is far smaller than ours, but its research and development expenditure is about equal to ours.
3. As a nation, we devote far too small a proportion of our total income to research and development activities. Moreover, our expenditures are overly concentrated in applied research and development to the neglect of basic research. "The nation could profitably devote more than 1 per cent (of the national income) to these purposes; it cannot safely spend less." [33]

Thus, the record of the U.S. economy in the field of research and development was not at all distinguished during most of the nation's history. Free enterprise and the price system did not place a high premium on pushing back the frontiers of knowledge.

The role of the United States in technical research changed sharply following World War II. A variety of factors—mainly the huge national defense budget, the stress on new weapons and space exploration, and the quest for peaceful uses of atomic energy; the dramatic scientific achievements by the USSR and its manifest superiority in certain fields, particularly in rocketry; plus tax incentives for private corporations to engage in research and development—saw research activities boom. The United States has become clearly the leading spender for research—both relatively and in absolute terms—in the world. The best data available (still not precise by any means) shows that in the United States approximately 2.8 percent of GNP is devoted to research and development; in the UK the figure is 2.1 percent, in the USSR and France, 2.0 percent.[34]

Even when the American economy was not generating new technical ideas to the extent either possible or desirable, it was the world leader in assimilating and putting to use the basic research findings of the entire world. This phase of technical progress must not be depreciated. Pure research is doubtless the most glamorous and potentially valuable source of new knowledge and the basis for new techniques. But a huge gap exists between what is known and what is put to active use. It is in this latter

---

[33] "Science and Public Policy," report by the President's Scientific Research Board, August 1947, I, pp. 4-5, 5-6, and 26.
[34] National Industrial Conference Board.

sphere that the United States has been outstanding—at least up to the present.

It is impossible to measure all aspects of economic progressiveness. Estimates of the rise in productivity—the extent to which methods of production become more efficient—can be made. These will be reviewed for the United States.

The rise in labor productivity of U.S. industry (the private sector) was about 2.3 percent between 1909 and 1963; in recent years, the increase has been substantially greater. (Between 1947 and 1963, the rise was 3.2 percent; between 1960 and 1963, 3.6 percent.) An annual increase of 3 percent in productivity would mean a doubling of output *per person* in approximately twenty-three years. (The annual rise must be "compounded.") In recent years labor productivity has risen far more in the agricultural than the nonagricultural sector. For example, the increase in agriculture between 1947 and 1963 was 6.1 percent per annum, whereas it was 2.6 percent in nonagricultural activities.[35]

As indicated earlier, most nations that have made a start toward industrialization have been able to increase productivity much more rapidly than the United States. In part, they have been able to do so by imitating our production methods, and in part, they seem to have generated efforts and created special arrangements (some of which will be discussed later when we describe the French economy) that accelerate economic growth. Nevertheless, the United States economy certainly cannot be described as unprogressive. From a relatively mediocre position, it has become a world leader in this respect. But its rise to eminence can not be attributed solely to the price system or free enterprise. Research activity is a central core of the government subsystem of the U.S. economy. As Table 9 indicates, almost two thirds of current R & D activities are paid for directly by the federal government.

ACHIEVEMENTS OF THE AMERICAN ECONOMY

Our discussion of the economy of the United States thus far has been inconclusive. At every point, we found no reliable criteria that could be applied to evaluate its performance; even where criteria did exist, the data needed to apply them were lacking. As a result, the preceding discussion has consisted primarily of a listing of its shortcomings and achievements without any attempt to make over-all judgments. Is there no way in which we can summarize the combined influence of all aspects of the present-day American economy?

---

[35] National Industrial Conference Board.

Table 9. Sources of Funds for Research and Development, 1953-1962

(in millions of dollars)

Business year	Federal government	Private industry	Universities and colleges	Other nonprofit institutions	Total
1953-54	2,740	2,240	130	40	5,150
1954-55	3,070	2,365	140	45	5,620
1955-56	3,670	2,510	155	55	6,390
1956-57	5,095	3,325	180	70	8,670
1957-58	6,390	3,450	190	70	10,100
1958-59	7,170	3,680	190	90	11,130
1959-60	8,320	4,060	200	100	12,680
1960-61 (prel.)	9,010	4,550	210	120	13,890
1961-62 (prel.)	9,650	4,705	230	155	14,740

SOURCE: *Statistical Abstract of the United States 1963*, p. 543.

Standards for Judging an Economy as a Whole

Economic welfare ordinarily is measured by the output of an economy for each person who must be supported. This measure has important shortcomings, but it is the best available and so will be used here.

Personal experience indicates that the average American has far more goods and services than he had even fifteen years ago. And, looking back over a longer period, the level of living in this country has soared. That it has increased greatly over long periods of time attests to the ability of our economy to improve living conditions. Such evidence cannot be used to demonstrate that the economy is "efficient," however. To judge the efficiency of anything requires a comparison of alternatives. We must compare what was done under our system with what might have been achieved under another system. Though such comparisons cannot be made easily, if we are to evaluate our economy, we must make them as best we can.

Two types of comparison might be made: comparisons of absolute levels of living and of rates of increase in levels of living. Overlooking the difficulties of measuring living levels in nations that consume different kinds of products, we must nevertheless ask whether differences in living levels—or in their rate of growth—are attributable entirely to differences in the efficiency of economic systems. Nations differ in many other respects. The very high living levels in the United States may be due to circumstances other than its economic system; similarly, the slowing down in its rate of growth in recent decades also may not be the responsibility of the economic system. One can be certain that living levels and the rate at which they change are influenced by a variety of economic and noneconomic circumstances.

Advantages Enjoyed by the United States

The United States enjoys the following advantages over most of the world's developed nations, possibly accounting for all or part of our high level of living. First, the United States is well endowed with such natural gifts as rich deposits of raw materials, rivers for easy transportation, excellent water-power sources, highly fertile soil, and a temperate climate. Second, the United States is free from the ravages and losses of war. While most other nations had to remain prepared against military aggression for more than a century, the United States maintained only insignificant token military forces. During the last two world wars, many nations in the world were heavily damaged by direct military conflict; the United States, on the other hand, greatly expanded its industrial resources during those wars. Combat losses, generally concentrated among the cream of a population, were a far smaller percentage of the U.S. population in World Wars I and II than they were in the other belligerent nations. Third, most Americans are descendants of those venturesome and intelligent persons who saw in emigration a chance for advancement. These persons risked a dangerous and acutely uncomfortable voyage to these shores; many of them undertook a hazardous journey within the United States to a dangerous frontier; many assimilated an unfamiliar language and culture. Those who survived these ordeals probably formed a more hardy and industrious population than was to be found in most other nations. Fourth, the large number of immigrants who settled in the United States represented an important economic gain, because many millions of immigrants were reared at the expense of other countries and came to the United States only after they were economically productive. These four advantages are surely not trifling. However, their precise importance cannot be measured.

In one respect, perhaps, the United States has suffered a slight disadvantage compared with other countries. Since the beginning of World War II, it has given very substantial sums to other nations for a blend of humanitarian and expedient reasons. When these sums are totaled for the period 1945 to 1962, they amount to a very large figure—specifically $71.8 billion in grants and $11.3 billion in credits (outstanding in 1962).[36] For the total period, however, they represent less than 1 percent of the nation's annual gross national product, and it is, consequently, unlikely that they have affected the performance of the U.S. economy perceptibly.

---

[36] *Statistical Abstract of the U.S. 1963,* p. 859.

Comparison of Levels of Living

Table 10 presents the best available indicator of the differences in levels of living that exist among various countries. *According to these data, the United States enjoys by far the highest level of living in the world.*

There are great difficulties, some of which cannot be fully overcome, in comparing living conditions in different countries. Such comparisons, therefore, must be considered only rough approximations. It is generally agreed that Table 10 exaggerates the margin of superiority of American living levels over those in other countries.

Comparison of Rate of Increase in Levels of Living

Available data do not permit a reliable comparison of rates at which levels of living have increased in different countries. Very few nations even measure their present total output accurately. In the United States the annual increase in per capita real disposable income between 1929 and 1956 averaged about 1.5 percent. This rate of increase is smaller than it was in the late 1800s and falls substantially below what is being achieved in some other nations—capitalist and other—at the present time. However, there is some reason to expect that the rate at which living levels improve in other countries will decline as these levels reach high ground.

Table 10.   Seventy-two Countries Classified by Size of Per Capita National Income, 1962

(in U.S. dollars)

Per Capita Income	Country	Per Capita Income	Country
$50-$99	1. Burma		15. Paraguay
	2. Indonesia		16. United Arab Republic
	3. Uganda		17. Brazil (1960)
	4. Tanganyika		18. Ecuador
	5. South Korea		19. Rhodesia and Nyasaland
	6. Pakistan		20. Communist China (1959)
	7. India		21. Morocco
	8. Congo		
	9. Kenya	$150-$199	22. Guatemala
	10. Nigeria		23. Syria
	11. Sudan		24. Malaysia
	12. Thailand		25. Tunisia
			26. Colombia
$100-$149	13. Philippines		27. Peru
	14. Ceylon		28. Iran

Table 10 (*continued*)

Per Capita Income	Country	Per Capita Income	Country
	29. Libya	$700-$999	51. Poland
	30. Honduras		52. Israel
	31. Turkey		53. Austria
			54. Hungary
$200-$299	32. Jordan		55. Netherlands
	33. Ghana		56. Finland
	34. Albania		
	35. Nicaragua	$1000-$1399	57. Iceland
	36. Portugal		58. Norway
	37. Yugoslavia		59. East Germany
			60. Belgium
$300-$399	38. Argentina		61. Soviet Union
	39. Cuba (1958)		62. Czechoslovakia
	40. Mexico		63. France
	41. Spain		64. England
	42. Greece		65. West Germany
			66. Denmark
$400-$499	43. Chile		67. Australia
	44. South Africa		68. New Zealand
	45. Japan		
$500-$699	46. Venezuela	$1400-$1999	69. Canada
	47. Bulgaria		70. Switzerland
	48. Romania		71. Sweden
	49. Italy		
	50. Ireland	$2450	72. United States

SOURCE: Computed from data in the *Monthly Bulletin of Statistics* (United Nations), August 1964, pp. 1-4, 158-159, 164-166. National income of the Communist countries was converted into the Western concept, which includes services. Official exchange rates were used in case of the Communist countries and free market rates in case of the non-Communist countries (whenever available).

The salient fact nevertheless remains that the American economy does provide the highest per capita output of material goods. Moreover, this large output does not arise from very long hours of work or the employment of large numbers of women and young and aged persons. The American economy clearly is among the most productive in the world and continues to grow in productiveness as Table 11 indicates. Industrial production in the United States has increased faster than in many other nations—if one measures from most interwar years. However, comparisons based upon output increases after World War II show an opposite result.

Table 11.   Index Numbers of Industrial Production
(1958 = 100)

	1938	1948	1953	1955	1957	1959	1961	1962
United States	33	73	97	103	107	113	117	126
USSR	18	27	59	74	91	111	133	146
France	52	55	72	84	97	101	114	120
United Kingdom	67	74	89	99	101	105	114	115
Sweden	52	74	83	92	98	106	120	122
Canada	32	62	84	92	101	108	112	121
Italy	43	44	70	84	96	111	142	156
India	56	64	74	85	96	108	129	138
Japan	57	22	60	69	99	124	186	201
Mexico	—	55	68	81	96	108	122	128
Israel	—	—	—	81	91	114	150	169
West Germany	51	27	66	85	97	108	125	131
Brazil	24	42	63	76	86	113	139	147

SOURCE: United Nations, *Statistical Yearbook, 1963*.

Summary Evaluation of the American Economy

Individuals can, and indeed do, violently disagree about the importance of individual defects in the present American economy. Lacking reliable measures of performance, these disagreements cannot be resolved. There cannot be any disagreement, however, about the necessity of providing some reliable measure of performance—whether it be altogether new or simply an improvement in the indicator we now use. Imperfect as our criteria for judgment are and even though only limited evidence exists on many points, it is clear that our economy is very productive. It is equally clear that considerable opportunity for improvement exists.

Several defects of the American economy can be traced to either of two basic conditions: insufficient competition and susceptibility to depression and inflation. These conditions, which are not new and may actually have declined in severity, have undesirable effects in many spheres. For example, when rivalry among individual firms is blunted by whatever means, businessmen feel no irresistible pressure to produce the things that consumers want. Their market position sometimes is so strong that they can compel the consumer to accept whatever they choose to offer him. Similarly due to the weakness of competion, some businessmen are not compelled to use the most productive methods available and are not even forced to keep abreast of technological developments. Also, some firms have grown to huge proportions—occasionally by superior efficiency, but no less often by cooperation or collusion or by the use of rough-and-ready market practices. They often are able to treat their suppliers, labor, and distributors with relatively little regard.

As a rough rule, the price system and capitalism are efficient to the extent that rivalry is unrestrained—save in ways in which the public might be injured. This rule can be derived directly from the rationale underlying the American economy. It makes sense only to the extent that keen rivalry operates in markets for the sale of goods and services. To a considerable, but not accurately measurable, extent, American product and labor markets are shot through with monopolistic arrangements and with conventional methods of doing business that represent serious departures from unbridled competition.

The second major shortcoming of the American economic system, already mentioned but deserving greater emphasis, is its instability. The susceptibility of the American economy to business cycles—depression, recession, but also inflation—is possibly its greatest defect. Various defects of the American economy beyond the obvious direct waste of manpower through idleness can be traced to economic instability. Business cycles color the attitudes of businessmen, for example, and discourage investment that might substantially improve the efficiency of production. Individuals are compelled to accept almost any type of employment during depression and may for a variety of reasons fail to shift to occupations in which they would be more productive. Persons who are capable of acquiring the highest type of skill may be compelled to accept employment as unskilled workers because they reached maturity during a depression and their parents were unable to finance additional training for them. In these and many other ways, business cycles prevent the American economy from realizing its full potential efficiency.

Several measures have been devised to reduce the likelihood that the economy will suffer a major depression; also, changes have been made in the structure of the economy that may reduce its vulnerability to downswings. Just how effective these measures and structural changes will prove to be is a matter of conjecture. Doubtless much more is known about depression's causes than ever before, and there is growing readiness to apply remedies that were politically unfeasible not long ago. On the other hand, as the nation's total output has grown, so that a larger proportion represents optional purchases and more of the national output consists of highly durable products, permitting buyers to defer purchases without great sacrifice, the economy may have become increasingly vulnerable.

The highly disturbed state of the world economy makes hazardous any projection of the unparalleled stability of business in the United States since world War II. *It may turn out that the dread business cycle has been conquered or at least tamed. At this writing, it seems prudent to regard the U.S. economy as vulnerable to cumulative cyclical changes, sometimes resulting in depression and sometimes in inflation.*

It must be emphasized that all other known economic systems also fail to unleash the full productive efforts of individuals and business organizations. They too, therefore, suffer from the equivalent of imperfect competition. Economic instability, however, seems more characteristic of the United States than of the Soviet Union and France. This defect, however, may be amenable to correction. Virtually every elementary economics textbook describes a variety of measures by which cyclical fluctuations would be checked. Moreover, these measures are altogether consistent with the underlying rationale and principles of a free enterprise economy.

Somewhat related to the instability of the U.S. economy is the persistence of particular forms of unemployment. By the early 1960s it had become clear that certain types of workers could not find jobs in the numbers that such jobs were being sought. In particular, unskilled and semiskilled workers—and more especially those who belonged to minority groups or were young—found jobs very hard to get. There seemed to be a pool of unemployment representing about 5 percent of the total labor force; though members of this pool were not always the same persons, many did find themselves out of work for many months at a stretch.

Another shortcoming of the American economy—one that it shares with some others—is an agricultural problem. Paradoxically, the chief difficulty with American agriculture can be traced largely to excessive output, the result of rapid increases in productivity (though a large number of farms are relatively inefficient, as has been shown). With the exception of the years during and immediately after World War II, American agriculture has been afflicted with a condition of excessive output *relative to existing moneyed demand.* (However, farm output is not excessive relative to the need for food in this country.) As a result, farm crops as a group have sold at prices so low that many farmers do not obtain a decent reward for their efforts. To meet this situation, Congress has subsidized farmers by price supports and nonrecourse loans; in 1956, it undertook a "Soil Bank" program whose purpose is to take some farmland out of active cultivation.

Poverty is another problem. It is not easily defined, mainly because it is a psychological, or relative, state rather than a directly measurable condition. In his stirring book, *The Other America,* Michael Harrington deals with the problem of poverty in great depth and very perceptively.[37] He defines the

---

[37] See Michael Harrington, *The Other America* (New York: The Macmillan Company, 1962).

poor as "the dispossessed in terms of what the rest of the nation enjoys." They are to him, "internal exiles" who almost inevitably develop attitudes of defeat and pessimism and who are therefore excluded from taking advantage of new opportunities. The poor are "those who are denied the minimum levels of health, housing, food and education that our present stage of scientific knowledge specifies as necessary for life as it is now lived in the United States." These people "live on the fringe, the margin. They watch the movies and read the magazines of affluent America, and these tell them that they are internal exiles." Given this concept of poverty, with which the authors agree, poverty can increase in severity even while the poor receive larger incomes; whether a person's income makes him poor or rich depends upon what others have and what it is possible for him to have.

Many estimates have been made of the proportion of U.S. families that are poor. They vary widely. Harrington sets the figure at between 20 and 25 percent during 1958-1959. He writes that, "From my point of view, they number between 40,000,000 and 50,000,000 human beings." [38] Lampman estimates that 19 percent of the population (or 32 million persons) were poor in those years. The AFL-CIO estimate concluded that 41 million or 24 percent of the population had demonstrably substandard incomes.

Congress passed, by a slim majority, a bill in 1964 designed to attack this problem, calling for an expenditure of less than $1 billion. Although this legislation represents progress, it can scarcely do more than dent the problem. Its legislative history also suggests that the population has relatively little interest in and feeling of responsibility for the poor.

One facet of poverty in the United States is deeply entrenched and has many unfortunate sides. It may be described as the Negro problem. We shall comment here only on its chief aspects: pay scales, economic opportunity, and unemployment. (Later, we shall touch on some of the political, social, and psychological aspects of this problem.) Despite substantial improvement in relative income position since the late 1930s, the incomes of Negroes are very substantially below those of whites. In 1939 the average (median) wage and salary income of nonwhite males was about two fifths of the average white income; in 1960 it was almost three fifths. Though narrowing, the difference remains great. Most of this improvement took place as a direct result of World War II. These data suggest that when the demand for labor is very strong, discriminatory patterns tend to break down.

Unemployment falls disproportionately upon the Negro. During the fifties and sixties, Negro unemployment rates have been at least twice those of whites. The outlook is particularly bleak, for technological change hits the Negro hard in two ways. First, it reduces the demand for precisely the kind

---

[38] Harrington, p. 182.

of labor that the Negro offers—unskilled industrial labor; second, it increases the demand for the kind of labor that the Negro cannot offer in large amount—skills requiring considerable education.

Educational opportunities for the Negro have been substantially poorer in just about every part of the nation than for whites. Their schools have been far inferior to the average. Moreover, a whole set of forces limited the amount of time that the average Negro was able to attend school. Even more, his educational opportunities within the home are limited, creating a persistent and expanding gap between the whites and the Negroes. The Negro seems to be trapped in the vicious circle of having low income which limits him to low education which perpetuates his low income status. This circle, perhaps more than anything else, explains the differences in income and employment rates that have been sketched.

Most people in the United States assume that their homeland is the most democratic in the world. Democracy is one of the main "in" words of this country and has been so for many decades. Americans went to war in 1917 and 1941 to "make the world safe for democracy." Many youngsters will separate countries into the good and the bad according to whether or not they are democratic. One ugly blotch on the record of the United States is the treatment of the Negro in the political, as well as in the economic, sphere. The plain fact is that most Negroes in the South do not and many dare not vote, though modest improvement have been recorded in recent years and further progress can be expected. Also, violence and terror accompanies the forward steps that are made. In certain states of the nation, a minority controls the political system and subjugates the majority by the threat of force and by occasional acts of extreme violence and outright terrorism.[39]

Thus, the record hardly supports the contention that political democracy is a natural concomitant of capitalism. On the contrary, to the extent that capitalism is unable to provide employment at good wages for even its least privileged citizens, the growth of political equality will be slow. As much as civil rights legislation may help the Negro minority, its greatest hope for substantive—as opposed to formal—equality lies in the creation of a very high level of demand and full employment.

Is the solution for poverty to be found in further income redistribution? Although some improvement in the condition of families at the very bottom of the income pyramid would seem possible by this means, a full solution must be expected mainly from other sources. In particular, the elimination of poverty will come, if at all, from a substantial increase in welfare expend-

---

[39] Another nation that has a capitalistic system—South Africa—likewise oppresses Negroes. There, however, enormous inequality of opportunity is enforced by the white-dominated national government to perpetuate the inequalities that now exist and to deprive Negroes of active participation in the political system.

itures (discussed above), from economic growth, the elimination of unemployment, and the spread of economic opportunity. The total income produced in the United States under current conditions of prosperity—when one hears so much about the nation's affluence—would not provide all Americans with a "decent" level of living even if equally divided.

NONECONOMIC EFFECTS OF CAPITALISM

People usually judge a foreign economy by its noneconomic as well as its economic characteristics. In evaluating the Soviet Union, for example, among the first things mentioned by Americans is its undemocratic character. By democracy we designate a political rather than an economic condition. Other criticisms frequently made of the Soviet Union are that it uses forced labor camps and that it infringes upon religious liberty. These conditions also are essentially noneconomic.

Even as the Soviet economic system is held accountable for certain political and social conditions, so, too, capitalism seems responsible for many of the social and political conditions that prevail in the United States. A full evaluation of an economic system therefore requires consideration of the noneconomic circumstances to which it gives rise.

Unfortunately, one cannot determine reliably how much of the political, social, and psychological environment in any country results from the characteristics of its economic system and how much is due to other causes. Present arrangements grow out of past conditions. Even after a violent revolution, a nation does not change its entire character. Many writers, for example, assert that the objectionable characteristics of Soviet communism are due to the Russian heritage of dictatorial monarchy, absence of civil liberties, and the habitual use of harsh and lawless methods by the authorities.

Countries with ostensibly the same economic system (namely, the United States, the United Kingdom, Canada, Japan, Germany) differ significantly in their noneconomic characteristics. Clearly, the economic system alone cannot be held responsible for all political, social, and attitudinal circumstances. In the discussion that follows, only those noneconomic features of the United States that might be attributed to its economic system will be considered. (Little space is accorded these subjects because the authors are economists and intend this book to deal primarily with economic matters.)

Predominant Personal Attitudes

Perhaps the most serious indictment against capitalism concerns its effect on personal attitudes. Some people maintain that while capitalism in the United States has provided a relatively large output of goods, it has also produced attitudes that make us dissatisfied and unhappy. The attitudes attributed to capitalism that are said to result in general dissatisfaction among Americans can be grouped under the heading of "materialism." Materialism (in the nonphilosophical sense) is an outlook on life that puts a high premium on the acquisition, possession, and use of material objects of wealth. It thereby weakens personal spiritual values, sympathy with others, and any desire to perform community service. Materialism contributes no philosophy that provides a satisfying purpose to life nor does it help individuals to adjust happily. It weakens the influence of religious and moral teachings without offering any satisfying alternative.

American capitalism, however, can be credited with a major contribution to a happy outlook by making most people believe they possess great and almost equal opportunities to advance themselves and can succeed if only they try. This attitude gives people hope and also flatters them into a feeling of basic equality and personal dignity. It also probably encourages people to make more strenuous efforts to improve themselves than they might otherwise make, and they probably gain lasting satisfaction from the achievements that result from their efforts.

Political Effects

One of the major noneconomic claims for capitalism is that it results in political democracy. Where capitalism has prevailed, ordinarily most people have had equal voting power. Partial offsets against this major claim for capitalism are to be found in the charge that capitalism mars the quality of democracy in several ways. First, disproportionate political power is exerted by those who control large economic resources. Second, the electorate is apathetic and badly informed.[40] Third, political power is exerted primarily by groups organized along economic lines, and these groups pursue policies that restrict rather than enlarge output.

In assessing the political effects of capitalism, one primarily wants to

---

[40] An indication of public apathy and misinformation about public issues generally is obtained as a by-product of public opinion polls. When people's opinions are asked about some public issue or personality, the pollsters also learn how many were never aware of the issue or never heard of the person.

The *Public Opinion Quarterly* carries all available results of polls in the United States based on a national cross section. This topically arranged summary is among the most interesting and illuminating sources of information one can hope to read. The Winter 1963 issue of the magazine turned up the following evidence of lack of information: (1) The initials F.B.I. had no meaning for 16 percent of those polled (Winter, 1949-1950). (2) In March 1953, 46 percent did not know or had incorrect ideas about what is meant by the term "price supports." (3) In December 1961, 83 percent did not know or had incorrect ideas about what is meant by the "fallout" of an H-bomb. (4) In January 1955, 59 percent had not heard or read anything about the term "peaceful coexistence." (5) In December 1961, 78 percent had not heard or read about the European Common Market.

know if capitalism in the United States has resulted in a government that represents the true interests of the people and responds to their wishes as well as another equally productive economic system might. We cannot assume that only capitalism results in democracy or that only capitalism fails to realize fully the benefits of democracy. Indeed, most countries that are at least partly socialized—for example, the United Kingdom, Sweden, Denmark, Norway, Uruguay, and New Zealand—enjoy a democracy that certainly is no less vigorous than our own.

Social and Psychological Effects

Capitalism over most of the world and particularly in the United States has been associated with minimum restraint on occupational selection, personal expression, and free choice of a "way of life." Psychologists are agreed that the absence of restraint contributes to healthy mental balance, personal happiness, and to successful social adjustment.

There are, however, social and psychological effects of capitalism that are not to its credit. These will simply be listed without discussion. First, most people in the United States live under heavy nervous pressure; they feel economically insecure and fear that their prosperity can quickly be turned into pauperism; the employee often fears that he can be fired from his good job "out of the blue" without much cause. Second, employees are subject to the arbitrary power of their employer; in this sense, no worker is completely free. Employers have, in addition to their power to fire, the ability to injure employees by giving poor references to other potential employers. Strong unions check the employer's power but sometimes create another arbitrary power over the individual worker. Capitalism makes of the pursuit of money the highest goal and the most engrossing activity for most people. It often creates a conflict between family and community obligations and business success. Finally, it produces a mass culture (movies, T.V., magazines, comic books) that tends to stultify rather than raise public taste and sensitivity.

CONCLUSIONS

The foregoing description and evaluation of American capitalism are admittedly sketchy and superficial. To describe and evaluate an economic system is immensely complicated. This chapter has done little more than raise the major questions that must be answered before we understand our own economy.

Doubts have been expressed about the extent to which the rationale for capitalism applies to the present economic system in the United States. Many criticisms of the American economy have been made. However, capitalism has been evaluated here by "absolute" standards. When a condition has been criticized, it does not follow that other types of economy excel in that respect. Conditions termed defects call for improvement if measures for improvement exist. Some of the defects indicated can surely be remedied.

Apart from the unquestioned productiveness of the American economy, two salient facts deserve emphasis: first, the economy has undergone fairly dramatic change in the last two decades; second, it seems to be less unstable than ever at this point.

Most of the changes in the economy can be attributed to piecemeal efforts to adapt economic arrangements to meet the individual problems that have arisen, and to accommodate to changes in prevailing attitudes and value judgments. Since the early 1930s, American capitalism has become a semiwelfare state. At present, most people expect the government to take measures—drastic if need be—to combat major downswings; social security, however limited in amount, is growing both in amount of benefits and coverage; the volume and variety of publicly provided social services is also increasing. The distribution of personal income has become more equal; business owners and managers acknowledge a responsibility to others besides their stockholders. With government encouragement, unions have grown enormously in bargaining power, influencing both the distribution of income to some degree and adding greatly to workers' feelings of security and self-respect.

Relatively few persons would contend that the American economy functions less well these days than it did in the past. Since the onset of World War II, the economy has suffered only minor recessions; technology has developed at a very rapid pace; businessmen have sometimes shown a readiness to make huge investments in plant and equipment; and prices have remained more or less stable. The American economy is, however, criticized on three main scores at present: first, the slowness of its growth; second, the large number of its permanently unemployed; and third, its wasteful and amoral selling practices.

CHAPTER 3

THE ECONOMY OF THE SOVIET UNION

The preceding chapter has described an economic system with which most readers are quite familiar. The Soviet economic system, on the other hand, is a mystery to the vast majority. This mystery has lessened now that Soviet authorities have somewhat relaxed their secrecy precautions and as a large number of specialists have become engaged in studying the Soviet Union. Even when this considerably augmented information is pieced together, however, the picture formed will remain indistinct in some particulars.

The following description of the Soviet economic system is as up to date as the authors could make it; however, it necessarily is somewhat behind the times. Descriptions always lag behind circumstances, but in the case of the Soviet Union the lag is particularly serious. Major changes and reforms are more rapid in the USSR than in non-Communist countries. Also, because the USSR does not treat its economy as "an open book" in all respects, some of its facets are known only in outline—the economics of defense industries, for instance.

APPROACHES TO A STUDY OF THE SOVIET ECONOMY

The fundamental purpose of this discussion is to explain the functioning of the Soviet economy in most realistic terms, with special emphasis on its unique features. More particularly, the aim is to make clear the ways and means by which a centrally planned economy of the Soviet type solves the basic economic problems of deciding what to produce and how much, by which means, how to get people and resources into the "right jobs," how to distribute income, and how to make the economy technically progressive. When this undertaking is completed, the accomplishments of the Soviet

Union under its economic system will be reviewed briefly. The discussion is not organized along historical lines and does not probe into future developments.

DISTINGUISHING FEATURES OF THE SOVIET ECONOMY

The Soviet economy is similar to the American only in that most of the population work under the supervision and direction of others to produce goods and services for consumption and various other uses, and that resources available for such production and consumption are limited at any given time and must therefore be used economically and efficiently. Beyond this basic similarity, it differs in many essential respects, and especially in how production and distribution are organized and how efficiency and economies in the use of resources are achieved. We shall concentrate upon the features of the Soviet economy that are different from the American, for by contrasts both economies will become clearer.

Principles Underlying the Soviet Economic System

The Soviet economic system is, in most respects, entirely different from the American economic system. In a point-by-point comparison with the description of the latter in Chapter 2 the *basic characteristics of the Soviet economic system can be summarized as follows.*

1. According to the Constitution of the Soviet Union (Art. 6), "the land, its mineral wealth, waters, forests, mills, factories, mines, rail, water and air transport, banks, communications, large state-organized agricultural enterprises (state farms and the like), as well as municipal enterprises and bulk of the dwelling houses in the cities and industrial localities, are state property, that is, belong to the whole people." *State ownership means that only the government can decide how these things are to be used; they cannot be bought or sold, or owned privately.*

2. *Soviet citizens are not permitted to own profit-making private property or to engage in commercial private enterprise.* They cannot go into business, open a shop or own a farm; they cannot own stocks for there are none in the Soviet Union. *On the other hand, consumer goods are privately owned in the Soviet Union.* Soviet citizens can own as many suits, televisors, jewelry, saving accounts, summer homes, and automobiles as they can afford and can find in the government-regulated market. They can also inherit them and sell them to each other, if they wish, but only as personal items for personal use, and one at a time, for prices that are not much higher than those prevailing in the government-owned stores. *Private profiteering is prohibited under the Soviet laws and is severely punished. It is*

also genuinely despised by most Soviet people on moral and cultural grounds.

3. Since, with the sole exception of collective farms, which are cooperatives, and some consumer and handicraft cooperatives, all enterprises in the USSR are government-owned and operated, their managers are public employees, not private owners or employees of private owners. Soviet managers work for salary and bonuses, not for private profit or stock options. The government frequently shifts them from one job to another, so that the enterprises which they manage are not in any sense "their own." As a result, the basic goals of managers' activities in the USSR are different from those known in the United States. *In their business activities Soviet firms strive, above all, to fulfill the national economic plans established for them by the government.* For outstanding performance in the fulfillment of government plans, the government pays bonuses to managers and workers, makes promotions, bestows medals of honor, gives wide publicity in the press, over the radio and TV (which all are government-owned, of course). All these arrangements have been devised as substitutes for the capitalist profit motive as we know it in the United States. ("Profits" are planned and calculated by Soviet enterprises along with "costs"; but Soviet enterprises do not own their profits—they all rightfully belong to the government. Some bonuses, though not all, are paid by the government to the managers and workers out of the enterprise's profits; *but these bonuses are paid for fulfilling the plans, not just for "making" the profits.*)

4. *Major economic decisions concerning what to produce in the country as a whole or in some part of it, as well as in each individual enterprise, in what quantities and qualities, by which method, by which deadline and so forth, are made in the USSR by government planning agencies, not by enterprises themselves. These decisions, specified in varying but great detail, are communicated to the enterprises by the government in the form of economic plans, which the latter are obliged to carry out.* For the most part, Soviet enterprises do not purchase or order raw materials, machines, or other important commodities freely from each other, and neither do they sell them in a free market. They cannot freely approach a bank and ask for credit to invest in capital construction. It is rather the government planning authorities that tell one enterprise to conclude a contract with and to deliver its products to another enterprise in stated quantities and at government-fixed prices. And it is also the government that not only permits the bank to extend credit to an enterprise, but also permits the enterprise to apply for such credit. *In other words, there is no free enterprise in the Soviet economy, as it is known in the capitalist market economies.*

5. *All basic goods and capital investments in the USSR are allocated directly by the central government authorities, in accordance with and within the framework of some plan.* Free enterprise is simply unconstitu-

tional in the planned sector of the economy, for Article 11 of the USSR Constitution postulates: "The economic life of the USSR is determined and directed by the state economic plan." The planned sector embraces more than 90 percent of all goods and services produced and distributed in the USSR.

6. *Competition as we know it in the United States does not exist in the Soviet economy. The government has virtual monopoly over almost everything in the economy.* The Soviet economic system is perhaps best characterized as a *total state monopoly,* for according to Lenin there is no difference between socialism and a total state monopoly "serving the people." Soviet government-owned enterprises are not independent "public corporations," as, for example, the TVA is; they possess but a very limited business autonomy. Competition against government interests is naturally prohibited by law. Competitive products and services are sometimes produced by different Soviet enterprises, but if one plant produces a better product than another plant, the latter plant is told by the government to learn from and to adopt the product of the more efficient plant. Some competition undoubtedly exists also inside the government planning agencies among various individual projects, pressure groups, and local interests for the allocation of scarce resources, but this is not the same thing as the competition among independent firms in a free market.

7. *By virtue of its ownership of the means of production and distribution, the government in the Soviet economy appears and acts as a big business enterprise, a giant corporation embracing nearly the whole economy.* Individual enterprises in the USSR completely differ from firms in a market economy; they rather resemble constituent parts of such firms—departments, subsidiaries, or individual plants of a corporation. *All major economic relations and interactions, the allocation of resources and distribution of orders, price setting and the flow of funds take place in the Soviet economic system as if inside one single enterprise.* Similar relations exist *inside* big U.S. firms; resources in them are allocated by top management so as to maximize the profits of the company as a whole—not necessarily of each of its individual plants. This situation conforms exactly with the principles of Soviet economics, and explains why it is helpful to view the Soviet economy as a single enterprise.[1]

---

[1] Kenneth E. Boulding has jokingly suggested a new term to designate the Soviet-type economy: "ecorg." Said Boulding: "It is a nice word and it means 'an organization which is organized by budget rather than through the market.' And if you were to make a list of the ecorgs in the world roughly in the order of their, whatever is the equivalent of the GNP, it would run something like this: The Soviet Union, the People's Republic of China, the Pentagon, Czechoslovakia, General Motors, Yugoslavia, General Electric, Bulgaria, General Dynamics. When we get way down the list, we get to Albania sandwiched in the middle of the minor corporations." In N. Spulber, ed., *Study of the Soviet Economy* (Bloomington: Indiana University Press, 1961), p. 124.

8. *The giant Soviet government enterprise works "for profit" in one sense. It seeks a surplus, or a net income, to continue and to expand its operations and to increase its output to satisfy the country's growing population and its various other needs (defense, space explorations, foreign aid).* Its "profits" consist of the income above costs of its subsidiary enterprises. As said above, profit in the USSR does not belong to the plant or the factory producing it; it is owned and redistributed by the government. Some plants and factories in the USSR continuously work at a loss; the government subsidizes them from the profits of other enterprises. Soviet enterprises can never go bankrupt, unless closed by the government. But the Soviet economy as a whole must undoubtedly be profitable. The government finances its new capital investments, builds new plants and factories, expands production partly from such profits, and partly from taxes.

9. *The Soviet Union is guided by the principle that the economy should be directed toward socially prescribed goals, and that government planners should devise the best measures possible to attain them.* By "socially prescribed goals" are meant objectives set down for the country as a whole by the Communist party. These goals are decided upon "arbitrarily" by individuals in political power, "arbitrarily" inasmuch as they are conscious choices among alternatives and could have been decided differently. "Prescribed goals" are perhaps clearest when contrasted with the goals of our own economy. In the United States most output goals are not centrally determined; *they just happen to be* as the result of decisions made by many persons operating more or less independently of each other and of any central authority. In the Soviet Union, however, virtually all matters relating to the use of economic resources (including research services, the arts, training in colleges and technical schools, and the like) are determined by the Communist party, whose major function it is to decide on such matters. The over-all goals of Soviet economic system, according to Soviet Constitution (Art. 11) are "to increase the public wealth, to steadily raise the material and cultural standards of the working people, to consolidate the independence of the USSR and strengthen its defensive capacity." *In practice so far, the actual goals of topmost priority were rapid industrialization, technical modernization, and military build-up, rather than a maximization of people's living standards and culture. The maximization of consumption has been deliberately retarded and postponed in order to save resources for very rapid industrialization.*

10. *As in the United States, most individuals in the Soviet Union strive to better their livelihood by obtaining a maximum income; but according to the prevailing morals and laws, that income must stem only from work, not from ownership of property or from resale of goods.* Like Americans, Soviet people are basically free to choose the jobs they want; no one orders where they are to work, or for how much and how long. However, the great

majority can find employment only with the government, its enterprises, or with collective farms; only a minute portion of the population (some artisans, writers, painters, lawyers, physicians) can find support in self-employment. Any kind of business self-employment is of course prohibited in the USSR. In principle, all working individuals in the USSR are compensated in accordance with their skill and productivity. However, their basic rewards are determined by the government, not by free play of demand and supply for and of their services, and neither by the pressure of the labor unions.

11. *Soviet people are also entirely free to spend their incomes on immediate consumption or save them for future consumption as they wish.* They cannot invest their incomes to earn profit, however. Furthermore, the freedom of Soviet consumers choice is almost completely limited by the quantities and qualities of goods offered by the government enterprises and the prices set by the government. (There is no direct rationing in the Soviet Union, but a rationing effect is achieved by means of planning in kind and government-fixed prices. This is explained below.)

12. *The collective welfare of society is both the right and the duty of the state in the Communist countries.* On one hand, the state is capable of manipulating the well-being of society, limiting it to a bare minimum or expanding it to a maximum, for such is its right and power. On the other hand, however, the state is also obliged to expand social welfare, to look after people's well-being, and to furnish them with work and income. It assumes this obligation because it has nationalized the economy and has deprived people of all independent means of livelihood by having taken over the right to property of their own. The guaranteed right to a job, the development of collective consumption and social welfare are, therefore, central features of the Soviet-type economic system, which includes such institutions as free of charge, socialized medicine, tuition-exempt education in schools of all levels and vocations, many free resorts and rest homes, sometimes also free food for workers and collective farmers in communal mess halls, free transportation and many other services.

Soviet Goals

To understand the Soviet Union requires, perhaps above all else, knowledge of the goals pursued by its leaders. To explain most people and arrangements, the best clue is their fundamental purposes and objectives. In the case of the Soviet Union, we must ask what those persons who exert dominant control over the country want to achieve both for themselves and for the country as a whole. To answer these questions requires an exploration of the Soviet political system to determine what persons possess dominant power. Then it is necessary to speculate about their motives. These matters are touched upon at various points in this book though they have not been explored exhaustively and therefore no firm conclusions have been drawn. At this point, it should suffice to state that, in the authors' opinion, the Soviet Union is a dictatorship of a relatively small group and the political power is lodged in the Central Committee of the Communist party. The goals *stated* by the highest Soviet political authorities fall under the head of creating a Communist society[2] and include the following:

1. Expansion of the industrial productive capacity of the USSR to surpass that of the United States by 1972. This expansion is sought as a base for a rapidly increasing level of living and as a foundation for military power, which the leaders state they desire for defensive purposes.
2. Reduction in hours and unpleasantness of work.
3. Improvement in education and a raising of cultural levels.
4. Elimination of economic and social differences between the city and the countryside, and different regions of the country.
5. Improvement in national health standards.

Whatever their real purposes, the Soviet leaders say they have no interest in territorial expansion. (Their aspirations with regard to expansion undoubtedly have changed as their power position has improved.) In their view, they have grown from an encircled backward country (prior to World War II) into a first-rate power whose friends are numerous and strong. The Soviet bloc accounts for about one third of the world's population.

The *stated* objectives of the Soviet authorities are similar to those of many Western political leaders and opposite to those of Fascist and other right-wing groups. They eulogize the virtues of democracy and demand the participation of all persons in matters pertaining to their jobs and their community. Moreover, most of these principles are explicitly incorporated in the Constitution of the Soviet Union. In describing their relationship with other Communist countries—which many outsiders consider to be one of ruler and ruled—they speak of it as cooperation and mutual assistance. Thus, in many respects the statements of the top Soviet leaders are similar and even identical with those of the Western democracies. However, the behavior of Soviet leaders also differs substantially from their stated goals and principles.

One feature of the five listed objectives should be noted: they are likely to conflict. For example, the authorities must constantly choose between increased output and reduced hours of work; between devoting additional resources to improvements in health and literacy and using them to increase industrial output. Consequently, one must know more than the objectives

---

[2] See *The Program of the Communist Party of the Soviet Union* (Moscow: Foreign Languages Publishing House, 1961).

pursued; he must also know with what relative urgency each goal is felt by those who possess power to decide.

The objectives attributed to the leaders of the Soviet Union by their critics include the following: to retain political power as long as possible by whatever means are necessary; to exploit the people they govern to obtain good lives and luxuries for themselves; to impose their will upon the rest of the world in order to expand their power; to spread communism and eliminate the threat to it that comes from the non-Communist world.

Certainly, it is dangerous to judge people's motives solely by the things they say. What they say, however, should not be ignored entirely. The Soviet rulers may be tyrannical, cruel, hard, shrewd, and power-hungry men. They must nevertheless be distinguished from politically powerful men in non-Communist nations. Those who rule the Soviet Union have doubtless been strongly influenced by the doctrines they learned and preached. They are likely to have absorbed and accepted most of the views espoused by Marx, Engels, and Lenin. Therefore, their motives are to be understood in considerable measure by understanding Communist doctrine.

These men unquestionably hold many views and personal objectives that are not covered by Marxian theory one way or another. They may not accept Marxian doctrine in totality. One would suppose that they are motivated in some measure by such purely personal goals as the attainment of high office, the wish to lead a comfortable and secure life, and the like. *However, in the absence of evidence to the contrary, it is safest to assume that the persons exercising the political power in the Soviet Union believe in the writings of Marx, Engels, and Lenin and are under great pressure to make their actions consistent with the Marxian doctrines.* Abrupt and obvious deviations from those doctrines are almost certain to arouse criticism among other Communists and bring a fall from power—possibly even severe punishment.

To fathom the true motives and intentions of the Soviet rulers is one of the foremost tasks of our times. The key to their minds will not be found here, however. To study the Soviet economy it is not necessary to explore the objectives of the Soviet leaders any further. No matter what their most fundamental aims, there is no reason why they would desire to produce few goods rather than many, and why they would prefer to work long hours if they could produce as much in less time. *Accordingly, we can safely assume that the paramount economic objective of the Soviet leaders is to increase the output of goods and services as rapidly as possible with a minimum of sacrifice.*

To sum up, let us crystallize the difference in principles underlying the Soviet and the American economic systems. In the United States, everyone may do whatever he wishes within the law, and it is expected that the outcome will be better than could be obtained from any other method of organizing our economy. The goals of the American economy are not specified; we simply accept whatever happens as a result of the fact that all individuals independently pursue their own personal objectives. The Soviet Union states very specifically what it wants to happen and then takes the best measures it can devise to achieve its goals.

Structural Differences between the American and Soviet Economies

The institutional structure of the economy of the USSR is, for the most part, similar *in form* to that of the United States. However, the great bulk of all industrial and agricultural output in the USSR is produced, transported, and sold in enterprises owned by the state (see Table 12). The few peculiarly Soviet economic institutions, which are strikingly different from those employed in the United States, can be described as follows.

Table 12.   Estimated Structure of the Property Ownership in the Soviet Union, 1964

(percent of the total)

	State	Cooperatives and collective farms	Private
Banks	100%	—%	—%
Industry	98	2	—
Transportation	91	9	—
Retail trade	67	29	4
Agriculture: Land in use	57	42	1
Livestock	28	44	28
Urban housing	62	1	37

NOTE: Industry, transportation, and trade are represented here by the owners' shares in the total output, haulage, and sales respectively. Land is all owned by the state in the USSR; what is given here is the permanent use of it by the enterprises of particular form of ownership. Housing given here is only residential; in rural areas, almost all residential housing is privately owned.

Collective and State Farms

In agriculture the Soviet Union employs a unique arrangement known as the collective farm, or *kolkhoz*. Collective farms combine the features of a producer cooperative and a private enterprise, but are subject to government planning and strict controls. Each collective farm unites about 410 peasant families, on the average; it owns about sixteen tractors, eleven trucks, 345 cows and 800 pigs, and cultivates some 7500 acres of land. In 1963 there were but 38,800 collective farms in the whole Soviet Union;

yet, they employed 26.3 percent of the total working labor force in the country and used 42.5 percent of all agricultural land.[3]

Since only one fourth of collective farmers are skilled in some specialized job, the rest are periodically rotated on different jobs assigned to them by the farm management. Job rotation is undertaken in order to equalize the farmers' income, for difficult jobs are paid more than the light ones. Upon the completion of each job, the farmers are assigned a certain number of score points, called labor days, for which they are paid on the average one half in produce and one half in money earned by the collective farm from the sales of its produce to the state. At the end of the year, the remaining net income of the collective farm (after taxes and allocations for investments) is also distributed as a sort of dividend per total number of "labor days" earned by each farmer.

Each peasant family on a collective farm is also given a plot of land of about one acre in size on which it is permitted to operate a tiny private enterprise: it can plant whatever it wishes, own one cow, two pigs, or five sheep, and an unlimited number of chickens. The produce of this enterprise can be sold in the free market in the cities, the only free market that is permitted in the USSR. On the average, about 30 percent of a collective farm family's total income is derived in this way nowadays, the remainder coming from its share in the income of the collective farm.

The collective farm is a cooperative, even though it lacks autonomy in its management. Its chairman is often appointed from the outside and he generally listens less to the peasants than to the local Communist party officials. Production plans of each collective farm are subject to approval of the local county government and party committee. In its general economic plan, handed down from the county agricultural department, the state prescribes to each collective farm, how much of each crop and product it has to sell to the state during the year. The purchase prices paid by the government for collective farm produce are fixed by the central government and are not subject to negotiation. Most of these prices are relatively low, although in recent years they have been raised in an effort to provide increased incentives to the peasants to raise agricultural output.

In addition to collective farms, the Soviet Union has organized state farms, which are run more or less like state factories. There are 9175 state farms in the USSR as of 1963; they account for 44 percent of the total cultivated area in the country and employ 6.6 million workers. The average size of a state farm is more than 64,000 acres. They are much more mechanized than the collective farms, and their productivity is also much higher. Workers in the state farms are paid money wages as in industry, but in

---

[3] *Narodnoe khozyaystvo SSSR v 1962 godu* (National Economy of the USSR in 1962), Moscow, 1963, pp. 14, 225, 243, 246, 303, 330. Also *SSSR v tsifrakh v 1963 godu*, Moscow, 1964, pp. 107-108.

addition they are permitted to operate a tiny private enterprise of the same sort and size as that of the collective farmers. State farm workers fare somewhat better than the collective farmers in general. The preferential treatment of state farms by the Communist party is designed to tempt the collective farmers to abandon their traditional peasant way of life and voluntarily become employees of the state. A gradual transformation of collective farms into state farms has been under way since 1953 and is probably to continue.[4]

Money and Banking

Money in the Soviet Union serves as medium of exchange and a unit of account in the same way as in our country. Soviet prices, production costs, the government budget, and the like are calculated in money terms. Money is also used for personal savings, but only for future personal consumption. All that one can do with money as capital is to deposit it in a savings account with the State Bank and earn 3 percent interest per year, or purchase government bonds bearing a similar interest rate, or buy and resell some consumer goods (a car, a bungalow), but in very small quantities, for otherwise the transaction would be illegal black marketing, punishable under the law.

The Soviet banks differ from those in the United States in that they are a vital part of the centralized planning machinery. The Soviet banking system is highly centralized and specialized. There are, in fact, only three banks in the USSR today: (1) the State Bank of the USSR, which handles emission of money, short-term credit, all current and savings accounts, and serves as a depository for the state budget; (2) the Construction Bank, which handles long-term capital investments; and (3) the Foreign Trade Bank, which services all foreign transactions. All enterprises in the country, both state and cooperative, are obliged to keep all their funds in the State Bank. The banks are required to control all money transactions of enterprises, to compare them with the government production and delivery plans, and to withhold or extend short-term credit and other payments as necessary. The banks charge low rates of interest for all short-term loans (1 to 2 percent). All long-term industrial capital investments in new plant and equipment are nonreturnable, interest-free grants in the USSR. Collective farms pay 3 percent interest on their loans, however.

---

[4] Cf. J. F. Karcz and V. P. Timoshenko, "Soviet Agricultural Policy, 1953-1962," *Food Research Institute Studies,* vol. IV, no. 2 (Stanford, Calif.: Stanford University Press, 1962).

Soviet Trade Unions

Soviet leaders and law assume a harmony of interests in industrial relations because both workers and managers belong to the same social class. Although one might be skeptical about this notion, it is mistaken to apply a Western viewpoint to Soviet labor-management relations. For one thing, Soviet propaganda has hammered for forty years on the community of class interests of workers and managers and undoubtedly has conditioned the views of the population to some extent. Furthermore, as explained, the goals of Soviet managers are quite different from the goals of owners in the West. The profit motive is not the chief driving force for Soviet managers; their main goal is to fulfill and overfulfill government plans, and this is also the workers' goal because material incentives are all geared to this goal. In principle, therefore, both managers and workers have a common interest in achieving the goals of the enterprise.

It is not surprising, therefore, that under such circumstances Soviet labor unions are very dissimilar from unions in the West. The most important differences are these:

1. Soviet unions have neither the right nor any evident desire to strike against the management or the government. Strikes are not expressly prohibited in the Soviet Union, but they are not mentioned among unions' legal rights either. Ideologically, strikes are inconceivable for the above-mentioned reasons; practically, union-led strikes are almost impossible because Soviet unions are strictly controlled by the Communist party, to which they are expected to turn for help whenever serious conflicts with the management arise.

2. Wages are not subject to collective bargaining in the Soviet Union. As said above, they are fixed by the government, and *neither the local unions nor the management have any influence over them.* However, some local fringe benefits and issues involving material interests of the workers (for example, the method of calculation of bonuses in the plant, food prices in the plant's cafeteria—if that food is supplied by the plant's own farm) are subjects of collective bargaining.

3. Collective bargaining and agreements do not constitute the most important area of union activities in the USSR, as they do in the West. The contents of Soviet collective agreements are very different from those in the West. They do not contain wage clauses, for example, for reasons mentioned above. On the other hand, a contract may contain many paragraphs in which the union obliges itself to increase production by so and so many percentage points. At the same time, it will specify how the bonuses will be paid for this increased production. It also may state management's obligation to build a new sports stadium, a club house, or a housing project for

the workers. All collective bargaining in the USSR is between the local union and the local plant; there are no industry-wide agreements.

4. Soviet labor unions manage the state social security system (both disability as well as old-age pensions). All social insurance in the USSR, with the exception of that of collective farms, is financed by the government alone out of general taxes, but the management of this system is in the hands of the unions. Soviet trade unions also manage almost all health resorts, rest homes, sanatoriums, and homes for the aged in the Soviet Union, as well as many children's camps, sports stadiums, clubs, movie houses, public libraries, public beaches, and parks. In fact, the best vacation and recreational facilities in the country belong to the unions. Access to these facilities is one of the major incentives for belonging to the unions in the USSR.

Membership in the Soviet unions is voluntary, but nonetheless almost 95 percent of all factory and office workers belong to them. Some of the most important economic functions of the Soviet unions are these:

1. Unions participate with management in the drafting and periodic reviewing of production and construction plans, in the calculation of work quotas, and the establishment of piece-work rates, bonuses, and overtime work rules.

2. Without the union's consent, the management has no right to discharge workers from their jobs. The union committees review first all cases of proposed dismissals on whether or not they conform to existing laws. They also check on the management's observance of all labor laws in general, and are authorized to support the workers in court if the latter lodge a complaint against the management.

3. They have the right to criticize in public and to demand the dismissal or disciplinary action against managerial personnel who are careless of workers' rights or otherwise inefficient. New appointments to managerial positions in the plant must be done on consultation with the union.

4. In the settlement of labor-management disputes unions play a peculiar and unique role.[5] All disputes that arise in Soviet plants are viewed as taking place between *individual* workers and the management, *not* between the union and the management. A worker's complaint goes first to the labor dispute board of his plant. The board is composed in equal proportions of the representatives of the local union and the management; its decisions must be unanimous, but the complainant has the right of appeal. If the case is not settled by the board, or if it is appealed, it goes next to the local union committee. The latter tries to arbitrate between the worker and the manage-

---

[5] See I. Dvornikov and V. Nikitinsky, *How Labour Disputes are Settled in the Soviet Union* (Moscow: Trade Union Publishing House, 1959).

ment. If the arbitration fails, the union decides either for or against management. As the next and last step, the dissatisfied side has the right to bring the case before the court of law. Its judgment is final and undisputable.

The Right to Work

As mentioned before, the Soviet Constitution (Art. 118) guarantees to all citizens "the right to work." In practice this means but two things: first, equality of opportunity to a job, and second, security from arbitrary dismissal; it does not mean that the government is legally responsible for furnishing everyone with a job to his or her liking.

A Soviet citizen looking for a job must find it on his or her own. Various agencies may help him, but no one pays him any unemployment insurance during the time he is looking for a job. Unemployment insurance does not exist in the USSR because it is assumed that there is no unemployment and because the government prefers that the workers do not change their present jobs too frequently. Soviet workers have the right to quit their jobs by giving two-weeks notice. As a result, however, they lose their seniority rights, which are important in calculation of old-age pensions.

The right to work means first of all that if a worker finds a job and knows that he is suitable for it, the employer has no right to refuse him that job; the worker has the right to sue the employer, and the law will be on his side, if denied a position without lawful reason. In particular, the employer has no right to refuse a job to a worker because of the latter's race, nationality, or sex, or because a woman worker seeking the job is pregnant.

Second, the Soviet worker's right to work means that his employer has no right to fire him or to transfer him to an inferior job except under the extreme circumstances specified by the law and only if the local labor union consents.[6] The worker can be legally dismissed only if he is negligent in his work, is too frequently absent without reason, or is frequently drunk. (In case of illness the worker legally retains his job for four months and is paid.)

Especially important in this connection are Soviet regulations concerning group dismissals of workers that become necessary due to automation and other technological progress. Soviet labor codes provide specifically that in all such cases the employers—that is, either the plant or the economic council—are obliged to secure new employment for the dismissed workers in advance of their dismissal. One provision specifies that, if necessary,

---

6 The unions, indeed, defend the workers in case of unlawful dismissals. For example, *Trud* (Moscow) of February 28, 1959, reported that at the Zhdanov Heavy Machinery Works (Ukraine), in fifty cases when the administration proposed to fire the workers, the local union committee gave its consent only to ten, so that forty workers retained their jobs.

workers must be retrained in new professions at the employer's expense. In no case can the worker's pay in the new job be lower than it was in the old.[7]

Functional Differences

The American and the Soviet economic systems differ fundamentally in the degree to which economic decisions are made centrally and "arbitrarily." In the Soviet Union, only relatively minor decisions are made by persons other than Communist party officials and government planners. Decisions about the quantity and quality of goods to be turned out by each enterprise, the location at which commodities are to be produced or sold, and the methods to employ in production are all made by central agencies with reference to one or another master plan that is drawn up to embrace and knit the economy together.

Subordination of the economy to a national economic plan is not peculiar to the Soviet Union. France is just one example. Although the USSR pioneered in economic planning, since the end of World War II more than ninety countries have adopted and carried out more than 450 partial or universal national economic plans.[8] What is, however, unique about the Soviet Union is the enormous detail of its plans, the rigor of the measures taken to piece together and to realize their goals, the extent to which they take precedence over and dominate all economic decisions of individuals and the degree to which they are a legal obligation for every economic unit in the country.

Accordingly, a description of the structure of the Soviet economy does not provide much insight into its essential character. To understand the nature of the Soviet economy requires, above all, knowledge of two things: the goals of the Soviet leaders and the techniques of planning that are employed to reach them. We will know the Soviet economy only if we know how the plans are drawn up, how records are kept of progress of their realization, how plans are analyzed and when they are modified, the kinds of action taken when experience departs from the plan, and the types of data and criteria on which the plans rest. The Soviet economy is a system of highly detailed and obligatory economic planning, and in this respect it is, indeed, very different from what exists in the United States and in France. We shall turn now to the study of the organization of planning in the Soviet Union.[9]

---

[7] *Cf.* A. M. Kaftanovskaya and V. I. Nikitinsky, *Priyom na rabotu i uvol'nenie rabochikh i sluzhashchikh* (Moscow: Profizdat, 1959).

[8] The resolution of the 16th General Assembly of the United Nations, adopted unanimously on December 19, 1961, specifically recommends that planning should be studied for application in all developing countries.

[9] Among the general literature concerned with the functional aspects of the Soviet economy, see *National Policy Machinery in the Soviet Union*, Report of the Com-

Soviet Economic Government and Planning Agencies

State ownership of the means of production and distribution has made the Soviet government virtually the only economic enterprise in the country. It has unified in its hands both the drawing of plans and their execution, thereby making the government alone responsible for the economy's suc-cesses and failures. The Soviet government is therefore responsible for in-suring that its plans are fulfilled.[10] To achieve their fulfillment, it has estab-lished a very elaborate network of economic and planning agencies which prepare plans and carry them out in detail on a day-to-day basis.

The economic government of the Soviet Union is depicted in detail on the following page. First of all, there are four levels of territorial organization: (1) The federal USSR government on the top (called the Union); (2) the governments of fifteen national republics;[11] (3) the regional economic councils (*sovnarkhozy*), of which there were forty-seven in 1964; and (4) the provincial, municipal, and county governments. The legislative organs of each of the four territorial levels of government, called *soviets* (coun-cils), adopt economic plans and fiscal budgets as well as all other economic legislation for their spheres. In practice it appears that they usually only rubber-stamp the bills sent to them by the Communist party.

The executive organs of the Soviet government are (1) the USSR council of ministers, (2) the councils of ministers of the fifteen republics, and (3)

---

mittee on Government Operations (Washington, D.C.: Government Printing Office, 1960); M. Fainsod, *How Russia is Ruled* (Cambridge, 1959); R. W. Campbell, *So-viet Economic Power* (Cambridge, 1960); A. Nove, *The Soviet Economy: An Intro-duction* (New York, 1961); N. Spulber, *The Soviet Economy: Structure, Principles, Problems* (New York, 1962); A. Vucinich, *Soviet Economic Institutions* (Palo Alto, 1952); A. Bergson, *The Economics of Soviet Planning* (New Haven: Yale University Press, 1964); G. Grossman, "The Structure and Organization of the Soviet Economy," *Slavic Review* (June 1962); A. G. Frank, "The Organization of Economic Activity in the Soviet Union," *Weltwirtschaftliches Archiv* (No. 1, 1957).

[10] The Soviet government decree of April 28, 1958, called "Concerning the Re-sponsibility for the Nonfulfillment of Plans and Delivery Quotas," provides for mini-mum fines of up to three-month salary and maximum jail or labor camp sentences of from five to ten years, to be imposed by the courts of law on all managerial personnel —from a plant manager up to a cabinet minister—who may be responsible for the breach of production and delivery plans without excusable reasons. Cf. *Vedomosti Verkhovnogo Soveta SSSR*, no. 9, Moscow, 1958. See also chapters entitled Economic Crimes, in the criminal codes of the republics of the USSR, which deal with criminal offenses against the plans.

[11] Fifteen constituent republics compose the Soviet Union. Unlike the states in our federal union, they are predominantly inhabited by racially and culturally different na-tionalities, speaking many different languages. Russia is only one, though the largest, republic among them; the Russians comprise 54 percent of the total USSR population, according to the census of 1959. Constitutionally, Soviet republics possess considerably more prerogatives than our states, with especially extensive powers in the economic sphere.

THE STRUCTURE OF SOVIET ECONOMIC ADMINISTRATION
JANUARY 1965

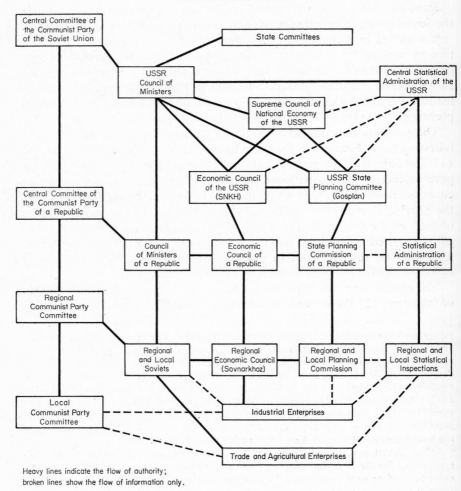

Heavy lines indicate the flow of authority;
broken lines show the flow of information only.

the executive committees of the local *soviets* in the provinces, cities, and villages. All these organs are responsible for the enforcement of economic legislation, including the plans and budgets within their territories. For this purpose, each has within itself or under its jurisdiction a number of economic and planning agencies. *All enterprises in the USSR are specifically assigned to one or another of these government agencies, which may be considered their ultimate planning and management bodies.*

Economic Ministries

The USSR council of ministers includes, among others, eleven ministries concerned with various sectors of the economy; there is a ministry of foreign trade, railways, electrification, finance, agriculture, and so on. The governments of the republics in their turn have about twelve economic ministries each, such as the ministry of domestic trade, automobile transport, paper industry, municipal economy. All these ministries plan and manage specific enterprises under their jurisdiction.

State Committees

In addition to the ministries, the Union and the republic governments have a large number (twenty-five in the Union government in 1964) of so-called state committees concerned with individual industries or sectors of the economy. The most important of them are the state committees on Wages and Labor, Coordination of Scientific Research, Automation and Machine-Building, and Defense Technology. Most of these committees are charged with the centralized planning of the technical modernization and development of their industries. For the most part they are not concerned with production, and the enterprises are not directly responsible to them. Many of these committees serve as advisory bodies to the planning agencies.

Planning Agencies

The planning agencies of the Soviet government on the Union and the republic levels are divided into those charged with the preparation of long-range plans and those responsible for the preparation and execution of the current, short-term plans. The preparation of the long-range plans (for five years and more) is vested in the State Planning Committee (Gosplan), while the preparation of the annual plans and their execution is centralized exclusively in the councils on the national economy (SNKH) of the USSR and of each of the republics. The SNKH are concerned only with *industrial* plans, while the Gosplans unify the industrial plans with those for agriculture, transportation, foreign trade, and finance. A coordinative agency supervises the work of both the Gosplan and the SNKH; it is the Supreme National Economic Council of the USSR.

Regional Economic Councils (Sovnarkhozy)

Regional economic councils are subdivisions of the SNKH of the republics. As mentioned before, there were forty-seven such economic councils in the whole of the Soviet Union in 1964; in some republics there were several, while others had just one. An average economic council in the Russian Republic produced a yearly output of more than $3.0 billion in 1962. It was thus equal to a large American corporation. In its internal organization it was similar to such a corporation, too, except that it was owned and strictly controlled by the government, not by private stockholders. All industrial enterprises within the territory of a regional economic council are directly managed by it, as if they were local plants and factories of a single company. The council tells them what they are to produce, in which quantities, at what cost, and by which deadlines; it also supplies the enterprises with the necessary raw materials, working capital, investments, and skilled labor; it controls the enterprises' profits and bonuses, and redistributes them among them on its own discretion. Thus, in many ways, the regional economic councils are the most important economic institutions in the Soviet industry.

Ground-Level Enterprises

The foregoing description of the economic councils should have made it clear that Soviet ground-level enterprises, although there are some 200,000 of them, are not at all similar to independent business firms in a free enterprise economy. Almost all rights and duties of Soviet enterprises are regulated, defined, and controlled from above; their freedom of action, financial independence, and entrepreneurial sovereignty are highly circumscribed. All their operative plans are approved and supervised by their economic councils, and their function is only to fulfill them as best they can. For example, a Soviet enterprise has no right to borrow money from a bank in excess of what is permitted in its plan, nor can it spend its funds for things not specified in the plan; in case of emergency, the manager has the right to spend no more than 5 percent of the daily cash revenue of his plant, and even then he must account for it the next day. This is all the freedom and independence possessed by a Soviet enterprise.[12] Within the limits of its plan, however, the enterprise has the right to (a) strive to lower its costs of production and (b) to overfulfill its production targets, if the goods it produces are in demand and if its economic council would furnish additional supplies. Incentives are geared to make the fulfillment and overfulfillment of plans, the reduction of costs, and the improvement of quality desirable both to management and labor. In all such cases, the enterprise is entitled to up to 6 percent of its planned profits and up to 60 percent of the above-the-plan profits to be automatically allocated to its so-called enterprise fund (the total amount of which cannot exceed 7 percent of the total wage fund, however). The enterprise fund is under direct control of the management, the local labor union, and the party committee, and is spent at their discretion. However, the rules of its expenditure are established by the govern-

---

[12] Cf., for example, *Prava rukovoditeley predpriyatiy i organizatsiy, sovnarkhozov, ministerstv i vedomstv v reshenii khozyaystvennykh voprosov: Spravochnoe posobie* (Moscow: Gosyurizdat, 1961), p. 149ff.

ment as follows: 20 percent of the fund must be invested in new technology, modernized equipment, and the expansion of output; 40 percent must be spent on workers' housing and recreation facilities; and the remaining 40 percent can be spent on individual bonuses, vacations at health resorts, improvements in mess halls' food and catering, and the like. A separate and quantitatively most important system of regular bonus payments is administered by the economic councils and ministries, not by the enterprises.[13] (Early in 1965, a growing number of Soviet economists and plant managers were clamoring in the press against the limitations on the autonomy of Soviet enterprises, and the Communist party and government had under their consideration a draft bill that would reduce the powers of the economic councils and would enhance the rights of the plant managers. However, the oncoming reform was not expected to bring about any dramatic changes in the nature of the Soviet system.)

Statistical Agencies

Of crucial importance for the functioning of the Soviet planned economy is the system of government statistical agencies; they are its nerve system because speedy and reliable information is indispensable to effective centralized planning. Statistical agencies in the USSR are highly centralized and completely independent of the rest of the economic government. All enterprises and government agencies in the USSR are obliged by law to furnish them with whatever statistics and other information they request. Enterprises send their statistical reports to these agencies regularly every week, and in some cases every day. These data are aggregated and analyzed at the statistical agencies' computer centers, and then reported to the planning agencies and the government.

The Role of the Communist Party

The Communist party is virtually omnipotent in the USSR over all the planning and execution of plans. Key economic decisions in the Soviet economy are made by nontechnicians—persons who are not necessarily educated economists or independent public servants. Planners fulfill only *technical* functions in the Soviet Union; they prepare plans—largely to specifications set down by others—and carry them out. *The most important decisions are made by politicians within the Communist party committees.* The decision-making apparatus of the CPSU, is organized on four abovementioned levels in accordance with the territorial principle. The rank-and-file membership of the party is organized in cells according to the place of work. The Central Committee of the CPSU, its economic departments and

---

[13] Cf. T. I. Ponizov, *Upravlenie promyshlennym proizvodstvom v SSSR* (Moscow: Ekonomizdat, 1963), p 58.

bureaus, as well as the Secretariat and the Presidium, represent the summit of all power in the Soviet Union. They must approve of all major elements in the annual and the long-range plans; they issue directives on what is to be included in the plans or how in particular the plans are to be carried out; they decide which industries are to have priority before others in the allocation of resources, and so forth. In a similar way, the central committees of the republic Communist parties exercise ultimate power within their republics and over the regional economic councils.

Local party committees in plants and factories as well as in the cities and provinces also play a decisive role in various local economic decisions. They supervise the work of all managerial personnel; organize the workers and collective farmers during campaigns to achieve one or another planned target; they have a voice in all appointments to executive positions, in the distribution of new apartments, in the allocation of consumer goods to the particular cities and regions, and so forth.

In practice the Communist party deals with every conceivable kind of problem. Its specific functions are hard to explain, however, because they are not defined in any clear-cut law or statute. *One thing is certain: the Communist party runs the Soviet economy. It makes all the basic decisions and can intervene in any and all matters that its leaders consider of importance.*

DETAILED ECONOMIC PLANNING IN THE SOVIET UNION

From the time that the Communists took power in the Soviet Union, they prepared for extensive planning of the economy, even though they had no specific plans ready. Before their present form of planning was devised, largely through trial and error, they relied upon very simple plans that affected only one or a few branches of industry. The first plan, known as the Goelro, was adopted in 1921 and was concerned almost exclusively with electric power generating capacity. The first five-year plan, adopted in April 1929, was extremely detailed and set output goals for hundreds of products. Since then, Soviet planning procedures have been broadened and strengthened; they continue to be modified in efforts to make them more efficient. The following pages do not deal with the historical development of planning in the Soviet Union, but try to make clear how it operates at present.

Is Economic Planning Complicated?

Why has the very possibility of efficient economic planning been questioned by some economists? [14] Because, it is contended, so many factors should enter into the decisions about what, how much, when, and how to produce that human beings are incapable of deciding these matters "correctly." Moreover, even if these decisions could somehow be made correctly, they would require, first, so much time that the plans would always be out of date and, second, the labors of so many people that little could be produced besides economic plans. Especially before the invention of electronic computers all this appeared to be true, particularly if one defined "correctly" in some strict sense.

A good economic plan takes account of social goals, the preferences of buyers for products, and the occupational choices of productive factors. Put more simply, a good plan would respect the desires both of consumers and of producers. But how can one obtain full and reliable information about the desires of consumers and producers? We shall see presently how the Soviet Union has coped with this problem.

In addition to the difficulty of determining the relative importance of various products, and the attitude of workers toward different kinds of work, planners face complicated "technical" problems in drawing up a good plan. Plans must be kept in balance. There are several types of balance that must be maintained if the general economic plan is to be efficient. Certain balances will be termed *crosswise balances;* others will be called *backward balances.* An explanation of these types of balance will help to make clear why economic planning, although very complicated, is nevertheless feasible.

Crosswise Balances

Certain relationships must be maintained between various economic factors and circumstances. First, output goals set by an economic plan should require the use of all available productive factors—no more and no less. To call for less output than the available labor force and equipment could produce would result in underemployment—a mark of inefficient planning. To call for more output than the available resources could turn out would necessarily result in failure to produce all that had been planned, and might lead to unavoidable interruptions in production. But to use the labor force

---

[14] Perhaps the best known among them are Von Mises and Hayek, both famous Austrian economists. *Cf.* F. A. von Hayek (ed.) *Collectivist Economic Planning* (London, 1935); L. von Mises, *Planning for Freedom* (South Holland, Ill., 1962). Even some Socialists, under Hayek's and Mises' influence, abandoned their traditional belief in planning; *cf.* O. Lange and F. M. Taylor, *On the Economic Theory of Socialism* (Minneapolis, 1938).

exactly and also use exactly the supply of power, transportation, basic metals, and the like is vastly complicated. Soviet planners check crosswise balances of this type for thousands of items.

Another crosswise balance that must be maintained arises from the fact that production takes place in space. Planners must decide where output is to be produced. They must locate production with respect to the availability of resources and with regard to the cost of transporting raw materials to the site of production. Consequently, an economic plan must have geographical balance—with the output goals for each area calling for the supplies of factors that are or could easily be made available in the area.

Still another crosswise balance that must be achieved by economic planners is that between physical and financial conditions. In the Soviet Union money is used to facilitate almost all economic activities. Workers are paid in money and they purchase goods with money. It is necessary, if the economy is to avoid inflation or an accumulation of inventories, that money payments to individuals be kept in balance with prices charged. While the consequences of excessive and insufficient expenditure differ in planned and unplanned economies, they are undesirable in both. A perfect plan maintains an exact balance.

Backward Balances

Backward balances are relationships between the output of finished products and their input components. For example, the output of automobile wheels and tires must be kept in line with the output of automobiles. If almost completed cars were to remain unusable for lack of tires, or if far more tires were produced than were needed, the plan would be out of balance and resources would have been used inefficiently. If we remember, however, how many other inputs go into the output of an automobile (steel, aluminum, copper, glass, as well as lathes, tools, assembly lines, electric power, various types of labor and so on), and if we understand that all these ingredients could also be used to produce goods other than automobiles, and that they, therefore, must be equally balanced in all other uses, including the production of automobiles, airplanes, locomotives, tractors, rockets and what not, it may come home how truly difficult it must be to exactly dovetail all such backward balances. Backward balancing is much more complicated than crosswise balancing, but the final plan must be balanced out both ways.

A mere statement of the balances that must be maintained in a perfect plan shows that "perfect" plans are virtually impossible. It does not follow, however, that efficient planning is impossible or that planning is undesirable. Every economy falls far short of perfection.

Before the mechanics of planning in the Soviet Union are outlined, two general points should be recognized. First, if one conceives of planning as the formulation of plans "from scratch" by which the activities of all individuals and plants are directed, it will surely appear impossible. In practice, a planned economy is built in stages; planners are able to build on the present and the past. Planning primarily takes the form of projecting changes from the present. That, is, planners decide in what ways existing arrangements might be improved; they do not draw up a completely different set of arrangements. Second, plans are not made "once and for all." If it turns out that something is out of kilter, a correction will be made.

By patching up mistakes in the original plan, the planners may end up with an efficient plan. Once they have achieved an efficient balance of the various parts of the economy, it should not be very difficult to maintain efficiency even while some modifications are made in the economy. However, during the period when the economy is undergoing basic changes—such as a large relocation of industry, a transformation of an agricultural into an industrial economy, a sharp shift in the rate of capital formation, and the like—correction of mistakes would not be easy and would usually involve waste. On the other hand, even such basic changes would not require replanning from the ground up. *The ability to build on the past and to change things around if plans are out of line enormously simplifies the task of planning.* Indeed, without it, efficient planning would almost certainly be impossible.

What Are Soviet Economic Plans?

Economic plans are not unique to the Soviet economy.[15] Nevertheless, Soviet economic plans are quite distinctive and are prepared in a unique manner to deal with the very special problems and to achieve the particular goals pursued by the Soviet leaders. The nature of these plans and their preparation will be discussed in the following pages.

It is common to speak of the Soviet economic system as being directed by "a plan." In particular, foreigners frequently refer to the "five-year plan" as

---

[15] The description of Soviet planning that follows is for the most part based on the following sources: I. A. Yevenko, *Planning in the USSR* (Moscow: Foreign Languages Publishing House, 1961); G. Sorokin, *Planirovanie narodnogo khozyaystva SSSR* (Moscow, 1961); M. G. Kolodny, A. P. Stepanov, *Planirovanie narodnogo khozyaystva SSSR* (Kiev, 1963); M. S. Urinson, *Planirovanie narodnogo khozyaystva v soyuznykh respublikakh* (Moscow, 1963); Y. I. Koldomasov, *Metod material'nykh balansov v planirovanii narodnogo khozyaystva* (Moscow, 1959); G. I. Grebtsov, P. P. Karpov, eds., *Material'nye balansy v narodnokhozyaystvennon plane* (Moscow, 1960); H. S. Levine, "The Centralized Planning of Supply in Soviet Industry," in U. S. Congress, Joint Economic Committee, *Comparison of the United States and Soviet Economies,* 86th Cong., 1st sess. (Washington, D. C.: Government Printing Office, 1959). Exceptionally valuable original documents on Soviet planning have appeared in *Cahiers de l'Institut de Science Économique Appliquée* (Paris), No. 107 (supplement, Série G, no. 10), November 1960; and No. 140 (Série G, no. 18), August 1963.

the document that directs the Soviet economy. These statements show a certain misconception, for a whole hierarchy of plans are in operation at any time in the USSR. Each enterprise, each collective farm, mine, bank, and each district, province, city, economic council, and each national republic has its own plans. Each of these has not one, but a number of plans.

The Soviet system of plans is often pictured as starting as a single, all-embracing plan for the country as a whole and for particular industries, regions, and republics; also, it is viewed as being divided into annual, quarterly, and monthly plans for each area and enterprise—with all plans adding exactly to the total national plan. This too is a gross oversimplification.

Naturally, all Soviet plans apply to some particular period of time, but individual plans are not constructed for identical periods. In the main, five types of periodic plans can be distinguished: (1) perspective plans—which establish targets for up to twenty years in advance; (2) long-term control figures providing targets five to seven years ahead; (3) annual plans; (4) quarterly plans; (5) monthly plans. These periodic plans do not necessarily subdivide into plans for shorter periods, and subplans do not always add up into superplan totals. Thus, five- or seven-year plans are not usually subdivided into annual plans; plans of the republics include many details that are not part of the federal plans.

In other words, the Soviet economy is governed by an elaborate superstructure of economic plans. Some are superimposed upon others; some reflect special efforts in a particular sphere above and beyond the usual type of plan; and some represent revisions of old plans.

Soviet economic plans are primarily expressed in kind rather than in money terms. That is, supplies and desired outputs are expressed in tons, pounds, barrels, baskets, yards, numbers of units, rather than rubles. As a result, Soviet plans are extremely complex, for they involve specific programs for literally hundreds of thousands of particular items. Each of these must, in some way, be made to balance with all others so that all of the nation's productive resources are put to use and not left idle.

Soviet Long-range Plans

Important Soviet plans cover fairly long periods. Currently, the Soviet Union is operating under a Twenty-Year Plan for the Construction of Communism (1960-1980); a Seven-Year Plan for the Development of the National Economy of the USSR (1959-1965) is also in effect. The main function of such long-range plans is to point the direction and set the pace for the economy's development. Long-range plans lend historical perspective to planning and force the planners to think in terms of the evolution of society as a whole. If Soviet planners were to plan solely in one-year terms, they could only pursue very limited objectives; and, such plans would not be able to mold the fundamental character of the economic and social structure of the Soviet Union.

Soviet long-range plans represent directives to those who prepare plans for a shorter period. They set down broad objectives and weigh social, political, military, scientific, and international goals. They deal with such matters as the proportion of resources to be devoted to investment (the building of new plant and equipment) as opposed to consumers goods; output for military purposes; the speed at which various regions are to be developed; the degree of dependence upon imports, and the like. Individual enterprises also have long-term plans, including specific output goals for some five to seven years in the future. These goals are revised annually.

Although long-range plans are in many ways the most important influences on the direction in which the USSR moves, they generally set down specific tasks only for 40 percent to 60 percent of all industries.[16] They are much more general than annual plans. *Annual plans are the actual operational plans according to which the Soviet economy does its daily business.*

One of the most difficult decisions made by top Soviet authorities in their long-range plans concerns the relative effort to be devoted to consumers and capital goods. In order to become militarily strong and to develop a powerful industrial base for continuous economic expansion, Soviet leaders have placed overwhelming stress upon capital goods. They have held down the output of consumer products far below what consumers wanted. In this way they were able to release resources and manpower to build heavy industry and a strong military arm. Of late, consumers goods production has been expanded fairly rapidly—though a comparatively very large share of Soviet output continues to be made up of capital and other nonconsumer goods.

As mentioned before, Soviet long-range plans are prepared by the State Planning Committee (Gosplan) of the USSR and of each of its fifteen constituent republics. These plans are discussed and approved by the Communist party congresses.

The Preparation of Soviet Annual Plans

Detailed annual plans for the Soviet Union as a whole include at least the following parts: output and consumption plans, a financial plan, a capital budget, a labor plan, and the plans for individual regions. We shall discuss the preparation, adoption, and execution of output and consumption plans only. Later, the others will be sketched briefly.

Planning is a detailed process and unless one understands the process, he

---

16 *Cf. Voprosy planirovania i razmeshchenia promyshlennosti* (Moscow: Gosplanizdat, 1959), p. 27.

does not understand planning. One cannot simply assume, as many persons sympathetic to economic planning do, that "planners can figure it out." One must determine just what planners are able to accomplish and what lies beyond their grasp. To do this, one must explore the details of planning mechanics.

All planning in the Soviet Union can be divided into four stages. In the first stage, the highest political authorities set down the country's basic goals. The second stage calls for preparing programs that will achieve these general objectives. In this stage, specific output goals are set for a large number of products. The third stage is the adoption of the detailed plans. Finally, the last stage is the execution of the plan.

The First Stage: General Objectives

As explained, Soviet authorities pursue a variety of goals beyond purely economic objectives. These represent the starting point of an annual plan. The long-range plans provide most general objectives for the annual plans; others may be established by current decisions of the Central Committee of the Communist party and the Council of Ministers of the USSR.

Every Soviet plan, be it for the country, a region, or even a single enterprise, designates one or several "leading links." *These are top priority targets* on which resources and efforts are to be concentrated ahead of other goals. They are the most important targets of the annual plans. As a rule, they are designated by the Communist party well in advance of the preparation of the annual plans.

The Second Stage: Detailed Annual Plans

The primary concept that guides Soviet planners is that of balanced allocation and full employment of all resources. For example, at the heart of every year's planning in the USSR at present are 130 raw materials balances. That is, the total supply of 130 basic materials is forecast with considerable accuracy and subdivided among a vast number of specific uses. By dividing up the total estimated supply of these 130 items among the uses to which they will be put, the planners try to ensure an equality of supply and demand. More important, the supply is allocated among alternative uses in a manner designed to achieve what the planners consider a "balanced" division of that raw material.

As their first step, the planners calculate how much of each given material must be allocated to the "leading link" targets of the plan. Next they determine how much will be devoted to the targets with lower levels of priority, going down the list of possible uses until the total prospective supply is exhausted. In the process of this allocation of raw materials on paper, they ponder the benefits and sacrifices that would follow from shifting the materials from one use to another, or from substituting them for one another, wherever such shifting is possible. When the prospective supply of the raw material is thus allocated among the necessary uses, the "balance" of that material is established. The balance then appears as a statistical table listing the sources and quantities of supply and the uses to which that supply will be put; both sides, total production and total consumption, in the table balance out. As an illustration, we reproduce here the actual 1955 electric power balance for the USSR as a whole.

This procedure is employed by Soviet planners not only for raw materials, but also for the most important final products, including consumer goods, for the labor force, capital investments, and exports and imports. Two things are worth remembering about the Soviet planned balances. First, most of them are established *in kind,* in physical units, rather than in money and price terms. Second, the established balances are not necessarily final or rigid; in the process of the plan's fulfillment, the planners may change them as circumstances require. If something goes wrong, and the particular total plan cannot be fulfilled, the allocations to low-priority targets within the existing balance are shifted to the "leading links" to secure their fulfillment. In Table 13 the "leading link" of course is constituted by the industrial users of power, while those having the lowest priority are private households and agriculture.

The preparation of resource balances lies at the base of Soviet planning. However, economic planners cannot prepare such balances without obtaining a vast amount of information from the individual enterprises and low-level planning agencies in the republics. Let us accordingly, sketch the steps followed in preparing an annual plan in the USSR. The reader should recognize clearly that the following account of Soviet planning is *not* offered as an accurate description of how things are actually done; rather, it explains what Soviet planners are trying to do. They would be the first to admit that they have not perfected the planning process and that it is extremely complex and time-consuming. But they believe it clearly can be done and, with its imperfections, still substantially "better" than any other system. These are the views, it should be remembered, of highly intelligent men, many of whom have considerable information about other economic systems.

Draft Plans of Individual Enterprises. The preparation of an annual plan in the Soviet Union begins in May of the preceding year. At that time each enterprise prepares its own draft plan, starting with its past year leading links and estimating its own balances. That is, it sets down the output it proposes to produce during the following year and it specifies the materials needed to produce that output. In setting down its proposed output, the enterprise will be guided by (1) whatever relevant information or statements are included in its long-range plan; (2) current decisions of the Communist party committees about what is intended for its industry; (3) forecast changes in productivity—that is, what the plant and staff would be

Table 13.   Electric Power Balance on the Union Level, 1955

(in million kilowatt-hours)

Republics	TOTAL PRODUCTION	Imported from other republics	TOTAL CONSUMPTION	Used by industrial enterprises	Used by transportation system	Used by households, agriculture, and other sectors	Used by power stations themselves	Lost in relay network	Exported from the republic
Russia	115,700	300	114,700	79,200	4,300	16,700	7,900	6,600	1,300
Ukraine	30,099	1,242	31,339	22,913	469	3,901	2,113	1,943	2
Kazakhstan	5,698	25	5,605	4,361	121	770	188	165	118
Azerbaidzhan	4,640	—	4,405	3,354	77	409	188	378	235
Uzbekistan	3,880	—	3,614	2,748	31	494	60	281	266
Georgia	2,221	235	2,248	1,291	227	429	39	262	209
Armenia	2,215	—	2,215	1,808	38	216	5	148	—
Belorussia	1,870	—	1,870	1,105	51	427	164	122	—
Estonia	941	11	950	605	14	190	68	73	2
Latvia	928	—	926	498	23	251	46	108	2
Lithuania	574	6	580	310	14	168	36	52	—
Kirghiz	517	64	581	437	5	110	5	24	—
Turkmenia	413	—	413	274	14	96	11	17	—
Tadzhikistan	296	199	493	337	5	118	1	32	1
Moldavia	258	—	258	115	9	97	11	26	—
Soviet Union	170,200	—	170,200	113,300	5,400	30,300	10,900	10,300	—

NOTE: Some figures may not add up to totals because of rounding.

SOURCE: USSR Central Statistical Administration, *Promyshlennost SSSR: Statisticheskiy sbornik* (Industries of the USSR: A Statistical Handbook), Moscow, Gosstatizdat, 1957, pp. 20, 58, 74-100.

able to produce; and (4) information about buyers' demand often based on direct contact with its customers, including trade organizations.

In estimating the material requirements to produce that output, the plant will use its "norms." These represent measures of the amount of various *inputs* (raw materials, component parts, energy, labor) required to produce a single unit of output. These norms are carefully computed in the Soviet Union and represent a central tool employed by planners—both in construction of plans and review of plans made by others. As one would expect, these norms change as technology is improved. In the preparation of a draft plan, the plant manager will confer with the Communist party and trade union organizations represented at his plant. Ordinarily, they all will agree on the proposal that is sent on to the economic council for that area.

Activities of Various Types of Territorial Planning Agencies. When the regional economic council receives the proposals and requests from individual plants in that region, it scrutinizes them closely for internal consistency, compatibility with the draft plans of other enterprises in the area, and with the demand information at its disposal. Questions will be raised— possibly by telephone or letter—and a total plan for that region will be constructed. This draft plan will be passed by the economic council along to the republic economic council (SNKH), which will repeat the process for the republic as a whole. It will examine the proposed output and proposed requirements for resources. It too will communicate with the local economic councils and major plants in the event of questions, doubts, and disagreements. In the usual case, the plans submitted by the different economic councils will require some modification at the republic level. The republics will then submit their draft plans to the Economic Council of the USSR (Union SNKH). At this point a crucial stage in planning is reached; that is, the process of actually ensuring the balanced use of all resources for which balances are prepared.

Up to the point that a plan reaches the Union level, no republic can tell whether the supplies of materials will be completely adequate to the proposed uses of them because much of the supplies come from other republics. When all plans are assembled, several hazards exist. First, the resources available may not be sufficient to meet all requirements. More vexing, draft plans may call for too little of certain materials even while calling for an excess of others. For example, the compiled plans of all republics (economic councils and enterprises) may call for 5 million more tons of steel than will be available, 2000 tons less of aluminum than can be available, 10 percent more of coal than can be produced and 5 percent more of oil, and so on. Under these circumstances, the draft plans of some enterprises and economic councils necessarily will be frustrated if they try to carry them out. An excess of certain things will not compensate for a deficiency of others. Unless disparities between supply and demand are ironed out in advance, considerable potential production will be lost. It is the task of the Union SNKH to achieve balanced use of all materials in the USSR as a whole and in each republic. In pursuing this objective, the Union SNKH might call for greater expansion of some industries and a lesser growth of others. It might encourage certain industries to substitute one material for another; and, it might be compelled to cut back the output of certain products and regions. But it *must* achieve a balance, for unbalanced use of resources is wasteful and disruptive; it means either unused resources or undertakings that are unfinished for lack of materials or labor.

When the Union SNKH has completed its work, it passes the plan over to the Central Committee of the Communist party of the USSR for approval. The plan must also be approved by the Supreme National Economic Council of the USSR, an arm of the federal government.

When this approval has been obtained, the national economic plan makes its way back down the planning hierarchy. For example, the Union SNKH allocates to each of the 15 republics a supply of 130 basic raw materials. At this point, however, the 130 materials are broken down into 11,000 to 12,000 items. For example, steel, one of the 130 basic materials is subdivided into approximately 45 different types: sheets, plate, wire, rod, and so on. Similarly, petroleum, another of the 130 basic materials, is divided into 9 different types of lubricants and 167 other products.[17] The republic SNKH must in turn divide, in the same manner, the materials allocated to them among the individual regional economic councils that comprise the republic. All these planned allocations that go down the pyramid are now *obligatory*. Their recipients have no right to change them.

The economic councils then have the responsibility of allocating supplies of these 11,000-12,000 submaterials to individual enterprises. They perform this function by referring to the draft plans they have received from each enterprise. In those initial plans, each enterprise has indicated its requirements for these 11,000-12,000 items. The economic councils usually will not be able to give each enterprise precisely what it had requested initially. However, the initial request will be studied carefully in making the final allocation.

Ultimately, then, each individual enterprise will receive from its economic council an allocation of various raw materials and other means of production as well as an output goal, indicating how many units of some commodity it is to produce out of these resources. This is the enterprise's final plan, which it is obliged to carry out. In the same manner and along the same channels of communication and authority quarterly plans are worked out on the basis of the annual plan. Monthly plans are not sent very

[17] Other industries include the following numbers of items planned in kind at this level: chemicals—1128; heavy machinery—1623; electric machinery and appliances—4109; consumers goods—326, and so forth. Cf. *Cahiers de l'Institut de Science Économique Appliquée* (Paris), No. 140 (G, 18), August 1963, p. 45.

high up for approval, however; they are worked out between the enterprise and its economic council.

We have thus seen what Soviet economic planning strives mainly to achieve: the utilization of the total supply of productive resources—neither a shortage nor a surplus of any resource—and the balanced use of each resource. At the very end of the planning process, each enterprise knows how much to produce, what materials it will be given, where it can obtain these materials, the price that it will be charged for them and the price it will receive for its output.

The foregoing process clearly makes sense. Equally clearly, it is extremely complicated and time-consuming. Opportunities for error are substantial and many mistakes are made. It would be helpful to explore the responses of the Soviet planning system to the kinds of errors that arise.

Let us first consider the situation in which some basic material is produced in smaller quantities than was originally demanded in the plan. Thereupon, we will consider what planners do when some models of some product are produced in the wrong proportion.

Assume that the supply of refined copper fell short of what the planners had anticipated, what remedial action might the planners take? First, inventories might be depleted (inventories of most things in the USSR are extremely small, a fact that magnifies the impact of planning errors). Second, supplies of the product might be imported. Third, substitutions for copper might be improvised in certain uses, thus releasing copper for use where substitution would not be possible. Further, the output of selected items could be curtailed—thus releasing supplies of also other products than copper. The planners might redistribute these released supplies of steel, nickel, rubber, and the like or hold them in inventory so that when copper becomes available, the output of the curtailed item could be made up. The serious consequences of a shortage of basic material, as sketched, explains why the 130 basic materials are considered leading links and strenuous efforts are made to achieve their target output.

Let us now consider the remedies available to planners in the event that the output of different models of, say, refrigerators did not conform to customer demand. Let us assume that, for some unspecified reason, factory managers elected to produce an undue proportion of six-foot refrigerators and too few five-foot and seven-foot refrigerators. Would this error be detected promptly? How might it be remedied?

In the first place, consumers of five- and seven-foot refrigerators would be frustrated by the shortage in the shops. Soviet consumers would ordinarily indicate this fact in the special book kept by each major store in which complaints are recorded by customers. If a consumer was in urgent need of a refrigerator, he might accept the six-foot size even while registering a complaint in the store's book. (The books are later checked by government inspectors and complaints are analyzed.)

If a surplus of six-foot refrigerators developed, the managers of the stores with surpluses would eventually note this fact. Their reaction would be to refuse to accept further six-foot refrigerators and to notify both the trade ministry and their supplier that they had too many six-foot refrigerators and too few five- and seven-foot boxes. Such information would be conveyed to the appropriate economic councils which usually would direct refrigerator manufacturers to shift the proportion of their output.

It is not suggested that products are always produced in exact proportions that consumers wish to buy them or that disproportions in output are always eliminated promptly. Indeed, the Soviet press tells of many cases where there are gluts of individual models and sizes of a product while others are in surplus supply. However, these situations apparently are the exception rather than the rule. The means clearly exist for correcting such difficulties though they are not always used at the earliest possible moment and in precisely the best manner possible. On the other hand, every other developed nation's distribution system is also afflicted with such imbalances between production and sales of individual items—though not necessarily with equal frequency.

The Third Stage: Adoption of the Plan

With the approval of the Central Committee of the Communist party usually secured by December, the draft annual plan is introduced as a bill at the December session of the Supreme Soviet of the USSR. Whether or not the legislators in the Supreme Soviet can, or do, change something substantial in the bill is not known. The final summary version of the plan is voted into a law and is subsequently published in the press. It contains but from 25 to 100 explicitly stated targets of the plan. All the remaining target figures and supporting statistics (about 2500 more) are contained in an appendix to the law; this appendix is not made public. *Thus, the basic decisions concerning production and distribution of most goods and factors of production in the Soviet economy are undertaken without wide public approval or even knowledge.*

The same process of adoption of the annual plans is repeated in each republic of the Union. The draft plans are referred for approval to the central commitees of the republic Communist parties and then are voted into the laws by the Supreme Soviet of each republic. Sometimes republic plans contain more specific targets than the Union plans.

The Fourth Stage: Supervision of the Plan's Execution

In the Soviet view "fulfillment supervision" of economic plans is perhaps the most important step in economic planning. Certainly it is not less important than the drafting of plans.

The underlying principle of the Soviet planning philosophy calls for the plans to be fulfilled as exactly as possible. All Soviet plans are obligatory for those who have been designated to carry them out. If some output targets are not attained, the balances and the output plans of other enterprises and industries could be disrupted. The effect of the disruption of one plan often expands like circles from a stone thrown into a pond. For these reasons, they have constructed stringent controls and rely on supervision of what they call *planning discipline* to secure fulfillment of plans.[18]

Supervision of a plan's fulfillment is entrusted to several agencies. The planning bodies themselves at all levels—with their reporters at all plants throughout the country—probably are the best equipped to supervise the plan's execution. In addition, the State Bank reports deviations from the plan. It holds all deposits, and all payments among firms are required to be made on delivery by check. Thus, every delivery of goods is reflected in the State Bank's accounts. Imbalances in the accounts of firms are danger signals that require further investigation.

Local Communist party organizations also have the right and consider it their duty to supervise the fulfillment of plans by local enterprises and economic councils. The government-and-party Control Commission is, on the other hand, a special agency whose main function is to investigate all cases of possibly criminal disruption of plans as well as cases of corruption, profiteering, nepotism, and the like.

Criticism volunteered by individuals is another important form of plan fulfillment supervision. The Soviet economy relies heavily upon criticism and everyone is actively encouraged to submit carefully considered observations on every aspect of the economy. Departures from plan in any plant, especially those that can be traced to the shortcomings of some individual or department, are likely to excite comment. All newspapers maintain a special department for the investigation of complaints and publish those found valid and important. However, one must not assume that published criticism always has the effect of stimulating remedial action. Apparently there are methods by which some lax administrators can escape both the acceptance of blame and the need to remedy an objectionable situation pointed out in the press.

Plans undergo constant revision in order to correct original errors and to adapt to unforeseen circumstances. Perfect plans are not expected; accordingly, the need for revision is anticipated and regular procedures are prescribed for making changes in the original plan. The carrying out of an economic plan in the Soviet Union thus is accomplished by successive approximations.

---

[18] The overfulfillment of plans is also kept under control. These authors asked one top Russian planner, in a private letter, whether the overfulfillment of plans—which is particularly encouraged by the bonus system—does not disrupt the material balances in the same way as underfulfillment does. In his reply our correspondent pointed out that the overfulfillment of production plans is "permitted" only in case of selected goods, mostly those which belong to the "leading link" category.

The Financial and Labor Plans

As indicated, a total economic plan in the Soviet Union includes many parts. Thus far, we have described only part of a plan that sets output and consumption goals for goods and services. There are also a financial plan for the economy and "budgets" for capital and labor. *Each of these plans is subordinate to and closely tied in with output plans.*

The Financial Plan

The financial plan fundamentally translates the output goals into financial terms. Its objectives are to facilitate the achievement of output goals and to achieve a balance between prices of current output (supply) and expenditure (demand). The Soviet Union is a money economy and output plans must be translated into financial terms that allow the desired result. The financial plan incorporates the incentive system of the economy as well as the safeguards against "inflation" and "deflation." (These terms are put in quotes, for they mean different things in planned and in unplanned economies.)

The major components of the Soviet financial plan are the government budget, the credit plan, and the cash plan. The first aims to balance government revenues and expenditures, much like any government budget. It differs from the United States budget in that it applies to a far larger proportion of the economy; besides, it is always balanced. The credit plan governs the granting of short- and long-term credits by the banks. The cash plan controls the supply of money in circulation with the aim of keeping it in line with currency needs. It is based on an estimated balance of incomes and expenditures of the population and the enterprises. One of its most important components is the total wage fund for the country as a whole and for each republic and industry.

The Labor Plan

The labor plan indicates the supply of and requirements for labor. It includes estimates of additions to the labor force and additional total labor needs and a statement about the number of workers with particular skills that are needed to achieve the output goals. Except for the estimate of additions to the labor force, the labor plan is built up from reports by individual plants of their labor needs for meeting their output goals, and the estimated requirements for agriculture and new capital construction projects.

Regional Planning

As was mentioned before, all production, capital investments, labor supply, and finance plans which cover the Soviet Union as a whole, are subdivided into plans for each of the fifteen national republics; each republic in its turn subdivides its plans into plans for each regional council within its territory. This subdivision is not a simple matter, however. It is clearly one of the weak spots in the whole system of Soviet plans, for regional planning requires tremendously complex balancing of a very large number of factors. While for the Soviet Union as a whole, all balances may completely balance out, it is very difficult to effect this for each individual republic and region. The output of each republic or region is not consumed within its borders. One republic may produce a surplus of steel, coal, tractors, and wheat, for example, while it also has a deficit in aluminum, petroleum, cotton fabrics, and meat. It must export its surplus to other republics and make good its deficit by imports from them. To distribute the republic's total output of steel and total consumption of aluminum and other products by means of the balances in kind is not so difficult; the question arises, however, whether the total exchange among the republics *in value terms* adds up to a financial equilibrium. Otherwise, one republic subsidizes the others—gives up more resources than it gets—while some other republic gains at its expense. The same difficulty arises in exchange of goods among the regional economic councils within a republic; frequently, some councils do lose while others gain. Such imbalance gives rise to bitter complaints on occasion. There apparently is a tendency for those areas that export more output than they import to underfulfill their supply plans to other areas and to consume more of their output within their own frontiers than the plans specify. This phenomenon is called *localism* in the Soviet Union. It apparently represents a thorny problem in Soviet planning today because the methods to balance out the interrepublic and interregional exchanges have not yet been devised. Also, the arbitrary decisions of the Union authorities are sometimes resented and resisted.

Foreign Trade Planning

Two opposing principles guide Soviet foreign trade planning with the Capitalist countries and with the Socialist countries. In its trade with the Capitalist world, the Soviet Union apparently wants to be as independent as possible of imports from these countries. Imports from Capitalist countries are resorted to only when the product in question cannot be produced in sufficient quantities in the USSR or one of the Socialist countries, *not* simply when that product is cheaper abroad. Soviet authorities fear that if the USSR began to import everything that is cheaper abroad than at home, its economy would become dependent on the Capitalist economies and might become influenced by depressions and recessions in the world market, which might lead to dislocation and possibly to unemployment.

As far as exports are concerned, the Soviet Union seems to be willing to export heavily to Capitalist countries in order to earn the foreign exchange. Sometimes, it also resorts to sharp competition in order to win foreign markets. For example, it has sold oil, pig iron, coke, and automobiles, as much as 20 percent below the American export prices in Europe, the Middle East, and Latin America.

However, the Soviet Union seeks to expand trade as much as possible with the Socialist countries whenever it is cheaper to import and profitable to export. To this end, direct trade negotiations are conducted among the governments of the Socialist countries. The government planners of the Soviet Union and of the other Socialist countries come together periodically and compare the costs of production of different commodities in their respective countries. On the basis of selection of least-cost items, they decide to produce these items in the least-cost countries and to export them to those countries that agree not to produce these items themselves. Such decisions are subsequently incorporated into the national production and foreign trade plans of each country. This practice is referred to as the integration of the Socialist economies through the specialization of production and the dovetailing of their national plans.

In case of the balancing of foreign trade between the USSR and the Socialist countries, very similar problems arise as those among the republics and regions inside the USSR. In value terms, the trade of some countries runs a deficit, and they tend to shift their trade away from the USSR to the Capitalist countries. The Soviet Union's proposal to establish a single integrated economic plan for the whole Socialist bloc has not been accepted.

Pressures upon Planners

Thus far we have assumed that planners try to do the kind of job the Communist party would like them to do. Let us, however, inquire now into the motives and pressures that influence the decisions not only of planners but also of party leaders. They all are human, of course, and hence we may start with simple human motives.

First, it has been charged that government officials everywhere tend to avoid responsibility and initiative in decision making. This is also undoubtedly true of many Soviet planners as well as many Communist party officials. They tend to abide by past decisions made by others rather than advocate changes. That sometimes means, specifically, that planners tend to make simple percentage changes in output targets attained in the past rather than defend the introduction of a new product or propose a specific change in some line of production. The consequent danger of being proved mistaken in such initiative might be too serious for the planner to take the risk.

A more secure life for the planner is possible if he sticks to past decisions and strictly adheres to instructions sent from above.

While this argument doubtless is valid in many cases, there are also important incentives for and pressures on planners and party officials that operate in the opposite direction. If a planner were pretty certain about the success of his proposal, he would push it and, if successful, would indeed be able to attain recognition and possible promotion as a result. Many people desire advancement, bonuses, decorations, and publicity as much as they desire security. To gain such ordinarily requires novel suggestions and departures from familiar routines.

In the top Communist party and Soviet government quarters, the process of decision making as far as planning of the allocation of funds and the distribution of products is concerned "is full of contradictions and clashes of interests"—admits A. Mikoyan (in 1965 the head of state of the Soviet Union).

> This is not a strictly peaceful process. Each struggles for his particular plans and plant—inside the All-Union Gosplan and the Gosplans of the Union Republics, until a decision is reached. Most issues can be smoothed out by argument and figures, but sometimes the Government must make the decision.[19]

This decision is, presumably, an arbitrary one.

One finds reports in the Soviet government-run press of numerous conflicts of interests and activities of various pressure groups in and around the top decision-making bodies. Representatives of various national republics demand more investment funds from the federal treasury, economic councils lobby for the allocation of particular supplies, some factories push their new products for adoption in the national economic plan because their directors hope to be promoted and decorated as a result, and so forth. Such not very overt but nonetheless fierce competition is always present in and around economic decision-making agencies, and it undoubtedly influences the contents and the ultimate outcome of many a plan.

The Role of Prices in the Soviet Economy

The foregoing description of Soviet planning has made almost no reference to prices. Indeed, the chief decisions regarding what and how much to produce are made in terms of units of product and service and by the direct decisions of political leaders and planning technicians. The Soviet economic system, thus, is directed by the "visible hand" of the people in power rather than by the "invisible hand" of prices and competition.

However, almost all products and services bear a price in the Soviet

---

[19] Victor Perlo, *How the Soviet Economy Works: An Interview with A. I. Mikoyan* (New York: International Publishers, 1961), pp. 17-18.

Union. Moreover, money is used to pay for them. Money and prices perform the following major functions in the Soviet economy.

1. The authorities can pay employees in a manner that both provides clear incentives to work and relative freedom to use earnings as the employees wish. Any device other than money and prices would require an incredibly cumbersome system of direct rationing of products and payments in kind. Apart from awkwardness and inefficiency, this system would have greatly limited free expression of personal tastes and preferences.

2. The prices of labor and equipment determine selection among different methods of production. A comparison of the costs of alternative production methods is used in the Soviet Union to decide which method should be employed. Without a money yardstick, such a selection of production methods would necessarily be arbitrary—and most probably would be wrong. (The use of money costs will, however, be a poor measure of relative efficiency unless money costs do in fact measure a combination of sacrifices and opportunities foregone.)

3. Prices are also used in Soviet planning to decide on the desirability of substitution of one material for another, or one type of equipment for another, or for labor, whenever such substitution is possible or needed. Without prices to measure the cost of production, cost comparison would be impossible.

4. Money and prices are also used as an extremely efficient rationing device. That is, high prices both discourage and actually prevent people from purchasing large quantities of scarce goods. Conversely, low prices encourage consumption. Price adjustments make it possible to clear the market of products without employing direct rationing.

5. Prices are also sometimes used by the planning authorities to influence the proportions in which certain items are produced. The previous section explained that central planners divided available raw materials initially among 130 uses, then among 11,000 to 12,000, and so down the planning hierarchy, until these materials were allocated to each individual enterprise. However, out of these raw materials (and many other resource inputs) the Soviet economy produces many millions of different kinds of goods. (The Soviet government actually sets prices on 8 million different items.) It would obviously be extremely difficult for the central planners in Moscow to attempt to make direct specific decision as to which of the many kinds of goods each individual enterprise should produce, and in what specific proportions. Whatever decisions they might make would probably be mistaken, and the whole decision-making process would be extremely costly. Therefore, instead of deciding such matters high up in the planning hierarchy, these decisions are pushed down to the base of the pyramid. In most cases, it is the regional economic councils in the republics who make

the decisions as to what each individual enterprise must produce and how much. To retain a degree of control over such decisions, however, the central planners in Moscow retain for themselves the right to set prices on almost all goods and services. Neither the economic councils nor the plant managers have the right to change prices or to establish them on their own. What they can sometimes do, however, is to adjust their output to the existing prices. This does not happen too often, but this is one way in which prices influence output in the Soviet economy.

Every enterprise in the USSR operates within many direct constraints embodied in its plans. The manager is given an output goal for his plant by the economic council; this output goal is usually stated in physical units as well as in value terms (total value arrived at by multiplying the number of units by the price per unit). The different sizes, styles, colors, and models of the particular output sometimes will perhaps not be specified in the plan handed down by the economic council; the manager is then given the right to exercise his own choice in this matter. In such decisions, the manager would undoubtedly take prices into consideration. Suppose the manager of a plant that produces both refrigerators and washing machines is given the following plan by his economic council: Produce X units of refrigerators and Y units of washing machines; their total value must be $PX + PY = Z$ rubles. You will be given the following materials (in the amounts A, B, and C) to produce this output, and your wage bill must not exceed K rubles. Within these constraints, the plant manager may be left free to produce individual sizes and models of refrigerators and washing machines, and in any proportions he thinks best. Prices of all models and sizes have been set by the government, however, and cannot be changed. Under such circumstances, to the extent that the manager can produce efficiently, he will strive to keep costs low and to raise his profit. The latter will cast credit on his performance and his and his workers' bonuses will increase.

The Soviet Union has had some bitter experience with the operation of prices and of profit motive even within such a narrow framework as this. A factory in Odessa once produced trousers of the very largest sizes only because the profit mark-up on them happened to be the highest. To avert such malpractices, Soviet planners tend to do two things. On one hand, the economic councils are instructed to make their plans more and more specific and tell the managers what models and sizes they must produce in specified quantities or proportions determined by buyers' demand; on the other hand, the government has given the right to store managers and wholesale buyers to reject or return the unsalable goods to their producers and thus make them lose money.

If the goods in questions are consumer goods, the planners will sometimes lower or raise their prices in order to discourage or encourage their production in such an indirect way. Most usually, however, they will not resort to price changes because this involves a lot of costly paper work and also because they believe in principle that prices should reflect production costs rather than all the temporary and erratic fluctuations in the demand and supply situations. In spite of their rigidity, however, Soviet consumer goods prices have been found in a direct comparison to be no more "irrational" or "rational" than similar prices in the United States.[20]

Thus, the Soviet economy is very far from a fully operative price system. It uses other means to determine how much to produce and how to allocate its resources among different uses. Moreover, prices are set directly by planning authorities and do not reflect any "market forces." For example, an increase in consumers' demand for an item will not raise the price of that item and create a profit inducement to expand its output—which is generally the case under a full-fledged price system. Similarly, increases in the scarcity of raw materials or in the personal sacrifices involved in production do not directly and speedily result in higher prices for those items. Consequently, these changes in scarcity and real costs will not directly affect output. *Prices in the Soviet Union are tools in the hands of planners rather than an independent mechanism guiding the operations of the economy.*

The following principles underly current pricing policy in the Soviet Union:

1. There is a single factory price for each capital good, no matter where it is produced. Transportation costs are usually borne by the buyers.
2. There is a single retail price for each consumer product sold through the channels of state and cooperative trade wherever it is sold—with the following exceptions: Prices in rural stores are set 7-10 percent higher than in city stores. There are also several geographic price zones between which price differences are allowed.
3. Retail prices for most consumer products are fixed at a level intended to clear the market. Individual retail prices are intended to reflect broadly supply conditions relative to consumer demand. In some cases, prices are fixed to discourage consumption (vodka) or to encourage it (books, children's apparel and shoes).
4. The kolkhoz market, on which the output of collective farms that is not paid by or sold to the state is sold, still plays an important role in supplying city dwellers with food products. Prices on this market are "free" and reflect conditions of supply and demand.
5. Prices of new products are fixed at cost level, plus 5 percent profit for the enterprise.

---

[20] *Cf.* Vsevolod Holubnychy, "The Soviet Price System Based on a New Method," *Studies on the Soviet Union* (Munich), vol. II, no. 2, 1962.

In the Soviet Union, the prices of consumer goods and producer goods differ both in function and in the way they are set. Consumer goods prices are used primarily as a method of achieving the desired level of consumption. If consumers persistently do not buy the output of a product at the price originally set by planners, the price is eventually lowered; conversely, persistent shortages are averted by raising the price. Prices are not altered to correct temporary or local shortages or gluts, however.

Prices of consumer goods do not vary directly with production costs. Indeed, a large part of the price of almost every consumer product is accounted for by the "turnover tax." This tax, the equivalent of a sales tax, is the most important source of government revenue in the Soviet Union (40 percent of all revenue in the federal budget). It serves also as the most important source of capital for construction of factories and plants by the government. The rates of turnover tax are extremely high, as can be seen from Table 14; what is especially peculiar about them is that they are kept secret. Soviet consumers never know how much tax they pay whenever they purchase something; tax rates are not publicized.

Table 14.   Ranges of Turnover Tax Rates, Percent of Retail Price, 1963

Alcoholic drinks, tobacco wares, cosmetics, furs, caviar	99.9 %
Automobiles, gasoline, cameras, typewriters, phonograph records	50-75
Radios, televisions, refrigerators, washing machines, bicycles	20-40
Kitchen utensils, sewing machines, cement, wall paper, electric lamps, matches	33-66
Overcoats, leather shoes, woolen suits, silk dresses, shirts, lingerie	50-77
Electricity and gas	18-65
Sugar, flour, cereals, vegetable oil, margarine, macaroni, candies	49-70
Bread	24-27
Tea, coffee	10-12
Meat, butter, milk, cheese	0

SOURCES: A. Smirnov, *Ekonomicheskoe soderzhanie naloga s oborota* (Moscow: Sotsekgiz, 1963), pp. 89, 109, 113, 114; V. Kovylin, *Nalog s oborota po promyshlennym tovaram* (Moscow: Gosfinizdat, 1963), pp. 26, 66; S. G. Stolyarov, *O tsenakh i tsenoobrazovanii v SSSR* (Moscow: Gosstatizdat, 1963), pp. 178, 184, 188, 189; O. O. Nesterenko (ed.), *Natsional'ny dokhod Ukrayins'koyi RSR v period rozhornutoho budivnytstva komunizmu* (Kiev: Ukrainian Academy of Sciences Press, 1963), p. 198.

To see better how turnover taxes are used to determine the levels of consumption, let us assume that the top Soviet officials decide that the final output of the nation should be divided one third for capital goods and two thirds for consumer goods. On the other hand, assume that Soviet citizens would like to spend 95 percent of the income they receive—after income taxes—on consumer goods. (Such an assumption is conservative in the light of the low level of income in the USSR, which ordinarily results in an extremely high rate of spending.) If we assume that the Soviet national income is equal to roughly $100 billion, the conclusions would follow: the planners would want to produce consumer goods whose *cost* was roughly $66.7 billion; Soviet consumers would want to spend approximately $95 billion for consumer goods—or about 42 percent more than the consumer goods output costs. Put differently, Soviet consumers would attempt to buy on the average 42 percent more goods than were available—if consumer goods were priced at cost. Under such circumstances, to sell consumer goods at cost would give rise to a serious rationing problem to determine who should get the limited available supply. Inequities would be likely in the absence of direct rationing; and rationing is both costly and irksome.

Two measures might be employed to deal with this type of situation. First, additional heavy income taxes could be levied that would bring the population's disposable income down to the point where the consumers would have to spend about $66.7 billion; or, the prices of individual commodities could be raised (by means of sales taxes) so that the sales of each on the open market would just equal available supply. Also, a combination of both measures might be employed. For the most part, the Soviet Union relies on sales taxes, probably because they are highly selective as well as indirect and hidden. If they were to rely primarily upon income taxes, Soviet planners probably would find that consumer preferences did not conform closely with production capabilities, so that big disparities between the supply and demand for individual products would continue to arise.

Consequently, one must expect high levels of turnover tax as long as the authorities desire to devote a significantly smaller proportion of the nation's resources to consumer goods output than the citizens desire in their capacities as individual consumers. And, in the absence of rationing, the prices of consumer goods will not be based solely on cost.[21]

Many Soviet economists and planners are dissatisfied with the subordinate role of prices in their economy. They have written a great deal about the need to reform pricing arrangements so that they perform a larger func-

---

[21] To avoid possible misunderstanding at this point, the reader must remember that the initial basic distribution of Soviet resources between consumers and producers goods was made by the planning in kind by means of the material balances. Neither the price system nor the turnover taxes are the main instruments used by Soviet planners to allocate resources and limit consumption; the main instruments are the balances in kind. Prices and turnover taxes are merely used to equate *ex post facto* the population's income with the supply of consumer goods, and the country's total national income with its total output. This equilibrium is foreseen in financial plans, mentioned above.

tion in the planning process. Some Western commentators have inferred from this that the Soviet economic system might evolve into a price-regulated economy. The authors do not share this view, even while granting that prices may play a somewhat more important role in Soviet planning and the decision making in the future. It ought to be stressed, first of all, that not one among the many Soviet writers and leaders who have put their views on record has expressed a wish or an admiration for an economy in which prices fluctuate frequently and widely in accordance with current supply and demand. If Soviet planners were to make adjustments to all current surplus and shortage situations by varying prices, they would destroy the connection they seek to maintain between prices and costs of production, or "value," as they understand it.[22] *They prefer and are able to make adjustments in output and supply, rather than in prices, for they believe that this method is simpler, cheaper, and more certain to achieve the effects they desire.*

For ideological reasons as well, no Soviet economist proposes that the USSR become a price-regulated economy. To create a workable price system, managers of Soviet enterprises would have to be given full sovereignty to make decisions now made by the government planners; specifically, they would have to be free to set wages and prices on their products, and to freely compete among themselves. Uncontrolled competition can hardly be acceptable to the Communist party, however. In the first place, free competition would result in that the many technologically obsolete plants and industries would recurrently be forced out of operation, while the better equipped plants would at least temporarily profiteer at the expense of the poorly equipped ones. Workers of the obsolete plants and industries would become unemployed, and the employed workers would not get equal pay for equal work, although it would in no way be their fault that their plants would not be as well equipped and efficient as others. (This does not mean, of course, that the Communist party would not close obsolete plants just because of workers; all it means is that it is morally responsible for not letting the workers stay unemployed and suffer.)

Furthermore, with an effective price system, the distribution of resources in the economy would inevitably be largely determined by consumers' and managers' demand, rather than the Communist party's and central planners' preferences and priorities. In other words, the switchover of the Soviet economy to a full-fledged price system would obviously require a complete changeover in almost all the existing arrangements. For this reason, such a radical reform does not appear to be likely.

---

[22] *Cf.* Vsevolod Holubnychy, "Recent Soviet Theories of Value," *Studies on the Soviet Union* (Munich), vol. I, no. 1, 1961. See also Morris Bornstein, "The Soviet Price Reform Discussion," *Quarterly Journal of Economics* (Cambridge, Mass.), February 1964.

One real problem of which Soviet writers actually complain is that prices in the USSR are changed by the central authorities too slowly and infrequently. Major price reforms involving *all* prices take place only once every five to seven years. In the meantime, prices are changed on the average for only about 11,000 major products every fifteen months.[23] The costs of many more items change in the meantime because of technological improvements, increases in productivity, and planned changes in the composition of output and of inputs. Consequently, discrepancies between prices and actual costs develop, and planners may not be justified in using existing price data to compare actual costs of different materials and production processes. Of course, whenever discrepancies become too great, prices are changed. Nevertheless, many economists urge that price and cost changes be better synchronized than they are at present. Such a synchronization would undoubtedly solve a good deal of the present Soviet pricing problem.

Another frequent complaint by Soviet economists regarding present pricing arrangements is that the latter do not offer managers of Soviet enterprises enough incentive to improve product quality or introduce product innovations. Soviet planners are now experimenting with a novel and potentially interesting change in their pricing arrangements. Specifically, they have given the managers the right (as of 1964) to request permission to make a modified version of a product that they may regard as an improvement compared to their customary output; at the same time they may also ask for a price that would include more profit than the usual 5 percent margin over cost. At least one half of that extra profit would be used to finance the cost of further improvements on the product, while the rest, after taxes, would go for bonuses and other incentives. The right to charge such an extra large profit would continue for a limited time only. (They speak of a year or two.) Consumers would not be adversely affected by this premium price because the regular merchandise would still be available to them at the regular price. But if they showed preference for the new product —as revealed by the sales experience—the planners would presumably ask other enterprises to produce the new version too. Its initial premium price would subsequently be reduced to the regular profit level.

This change in pricing arrangements may herald the beginning of many similar innovations. A majority of Soviet economists, planners, and public officials are persuaded that they should make maximum use of the incentive motive within the basic framework of their planning system. As this example illustrates, considerable scope for broadening the function of incen-

---

[23] *Cf.* M. Mikhaylov, "Izmenenie v poryadke planirovania sebestoimosti promyshlennoy produktsii," *Planovoe Khozyaystvo* (Moscow), no. 10, 1962, p. 34. He says, however, that from the point of view of the enterprises even this rate of price changes is too fast; they would prefer even more stable prices.

tives still exists in the Soviet economy while retaining detailed planning based on output goals expressed in physical units.[24]

Similarities between prices in the United States and in the USSR should also be noted. As explained at great length, prices perform a very different function in the U.S. economy and in the USSR; however, they are important in the operation of both. In both cases, economic efficiency requires that costs and prices should accurately measure the economic sacrifice involved in production. (Temporary departures of price from cost do serve the dynamic function under capitalism, as explained, of attracting additional resources to industries where supplies of a product are short and by increasing output, which will eventually reduce profits). As was indicated, planners in the USSR bemoan the infrequency with which they can alter prices, and regard them as being out of date in many cases. *Interestingly, however, the same complaint is made about prices in the United States. The contention that large firms set "administered" prices—that they change prices infrequently and do not change them to reflect changes in cost and demand conditions—was mentioned in the preceding chapter.* The criticism of large U.S. firms that possess monopoly power and engage in collusion is partly based on the fact that prices are not proportional to cost in such instances; that is, prices do not, under such circumstances, perform the function of measuring the true costs to society of making different things. As a result, the methods of production employed may be less efficient than others that might have been used, and people will not purchase the goods that at equal cost to the economy, would have given them the greatest satisfaction.

Here again we have another example of the dangers of comparing ideal theoretical economies rather than those actually functioning. The Soviet pricing arrangements do seem cumbersome and may be clumsy and inflexible; but even the U.S. economy shows many of the same symptoms—

---

[24] Soviet writers consistently refuse to identify what they call incentive motive in their economy with profit motive, which applies under capitalism. The distinction may be too fine to be immediately clear, but it is, indeed, real and is worth knowing. Although in part derived from profits, bonuses and other incentive payments in the USSR never take the form of dividends or stock options and never result from the institution of ownership of the enterprise. For these reasons Soviet bonuses are not identical with capitalist profits. Moreover, Soviet bonus funds and the rules of payment are very closely controlled and regulated by the government. The bonuses in the USSR can never be reinvested by their receivers to produce further profits; they can only be spent on consumption. Last, but not least important, is the fact that in absolute amounts, Soviet bonuses are small compared to bonuses received by the managers of capitalist enterprises. Maximum bonuses for Soviet managers and salaried personnel are limited by law to 40-60 percent of the monthly salary, or to about $250 a month. In practice, however, this maximum is very difficult to attain; typical bonuses amount to only 10-18 percent of the salary (about $70) and are paid, on the average, in only three months of the year. *Cf. Pravda* (Moscow), February 2, 1965, p. 2.

though the causes and the extent are different. Furthermore, the French pricing arrangements that are discussed in the next chapter will also show the reader that price rigidities and the centralized price fixing are not uniquely peculiar to the Soviet-type system alone.

Efficiency of Planning in the Soviet Union

Efficiency of planning can be appraised on both technical and economic grounds. Technically defined, efficiency of planning calls for a comparison of goals and their actual attainment. This method is employed by Soviet officials themselves. Other possible criteria by which one might appraise planning efficiency are: internal consistency and the balancing out of plans, the speed with which plans are adapted to new circumstances, and the cost of planning.

The Soviet Union has not succeeded in achieving planned goals with exactness. Especially during the first two Five-Year Plans, some industries fell far short of fulfillment while others ran substantially ahead; even now, agricultural plans fail of realization by large amounts. Usually it is the consumer goods industries that underfulfill their plans, while the capital goods industries frequently overfulfill their assignments (mainly because they are the "leading links" and efforts to fulfill their plans are the greatest). The Fourth (1949-1950) and the Fifth (1951-1955) Five-Year Plans displayed a somewhat better correlation between the goals and their fulfillment than the earlier long-term plans, but nonetheless many industries fell short and others by far exceeded their targets. The Sixth (1956-1960) Five-Year Plan was officially abandoned in 1957 with the admission that it was badly calculated and could not be carried out. The Seven-Year Plan for 1959-1965 was substantially modified in 1962 and 1963. The fulfillment of the annual and quarterly plans for the USSR as a whole and the realization of various republic, territorial, and local plans as well as of the plans of the individual industries and enterprises likewise displays a very spotty performance. What does this record mean about the efficiency of Soviet planning techniques?

At first glance, it appears that Soviet planning is not very efficient. Frequent and large deviations of actual performance from planned goals appear to suggest that the goals were mistaken or the plans for achieving them were poorly conceived. More specifically, one would conclude that planners erred in their forecasts and estimates of the future, the plans were internally inconsistent and badly fit together. Deviation between plans and achievement might, however, have a very different explanation. We must go deeper and analyze the causes of deviations from plan.

Discrepancies between the initial goals of Soviet plans and the final performance in almost all cases occur because planners change the plans in the meantime. Such changes do imply, of course, that at the beginning the plan-

ners erred in their predictions of future events. (Some "errors" are to be expected; others that are due to political events and unexpected stresses abroad and at home should not be called errors at all.) At the same time, changes in plans also mean that errors were discovered and corrected. In the process of carrying out a particular plan, it might have been discovered that the initial goals were set too high and that they could not have been reached because of, let us say, an insufficient supply of raw materials due to an unforeseen natural calamity; or it could have been decided in the meantime to shift resources initially assigned to the fulfillment of this particular goal to some other use of higher priority; or some unforeseen economies were developed; or a technological invention was introduced, for example, and as a result, initial goals set in the plan could be surpassed at the end. In such cases, deviations from planned goals do arise; their presence does not signify any planning failure, however. On the contrary, whenever such deviations arise because of changes introduced into initial plans in the course of their realization, and whenever these changes eliminate initial errors or improve on previous calculations, they actually mean that the planners act efficiently and that planning is elastic and efficient. *What is most important for economic efficiency is not that predictions of the future be exactly correct, but that resources adapt to the everchanging needs as quickly as possible whenever a discrepancy between supply and needs occurs.*

The adaptability of the Soviet economy to such changes is in dispute. It seems to be very low in retailing, for example, but such slowness may result from Soviet efforts to concentrate changes in other sectors. Soviet planners clearly have the power of decision making and most of the information they require as the basis for decision; the data available to them is remarkably current.[25] Unless one analyzes each decision, or failure to make changes, and considers all alternatives, he cannot assess the adaptability of the Soviet economy.

Granted that it is difficult to find reliable data for appraising the efficiency of planning techniques, one does find unmistakable evidence that it falls far short of perfection. (The same statement applies quite as much to planning by large U.S. corporations.) The following general statements are based upon a large number of complaints that appeared in recent years in the Soviet press.

1. Output is defective in various ways; apart from complaints about generally low quality (which is not necessarily the fault of the planners), there are charges, for instance, that all clothing of a given size is sometimes made in the same color or style so that consumer has no effective choice.

---

[25] G. Grossman, *Soviet Statistics of Physical Output of Industrial Commodities: Their Compilation and Quality* (Princeton: National Bureau of Economic Research, 1961), pp. 29-30.

2. Goods produced are distributed faultily so that some areas experience a great glut while others suffer a shortage.

3. Replacement parts for durable goods are often unavailable and inaccessible.

4. Production is interrupted for lack of needed raw materials.

5. Machines are left idle, though they are of a valuable and scarce type.

6. Labor is not fully utilized because of "padding" of labor requirements.

7. Materials and other resources are hoarded by the enterprises.

Numerous criticisms of this type reported in the Soviet press indicate that planning errors do occur. However, they do not give a reliable indication of their quantitative importance. The examples cited may be isolated cases; on the other hand, they also may be representative of all economic activity.

One would expect gross planning errors to be caught even before a plan goes into effect, because it is possible to "test" plans on paper mathematically. If the components of a plan are out of balance, by summing the components on paper crosswise and backwards one would discover the errors. Formal planning errors, therefore, should be relatively small and not very numerous. On the other hand, there are no reliable tests that can be employed either before or during the planning period to determine whether individual products are produced in the proportions that give the greatest net satisfaction to their users. We can only conjecture about the frequency of this important type of possible planning error.

In assessing centralized economic planning in the Soviet Union, one should take account of the particular circumstances under which it has been employed. Specifically, Soviet planners did *not* simply substitute detailed planning for another type of system and then used their planning methods to run the same economy. *Planning was invoked to alter the Soviet economy at a rapid rate as well as to operate it at each stage.* Put differently, up to now, we have seen detailed centralized planning in operation only under conditions in which an economy was transformed rapidly from a peasant economy to a highly developed technological and industrial society. Once the basic economic structure of the USSR stabilizes, the nature of the planning problem will change.

In recent years, Soviet planners have made strong efforts to apply advanced mathematical techniques to economic planning. In addition, they have been experimenting with the use of large electronic computers and other types of automatic data-processing devices. There is great hope among those who look to planning to solve major economic problems that new mathematical techniques combined with the computers will vastly increase man's capacity for effective economic planning. Up to now, it appears that only minor applications of these new techniques have been made, but experimentation with them is extremely active; there are strong reasons to expect that the quality of Soviet economic planning will soon be improved as a result of these new developments.

A significant aspect of economic planning to be considered is its cost. The population census of 1959 reported that Soviet planning and statistical agencies employed more than 3.5 million full-time workers.[26] A rough calculation of the total *direct* cost of Soviet planning would be not less than $8 billion a year (plus losses due to planning errors, changes, and red tape).

Should one conclude from this that Soviet economic planning is prohibitively costly? The answer seems to be clearly negative. The available evidence suggests that the cost of performing equivalent functions in U.S. industry to those performed by economic planners in the Soviet Union is far greater. No exact comparative studies have been made on this point, but some suggestive evidence is, for example, that economic planning in the USSR requires fewer white-collar workers—relative to manual workers—in Soviet industry and mining than does capitalist industry. One study reported white-collar personnel to be 20 percent of annual workers in Soviet industry and mining in 1954-1956; for the United States the proportion at the same time was 29 percent.[27] On the plant level, the difference in favor of the USSR becomes even greater: In the USSR, the proportion of white-collar workers was 15 percent, while in the United States it was 26 percent.[28]

Another study, comparing Soviet and U.S. machine-building industries, found that the proportion of managerial and clerical personnel as a percentage of all employees was 3 percent in 1956-1959 in the USSR and 17.9 percent in the United States.[29] The chief reason for larger "bureaucratization" of the American economy compared to that of the USSR is that personnel and labor costs related to *sales efforts* are a major item in the American business enterprises, but very small in the Soviet ones.

The foregoing discussion completes our description of the Soviet planning procedure. With this general picture in mind, it is now possible to explain how planners decide what quantity of specific goods to produce.

---

[26] This total is approximately five times as much as employees in these occupations reported in the census of 1926, a time before centralized planning was established. *Itogi Vsesoyuznoy perepisi naseleniya 1959 goda: SSSR (Svodny tom)*.

[27] D. Granick, "Soviet-American Management Comparisons," in *Comparisons of the United States and Soviet Economies,* Joint Economic Committee, Congress of the United States, 86th Cong., 1st sess. (Washington, D. C.: Government Printing Office, 1959), p. 149.

[28] Granick.

[29] M. Boretsky, *The Soviet Challenge to U.S. Machine Building,* U. S. Department of Commerce, Business and Defense Services Administration (Washington, D. C.: Government Printing Office, 1962), pp. 16 and 44.

Setting Output Goals for Consumers Goods

Soviet authorities may aim primarily for maximum military power, for industrialization at the speediest possible rate, or what not. They nevertheless must determine the output of individual consumer goods. In this limited sphere they presumably should aim for the greatest amount of satisfaction for the population with a minimum of hardship in production. To achieve this objective, they must take into account the desires of consumers and the occupational preferences of workers.

Consumers' Preferences. Consumers in the Soviet Union are free to buy whatever they wish *from the goods available*. The chief point in doubt is how much their wishes determine what goods are made available. The following statement, by A. Mikoyan, first deputy premier and in charge of Soviet trade affairs at the time, suggests Soviet doctrine on this point:

> . . . The very essence of Soviet trade calls for an all-round study of popular demand and of the diverse requirements of the people;

> Trade must not be passive even in relation to the popular demand. It is the function of Soviet trade *to influence demand in the spirit of progress*. It should cultivate the taste of the consumers, bring new goods into use among the population, promote the sale of the most nutritious and wholesome food products, and also of useful, well-made and beautifully manufactured goods, which improve everyday life and enrich the cultural life of the working people.[30]

The sincerity of planners' desires to produce the things consumers want has been questioned. However, it is difficult to understand why planners should ignore the preferences of consumers if they do not conflict with the basic objectives underlying the plan. Soviet authorities do collect a great deal of information about consumers' purchases, stocks of goods, and desires. For example, since 1952, they have studied the purchase diaries maintained by a representative panel of 50,000 families. The data have been checked and processed monthly. Beyond this, they collect the following types of consumer demand information:

1. Scientific information about consumer "needs"—ideal patterns of consumption based upon medical, physiological, nutritional, and similar scientific research.
2. Censuses of inventories of goods possessed by consumers.
3. Current sales data.

---

[30] A. I. Mikoyan, "Measures for the further expansion of trade and for improving the organization of state, cooperative and collective farm trade," a report delivered at the All-Union Conference of Distributive Workers, October 1953, (Moscow: Foreign Languages Publishing House, 1954). Italics added.

4. Customer complaints.
5. The equivalent of market tests—exposure of new products to consumers' viewing for reactions.
6. Factory stores and fashion shows results.
7. Press comments received from consumers.

Foreigners who visit the USSR sometimes consider the government to be indifferent to or ignorant of consumers' preferences because of the poor kind of products in Soviet stores. When Soviet planners and economists are questioned on this point, however, they frankly say, at least in private, that they can design far better products than those now on the market but lack the means to do so. They prefer to invest in other things, at the present. *Also, they point out that a low-income and highly egalitarian society naturally does not produce goods of the highest quality; to do so would severely limit the number of persons who would share in the available short supply.* This important concept is most clearly exemplified in housing construction. In recent years the building of apartment houses has grown enormously. An inspection of the apartments, however, shows them to be quite small by U.S. middle-class standards. Also, the outside of these apartment houses shows clear signs of either relatively unskilled or hasty workmanship; in a short time they look a little shabby. To make larger and higher quality apartment houses might easily cut the volume and rate of construction by half or more. *Commitment to relatively low inequality of incomes and the meeting of the basic needs of all has led the Soviet authorities to set quality standards that are quite low in the eyes of, say, U.S. tourists. On the other hand, however, Soviet families from their own viewpoint are getting very modern, private, airy, and comfortable housing compared to what they have had up to now.*

Advertising is employed in the Soviet Union on a very small scale, partly to encourage the consumption of new and improved goods. Sometimes advertising is used to help clear the market of goods whose output was set higher than could be sold readily at the initial prices. Apparently advertising is increasing steadily, though it remains tiny compared to that in the United States.

Sacrifices in Production.   Together with consumers' preferences, planners on the SNKH level and below take relative production costs into account when they set output goals. They have at their disposal the recent cost experience and the projected costs of individual products and enterprises; their output decisions are influenced by this information. Costs of production are extremely difficult to define. They are even more difficult to measure, except in money terms. Labor represents by far the largest production cost in the USSR. The consumption of scarce natural resources and capital is another. How do the Soviet planners measure the costs involved in producing each product? To answer that question, we must know how the irksomeness and scarcity of labor in individual occupations are measured, and then learn how planners attach values to other scarce things used in production, such as natural resources, land, machinery, and loans.

Labor costs depend primarily upon wage rates. Great shifts have occurred in relative wage rates in the Soviet Union in quite short periods. The magnitude of these changes and the occasions upon which they were made suggest that wage rates do reflect the long-run conditions of supply and demand, the latter of course being that of the central planners. Wage rates are explainable by such basic conditions as the relative attractiveness of alternative employments, the location of the labor force in relation to the location of industry, the reluctance of workers to move to distant communities, and the real costs of acquiring skills. However, living costs are the most important determinant taken into consideration by the government wage setters.

The method by which the Soviet authorities determine the cost of nonlabor factors of production when they set output goals is not so clear. Prices assigned to machinery, raw materials, transportation, fuel, and the like seem to be based primarily, but not entirely, on labor costs; capital costs enter into the production costs of a product as depreciation charges based upon the initial direct cost of the equipment. Costs of materials enter as a whole.

The general principles of Soviet cost calculation do not differ significantly from those used in the United States. The major points of difference between them are these: No money cost is assigned to the depletion of natural resource deposits (direct costs of removing resources from the ground are, of course, included). Land bears no direct money cost. Investment in productive enterprises bears no interest charges, unless they are actually built on bank credit.

One must not overlook the fact that Soviet planners are influenced by a large body of Marxist economic doctrine. When they take factors into account in a general way, they may do so differently than would government officials in capitalist countries. Although there have been notable departures from Marxist doctrine in the Soviet Union, the views of Soviet economists clearly rest on concepts different from those of economists in other countries. They may accordingly have different notions from ours about what factors are relevant and important in determining the output of individual goods.

Output Goals for Capital Goods

Thus far, we have dealt with the determination of output goals for consumers goods. How is the output of individual producers goods set? We have indicated that broad directives determine what proportion of total resources is to be devoted to capital goods; the particular forms the resources are to take must be determined by planners and set forth in kind, in the detailed plan.

Capital investment during any period is governed by the capital budget, which lists specific capital projects. Major investment projects must be approved by the State Committee for Construction (Gosstroy); others are determined by the local planning authorities. Projects requiring approval of high party and government authorities usually are not purely economic in nature; sometimes they are of major military or political significance, as well as huge projects for land reclamation, the construction of large canals, and the like.[31]

Most capital projects are intended not only to increase output, but also to reduce the costs of production. Many enterprises desire new facilities with which to lower costs. Planners must select from a number of alternative capital projects. How is their selection made?

Soviet planners require individual economic councils and republics to defend their requests for new capital facilities. Among other supporting data, they must estimate the number of years in which a project "would pay for itself." For example, a plant might ask for 100,000 rubles' worth of equipment which would yield cost savings of 20,000 rubles annually. This project would be described as having a "coefficient of relative effectiveness" of 20 percent. Projects with the highest coefficients of relative effectiveness —meaning that they will pay for themselves in the shortest time—are given preference if other (political, defense) considerations do not outweigh this economic calculation. In effect, planners go down the list and approve those projects that will pay off most quickly; the exact number of projects undertaken depends upon the total amount of resources to be devoted to cost-reducing investment.

Some capital projects, typically the ones calling for the production of new products, are not intended to reduce production costs. The benefits of such projects cannot be measured by the time they take to pay for themselves. Some appraisal must be made of the "value" or "importance" of the new product to the nation. The planners compare the merits of competing claims and make their selection on the basis of considerations that necessarily are highly subjective. (Of course, decisions about investment in new products are subjective even when made by private businessmen in unplanned economies.)

---

[31] These decisions are among the most controversial and generate heated conflicts of interest. Recently, the planners of the Ukrainian Republic computed that 78 percent of capital created in their republic every year (turnover tax and profits) are transferred by the Union planners and invested in other parts of the USSR—in Siberia, Kazakhstan, etc. They charged that investments there are not recovered as fast as they do in the Ukraine and that as a result such capital transfers create losses for both their republic and the USSR as a whole. Cf. *The American Economic Review,* September 1964, p. 801.

In deciding what machinery to replace with improved equipment, planners use prices and money cost as an indication of the savings that would be achieved. In addition, they presumably are influenced by information about the amount of scarce factors of production involved in competing projects. That is, if they know that copper is critically short, they will favor projects not requiring copper, even though on a strictly monetary basis the copper-using project would have been preferable.

ALLOCATION OF THE FACTORS OF PRODUCTION

We have seen that the Soviet Union establishes output goals in enormous detail. To achieve these goals, the planners must somehow insure that the labor, professional and management skills, capital and land required are allocated in a way that makes this possible. We shall, accordingly, explore the mechanism on which the Soviet Union relies to allocate its chief factors of production.

The Allocation of Labor among Alternative Employments

Laborers in the USSR are free to enter any occupation; thus, they allocate themselves among employments rather than respond to orders from above. Much as in the United States, a Soviet worker "looks for a job." He is free to work wherever he can find someone who will employ him. Similarly, state enterprises, government offices, public organizations, and collective farms have the right to hire whomever they wish. Employers are, of course, limited by the employment plan for their enterprise which specifies its total wage bill and the number of positions. Employment opportunities, both in number and in type, reflect the output plans. In other words, the positions available are dictated by the kinds and quantities of things that the planners decide shall be produced. Within such limits, workers seeking employment enjoy freedom of choice.

Enterprises seeking employees inform the public of job vacancies by means of newspapers and radio and by notices in special window displays. In addition, recruitment departments exist in the various provincial, regional, and city governments for the purpose of engaging workers both for local and for out-of-town jobs. Enterprises suffering from shortages of labor use devices common to capitalist countries to win personnel away from other employers; namely, they offer monetary and other inducements—in particular, better housing accommodations.

The Soviet wage system is used by government planners to channel labor supply into the needed direction. By fixing comparatively higher wages for skills and professions that are needed most, planners create incentives for workers to seek employment in industries, regions, and jobs the planners want. The right to establish all basic wage rates as well as salary and bonus systems rests exclusively with the central government agencies, namely, the State Committee on Wages and Labor, the USSR Council of Ministers, and the governments of the republics. Within these agencies labor unions have a consultative voice on wages, but what they actually do or say there is not publicized. The regional economic councils and the management of individual enterprises have no right to fix or change the wage rates. However, they can manipulate with bonuses derived from above-the-planned profits and use them to stimulate labor efforts in the necessary direction inside the plants.

The planners use several other devices to ensure a sufficient supply of skilled workers and professionals to fulfill their output plans. (Such arrangements apparently are not needed to allocate semiskilled and unskilled workers.) First, they influence the number of persons given special vocational training and the kinds of vocational training offered them. Specifically, the authorities notify schools and vocational training systems of the number of students needed with particular types of training. Colleges and technical schools do not accept more applicants for a specific trade and profession than the number the planners specify—including some adjustment for "dropouts." The planners' requirements are not always filled because students possess freedom of choice of profession. Second, graduates from professional, technical, and vocational training schools (approximately 700,000 each year) are assigned to their first jobs by State Committees for Professional and Technical Education. These graduates are required by law to work at assigned jobs for a period of between two and four years depending upon the type of school they attended. Third, similar arrangements exist also for graduates of colleges and universities in the Soviet Union. One year before graduation, the government Commissions for the Allocation of Young Specialists inform each student of his or her future place of work, rank, and salary. Young specialists have a right to decline the Commission's placement, but only once. The Commission's second assignment is final and irrevocable. The graduates must work at the assigned places for at least one of the mandatory three years before they are issued their formal diplomas and degrees.

Soviet managerial personnel is also placed and transferred in a centralized manner, but mostly through Communist party channels. All leading positions in industry as well as in economic administration are manned by appointment on recommendation of one or another party committee. Since almost all managers are party members, they are subject to party discipline; the latter prohibits every Communist from changing or quitting his job without the party's permission.

The USSR uses another centralized institution for recruiting and allocating workers to jobs—the Chief Administrations for Resettlement and Recruitment of Workers. These organizations exist in each republic; a national plan is prepared for these administrations which establishes recruitment quotas broken down for each republic, province and county. A network of recruiters is engaged in meeting these plans.

One other feature of labor utilization in the Soviet Union is unfamiliar to the West: that is what is known as social mobilization for temporary jobs. Education and propaganda media are used to convince the public that they are obliged to perform work voluntarily "for society." For example, during the summer, students are urged to volunteer to assist in harvesting on suburban collective farms. This work is sometimes unpaid. Those who do not volunteer lose their political and moral standing in the eyes of their peers and of the Communist Youth League. Sometimes active campaigns are conducted to persuade volunteers to take more permanent jobs that are not adequately filled by ordinary methods. Examples include the opening up of virgin lands in Kazakhstan, the construction of new coal mines and hydroelectric stations. Volunteers to these jobs are paid regular wages and are given widespread publicity for their labors under adverse conditions in faraway places. Although most people resent such pressure to volunteer for relatively unattractive work, others accept it with as much enthusiasm as young people volunteer for the Peace Corps in the United States.

The Allocation of Capital

Capital, like other productive resources, is allocated in the Soviet economy in accordance with government plan. Indeed, no private investments in the means of production are permitted in the Soviet Union. Almost every single capital project is provided for directly in the plans drawn up by government officials. The only exceptions are a very small proportion reflecting the decisions of collective farms and other cooperatives. All new factories, railways, department stores, housing projects, and the like, are built at government expense; they remain government property and reflect decisions by government planners.

To a very large extent, capital investments are dictated directly by the output goals established by the planning authorities. That is, the decision to expand the output of certain products implies the need to create the facilities to produce those items.

At one level or another, decisions must be made in the Soviet Union about the particular types of plant and equipment to be produced—primarily on the basis of superior value to the economy. That is, the planners must decide which types of capital would offer the greatest yield. To make such decisions, they require a technique that will permit them to evaluate each investment. They have experimented with many methods for solving this problem. They do attempt to assign a value to alternative investments that is not different from the "rates of return" computed in the United States by private corporations for the same purpose. The main difference between the methods used by Soviet planners and American businessmen is that the first group takes a much longer and broader view of returns on investment. The Soviets are more patient to recoup their investments and attach a greater significance to *social* costs and *social* benefits, such as the development of the as yet nonindustrialized parts of the country, for example, Siberia.

The Allocation of Land

The allocation of land to various productive uses in the Soviet economy is also accomplished via the government plans, although in a considerably less centralized manner than the allocation of capital. Collective and state farms get planned quotas of how much of what they must *sell* to the government, rather than how much they must produce. Consequently, they are left in principle free to plan the allocation of their land and other resources to various crops and uses. All they need to do is to allocate their land in such a way as to meet the government sales quota and to have a maximum surplus product left for themselves after this sale to be distributed to the farmers or sold in the free market for a higher price than the government's.

All land in the USSR is the property of the government, even that used by collective farms, under private buildings, and in private courtyards and gardens. The land cannot be bought or sold and it carries no price; it can only be transferred from one user to another by government or court decree. The Soviet government does not collect any specific rent from collective or state farms, or from state enterprises and housing establishments in the cities, for the use of land. Whether the land is used efficiently or not is reflected therefore not in the rent but in comparative profitability and solvency of its users. Because land is "free," some farms are richer than others, although the government tries to equalize their incomes by means of progressive income taxes and larger delivery quotas levied on rich farms.

DISTRIBUTION OF PERSONAL INCOME

Socialists have always cherished equality of personal incomes as an ideal. In particular, they have denounced those with inherited wealth who do nothing productive. In view of their perennial criticism of income inequalities, it is especially interesting to see how incomes are distributed in the Soviet Union. Unfortunately, data available do not describe fully and accurately the size and the sources of personal incomes in the USSR. It is, indeed, paradoxical that the Socialist country should consider statistics on income distribution about as secret as statistics on the number of A-bombs it possesses. The chief reason for this secrecy might be that Soviet citizens are extremely sensitive to any sign of social or economic inequality.

Neither the Soviet people nor their government seem to have any objective criteria to set the boundary between social justice and injustice in income inequalities. They all recognize that some income inequality is inevitable and necessary under socialism. All types of work are not identical; difficult and complicated work has to be remunerated more than pleasant and simple work; incentives to increase production, to do the work better, or to take a faraway job usually show up in pay differences. But how much incentive should one offer? And even worse: The larger the incentive one has already paid, the larger must be the next incentive in order to be effective. Hence, the system of incentives inevitably expands income inequalities as time goes by.

Until 1931 the USSR consistently practiced income equalization policies: managers were paid almost the same wages as the workers, members of the Communist party were obliged as a rule not to take salaries larger than that of an average worker. Then Stalin concluded that equalitarianism kills incentives to improve production and to develop skills and education. He explicitly abolished income equality as a policy. Workers' wages were put on piece-work basis, salaries of managerial personnel were raised, bonus incentives were introduced, and the Communist party no longer required its members to feel and live like workers. The last more or less complete statistics on wages and salaries in the USSR were published in 1934. An American study of these statistics concluded that the principles of wage inequalities in the Soviet Union were the same as in the capitalist countries.[32]

Changes in income distribution since 1934 cannot be statistically ascertained. It is known, however, that in the course of the wage reform which started at the end of 1956, the Soviet government adopted a policy aimed at reducing income inequalities. In 1960 Khrushchev announced publicly that this was the policy of his government.[33]

An American economist who is friendly to the Soviet Union interviewed A. Mikoyan, Soviet vice premier at the time (1960), on this subject. He told Mikoyan that Moscow University students had told him that income inequalities in the USSR were "a very serious problem concerning which they felt too little was being done too slowly." Mikoyan's reply was revealing:

> The gap was natural when a peasant country had to create qualified technical help and intelligentsia. One had to have a big gap to spur all capable men to struggle to rise and learn. It was quite justified and necessary. This was not so great as the gap which arose after World War II. During the war and immediate post-war years, enterprises tried to establish very high pay for jobs for which they could not get people. In heavy industry, they raised

---

[32] Cf. Abram Bergson, *The Structure of Soviet Wages* (Cambridge, Mass.: Harvard University Press, 1946), p. 208.

[33] N. S. Khrushchev, *Ob otmene nalogov s rabochikh i sluzhashchikh i drugikh meropriyatiyakh, napravlennykh na povyshenie blagosostoyaniya sovetskogo naroda* (Moscow: Gospolitizdat, 1960), p. 26.

the pay of directors, qualified workers, and engineers very much. At that time people had ration cards for the food supply, so the gap in money wages didn't make so much difference in eating. Those with extra money bought in "commercial stores" at four to five times the regular price.

When there was a currency reform in 1947 and the rationing system was abolished, the problem really arose, even though low wages were raised somewhat. Because now the earlier excessive rise in the wages of leading personnel was fully reflected in purchasing power.

In the last few years, with the growth in the number of qualified workers and intellectuals, the large gap can no longer be justified economically, and begins to play a negative role. Now for the jobs with little pay it is difficult to get people.

Top salaries have not been cut much because it is easy to raise, tough to cut. Excesses have been cut, real excesses, but that affects only 100,000 individuals. But you cannot cut the pay of millions.

The main procedure is this: those paid well get no increases. Those in the middle get slow raises. Those on the bottom get big raises.[34]

What Mikoyan said was also partly known from other sources. In 1957 the statutory minimum wage rates for wage and salary earners in state enterprises were raised by about one third, from twenty-seven to thirty-five rubles a month. This adjustment affected more than 12 percent of all workers and employees. The plans called for further minimum wage boosts, but these were postponed until 1964-1965. Since January 1, 1965, the statutory minimum wage throughout the country is forty-fifty rubles a month ($44-55.50).

Also in the course of the 1957-1962 wage reform, average wages received by workers in industry and on the state farms increased by 4 to 26 percent by 1959 and were scheduled to rise a little bit more later.[35] The wages of lower paid workers were increased more than those of the rest. This produced a reduction of pay differentials between the highest and lowest grades. For example, while before the reform the ratio of the highest to the lowest wage rates in nonferrous metallurgy used to be 1:3.6, after the reform it became only 1:2.6; similarly, in the light industries it used to be 1:2.16, while after the reform it is only 1:1.8. And so in all other industries. The largest inequality ratio between the lowest and the highest wage rates today can be found in the iron and steel industry, where it is 1:3.2.[36]

Observe that these ratios apply only to wages of workers; they do not show the relationship between wages and managerial salaries. The Chinese Communists charged that, as a result of his bonus incentives policy, Khrush-

[34] Victor Perlo, *How the Soviet Economy Works: An Interview with A. I. Mikoyan,* pp. 48-49.

[35] V. F. Mayer, *Zarabotnaya plata v period perekhoda k kommunizmu* (Moscow: Ekonomizdat, 1963), pp. 136ff.

[36] Mayer, pp. 148, 150.

chev "has widened, and not narrowed, the gap between the incomes of a small minority and those of the workers, peasants and ordinary intellectuals," and that the "members of this privileged stratum" in the USSR enjoy "incomes that are dozens or even a hundred times those of the average Soviet worker and peasant." [37]

The few scattered statistics on wages and salaries of some particular types of workers and professional people that it was possible to collect from various sources are reproduced in Table 15. Since bonuses are not included in the wages reported, actual gross earnings may be about 15 percent higher, on the average, while the highest permissible bonuses for the managerial personnel may not exceed 40 to 60 percent of the monthly salary.[38] The reader should note the comparatively low pay of doctors and lawyers in the Soviet Union, and the very low pay of teachers. On the other hand, university professors are among the best paid people in the USSR.

This table shows an income differential of 1:25 between the lowest and the highest pay recorded, but probably these are not the highest earnings that actually occur in that country. Earnings of writers and artists are very high in the USSR, and so are the salaries of army generals, top government and party officials, and top scientists. Yet even if the Chinese charge were correct and income differentials were as great as 1:100, Soviet income inequalities are neither the same in size nor origin as those under capitalism. Top executives in many American corporations get salaries 150 to 200 times those of the lowest paid worker. In Soviet enterprises, according to a Soviet source, that maximum difference is but 1:10.[39] Some people in the United States receive many millions a year in dividends—perhaps 1000 times more than the wage of the lowest paid full-time workers, and 100 times more than the salary of the top manager. In the Soviet Union, such great income differentials do not exist; moreover, there are no such sources of income as dividends.

The maximum range between the very highest and the lowest income is not particularly revealing, however. What really matters is the proportion of the population that falls in each income class. On this question a Soviet source offers one small piece of evidence. It reports that the income ratio between the 10 percent of the highest-paid workers and employees in the USSR and the 10 percent lowest-paid was 1:5.8 in 1958.[40] Figured on family basis, including the income of the working wives, the 10 percent of families with the lowest income received one fifth of the income of the 10 percent of families with the highest income. The same 10 percent family ratio

---

[37] "On Khrushchev's Phoney Communism," *Peking Review* (Peking), July 17, 1964, pp. 14-15.

[38] *Kommunist* (Moscow), no. 13, September 1960, p. 28.

[39] Mayer, p. 160.

[40] *Voprosy Truda* (Moscow), no. 4, 1959, p. 147.

Table 15.   Base Wage Differentials in the Soviet Union, 1963

(U.S. dollars per year, before taxes) [a]

Statutory minumum, rural areas	$ 360
Statutory minimum, urban areas	400
Collective farmer (1962)	574
State farm worker	586
Office typist	588
Textile worker	679
Construction worker	746
Machine tool operator	746
High school teacher	824
Steel worker	872
Coal miner	1,092
Physician, M.D.	1,260
Lawyer	1,376
Average for all workers and employees	1,445 [b]
State farm manager	3,530
Technician	3,724
Engineer (oil industry)	4,238
Master foreman (machine-building)	5,028
Doctor of science, head of department in a research institute	5,730
Factory director (machine-building)	6,240
University professor	7,070
Cabinet minister, republic government	9,125

[a] Rubles convert into dollars at 1:1.11 ratio.

[b] Total wages received, *including bonuses*. All other figures in the table do not include bonuses.

SOURCES: V. F. Mayer, *Zarabotnaya plata v period perekhoda k kommunizmu* (Moscow: Ekonomizdat, 1963), pp. 141-144, 157-160. U. S. Department of Agriculture. Foreign Agricultural Economic Report No. 13, *Soviet Agriculture Today: Report of 1963 Agriculture Exchange Delegation* (Washington, D. C.: December 1963), pp. 38-43. B. Sukharevsky, "Rabochiy den i zarabotnaya plata v SSSR," *Kommunist* (Moscow), no. 3, February 1960, pp. 22ff. A. Volkov, "Sokrashchenny rabochiy den i uporyadochenie zarabotnoy platy," *Kommunist* (Moscow), no. 13, September 1960, pp. 28ff. E. I. Landin. *Realnaya zarabornaya plata i dokhody trudyaschikhsya* (Minsk: AN BSSR), pp. 58, 67. *Annual Economic Indicators for the USSR*, Materials prepared for the Joint Economic Committee, Congress of the United States, 88th Cong., 2d sess. (Washington, D. C.: Government Printing Office, 1964), p. 66.

in the United States, according to Soviet calculations, was 1:31 at the same time.[41]

---

[41] S. P. Figurnov, *Real'naya zarabotnaya plata i pod'yem material'nogo blagosostoyaniya trudyashchikhsya v SSSR* (Moscow: Sotsekonomizdat, 1960), p. 94.

Whatever the validity of these particular comparisons *there is no doubt that over-all income inequalities in the Soviet Union are considerably smaller than in the United States and in most other countries of the world.*

Income taxes used in the United States and many other countries as the vehicles of income equalization, are not important in this connection in the USSR. Neither are inheritance or gift taxes, which do not exist in the USSR. Soviet income taxes are very light. Wages up to sixty rubles per month are exempt; the maximum tax rate of 13 percent applies to wages 100 rubles per month and above, being unprogressive on higher incomes. Income taxes contribute no more than 8 percent to the total revenue of the Soviet budget. There is official talk of abolishing this income tax altogether one day and of relying exclusively on the turnover tax and the deductions from profits of state enterprises. In principle, such Soviet tax policies are less progressive than in the capitalist countries which rely heavily on progressive income taxes to reduce income inequalities; turnover taxes fall heavily on the low-income groups, of course.

Income equalization is greatly furthered in the USSR by the government's provision of vital social and welfare services free of charge. These include old-age pensions and disability benefits, the costs of which are completely borne by the government, free hospitals and doctor's services, free education from public school through graduate studies at the university, paid maternity leaves, subsidized low-rent housing, and so forth. According to Soviet calculations, direct cash payments consisting of pensions, disability benefits, paid leaves, stipends and grants supplement the income of an average urban family by as much as 20.4 percent, while free public services, consisting of education facilities, complete medical services, vacation resorts, recreation and sports facilities, rent subsidies, various urban facilities, old-age homes and funeral services, add another 26.6 percent to the total income of Soviet urban population. Altogether, the total wage fund of Soviet workers and employees is thus supplemented 47 percent by free government services.[42] Even if these official statistics are perhaps inflated for propaganda purposes, there is no doubt that all these government services considerably increase the real income of Soviet citizens. They especially help the lower- and middle-income groups, for whom social and welfare services represent a large proportion of their money income.

PRODUCTIVE EFFICIENCY

Responsibility for, and considerable incentive to achieve, productive efficiency in Soviet enterprises is lodged with the plant manager. Central planners also indirectly influence productive efficiency, for they allocate the money for production costs.

---

[42] Figurnov, p. 67.

In selecting methods of production, plant managers are directed to keep money costs to a minimum. Thus, the internal operations of each firm are guided by price considerations. In an effort to use money costs as a reliable indicator of production efficiency, the Soviet planners lay important stress on developing the science of cost accounting.

The compensation of Soviet factory managers and workers is linked to their ability to reduce production costs below those set in the general plan. They obtain financial bonuses based upon profits earned by the enterprise as a result of cost reduction.

Managers are urged to stimulate worker compensation in an effort to raise output. Since most workers are still paid by a piecework system, a strong financial incentive to increase efficiency is provided to workers. In addition, a larger proportion, approximately 50 percent, of the above-the-planned profits obtained by an enterprise goes into the "enterprise fund," which is used to expand industrial facilities and to provide cultural, social, and welfare services for workers. (The remainder is returned to the state, after bonuses to workers and executives have been paid.)

The efficiency of each Soviet plant reflects the zeal and intelligence of the plant manager, the quality of the industrial equipment, and the industriousness of the labor force. Very wide differences in productive efficiency exist from plant to plant. Competition drives inefficient plants out of use in capitalistic countries, but not in the USSR. Information is exchanged freely among plant managers in the Soviet Union, and the results of technical research are made available to all who are interested. Moreover, improvements in plant design and layout and general productive arrangements are, as a conscious policy, disseminated from plant to plant. As a rule, efficient plants help backward plants to modernize.

Productive efficiency is high even by American standards in the best-run Soviet plants[43] but in most it falls far below American standards. No overall assessment can be made with confidence. However, labor productivity in Soviet industry was estimated by Soviet statisticians in 1962 to be between 40 and 50 percent of that in the United States; in 1913 it was only 11 percent of that of the United States.[44] Some American studies show lower results; they place Soviet labor productivity in industry at about one third of that in the United States in 1956-58.[45] The rate of growth of labor productivity in the USSR has been considerably greater than in the United States. According to the same American calculations, between 1951-1961 it grew

---

[43] Especially in steel, heavy machine-building, electric turbines industries, and in hydroelectric power stations, as reported by the American delegations that studied them on the spot.

[44] *Narodnoe Khozyaystvo SSSR v 1962 godu,* p. 72.

[45] G. Schroeder, "Soviet Industrial Labor Productivity," in *Dimensions of Soviet Economic Power,* Joint Economic Committee, Congress of the United States, 87th Cong., 2d sess. (Washington, D. C.: 1962), part I, pp. 154-155.

on the average by only 3 percent per year in the United States, as compared to 5.2 percent to 7.1 percent in the Soviet Union.[46]

For the most part, however, labor productivity measurements do not fully reflect productive efficiency of an economic system because they do not take into account unemployment and underemployment of labor and capital equipment. There is no doubt that unemployment in the United States is consistently far larger than in the Soviet Union. There are no permanently unemployed in the Soviet Union; everyone who wants to work can find a job, although it takes on the average about three weeks to find one. There is also underemployment of the employed labor force due to inadequate supply of raw materials, bad planning, and the like. Thus, a condition analogous to unemployment does exist in the Soviet Union, in that there is a loss of output due to partial idleness of labor. However, the burden of unemployment does not fall in one segment of the population. Moreover, unemployment or underemployment is not cumulative as it is in capitalist countries.[47]

The efficiency with which capital equipment is used in the USSR—capital productivity—as measured by the output per unit of equipment and/or by the time the equipment is in use, is usually far higher in the Soviet Union than in the United States. In an effort to secure maximum output from industrial plant and equipment, a good part of Soviet industry works around the clock in three labor shifts, while the remaining part works at least in two shifts, that is, twelve to sixteen hours a day. And these are not merely seasonal efforts, as is sometimes the case in the United States. This means that the available productive capacity is utilized more fully in the Soviet Union than in the United States. This is also true about the individual types of equipment for which comparisons have been made. For instance, in the Soviet trucking industry, trucks are in use more per day and per year than in the United States. As a result, haulage per truck (per time worked and per unit of distance traveled) is larger in the USSR than in the United States, in spite of the fact that trucking in the USSR is generally much less developed than in the United States. The same is true about the use of railroad locomotives and freight cars in the Soviet Union and in the United States.[48]

Generally speaking, these findings should have been expected. The Soviet Union is still economically underdeveloped compared to the United States.

[46] Schroeder, p. 149.

[47] See A. R. Oxenfeldt and E. Van den Haag, "Unemployment in Planned and Capitalist Economies," *Quarterly Journal of Economics,* February 1954.

[48] E. W. Williams, Jr., "Some Aspects of the Structure and Growth of Soviet Transportation," *Comparisons of the United States and Soviet Economies,* Joint Economic Committee, Congress of the United States, 86th Cong., 1st sess. (Washington, D. C.: Government Printing Office, 1959), part I, p. 184.

It still has an abundance of labor relative to a shortage of capital; its labor is much cheaper (real wages are much lower), and relatively far cheaper than capital equipment—all as compared with conditions in the United States. It is not surprising that under such conditions labor is used less and capital more efficiently in the USSR than in the United States. (For the same reasons we must expect, for example, that labor in China is much less productive than in the USSR, while capital equipment—where there is one truck or one machine tool per thousand workers—is far more productive than in the USSR or even than in the United States because it is used so much more intensively.)

Labor productivity and efficiency in Soviet agriculture is relatively far lower compared to the United States. According to Soviet official calculations, labor productivity in Soviet agriculture in 1958-1962 was from 3 to 3.5 times lower than in the U.S. To produce a ton of food grains Soviet collective farms spend 7.3 times more labor than American farmers do; to produce a ton of beef they use 14.2 times more labor (1956-1957).[49] The reasons for such low efficiency of Soviet agriculture are fourfold. First, too many peasants in the USSR still live off the land. They must be given some work because they have no other means of subsistence. Second, mechanization, electrification, and the use of chemicals in Soviet agriculture is much below American standards. Per unit of area under crops, the Soviet Union has 4.7 times less tractors and 2.1 times less combines than the United States (1958); an average American farmer uses 520 times more electric power during the year than a Soviet farmer. Third, climatic conditions and soils in the USSR are much worse than in the United States. Only Ukraine and North Caucasus have conditions similar to the main agricultural areas of the United States. Fourth, incentives in Soviet collective farms are undoubtedly smaller than in the American farming.

The productivity of capital equipment in Soviet agriculture is higher than in the United States for the same reasons as in industry. Tractors and other farm machines in the USSR work almost twice as much during the year and they cultivate almost five times as much land each as in the United States.

It is also worth noting that the Soviet Union pursues a peculiar policy in the use and replacement of its plant and equipment. The planners frequently decide not to replace the relatively obsolete equipment, but continue its use along with modern equipment inside the same plant. Or they build an ultra-modern, automated plant and let it produce side by side with the old one without closing down the latter. Under competition this obviously would be impossible, but the planners reckon that as long as the old equipment produces output that covers its direct costs, they save time and production is not interrupted by not overhauling obsolete plants, while resources spared

---

[49] *SSSR i SShA* (*Tsifry i fakty*). (Moscow: Gospolitizdat, 1961), pp. 57, 80, 83, 84.

from replacement are used for other purposes. This policy is reflected in the fact that Soviet capital depreciation charges are much smaller than in the United States; in the USSR they are 6 percent a year on the average, while in the U.S. they are 17 percent and more.[50] These figures imply that American enterprises replace their plant and equipment considerably faster than do Soviet enterprises. However, Soviet economists believe that such American practices are wasteful. This contention is open to debate, of course, in view of the much higher cost of labor in comparison with capital in the United States than in the USSR.

Another aspect, this time organizational, of Soviet efficiency has been discussed by Allen Dulles, the former CIA director, as follows:

> Once they have determined upon a high priority project—and they have fewer echelons of decisions to surmount than we before the final go-ahead is given—they are able to divert to this project the needed complement of the ablest technicians in the USSR which the particular task demands. They can also quickly allocate the necessary laboratory or factory space and manpower required. Today, although their overall resources are far less than ours, they can allocate what is necessary if the priority is high enough. They cannot do everything at once, and they do not work on as many competing designs as we. But in many of the technical and military fields the leadtime from the drawing board to the finished product is less with them than with us. This seems to be true despite the fact that, generally speaking, the technical competence of our labor, man for man, exceeds theirs.[51]

TECHNICAL PROGRESS

The Soviet Union started from a far lower technological base than most West European countries and the United States, and has been able to adopt, directly or with modification, most of the technology developed in the West. Before World War II almost one fourth of all machinery, equipment, and engineering know-how used in Soviet industrialization was imported from the West at very high cost to the Soviet Union. After the war the Soviet Union pursued a thorough program of copying Western technology, and with one swoop purchased nearly 100,000 old patent drawings from the United States Patent Office at twenty-five cents a copy. The advantage of being a latecomer has become less pronounced as the technological gap between the USSR and the West has narrowed. The USSR had to undertake

---

[50] *Cf.* Vsevolod Holubnychy, "Problemy 'osnovnoy ekonomicheskoy zadachi' SSSR." *Uchenye Zapiski Instituta po Izucheniyu SSSR* (Munich), vol. I, no. 1, 1963, p. 68.

[51] *Comparison of the United States and Soviet Economies: Hearings,* Joint Economic Committee, Congress of the United States, 86th Cong., 1st sess. (Washington, D. C.: Government Printing Office, 1960), p. 3.

independent technological progress at larger cost than before. Lately this progress has been rapid especially in areas of high interest to the Soviet government—in particular, industries related to military production and space exploration. In these fields the Soviet government cannot copy others, but must develop something new and different for itself. In a number of civilian fields also, the Soviet Union has recently achieved a considerable number of firsts. It was, of course, the first to put an artificial earth satellite into space and followed this with the first man in space. It was also first in the world to put into operation an atomic power station and an atomic-powered civilian ship, an ice-breaker. It was also first to make commercial use of jet airliners. In certain fields of industrial technology the USSR is leading the world today, for example, in the methods of continuous casting of steel, in electric and vacuum welding, and in extra–high-voltage power transmission. In general, however, it is still considerably behind the United States in technological development, though it is catching up very fast.

As in all other important economic decision making in the USSR, it is the top Communist party and government planners who determine what proportion of the country's resources to devote to technological development and scientific research, toward what particular projects these resources should be directed, and what new inventions and innovations are to be put into production. There is no doubt that decisions to develop powerful rockets and to put astronauts into space, or to produce the superpowerful 100-megaton hydrogen bombs, which cost so much, were made in the Presidium of the Communist party of the Soviet Union—that is, at the very pinnacle of the power pyramid. In other instances of lesser significance, the Central Committee of the Communist party issues directives to develop certain machines[52] or to adopt certain technologies.[53]

The day-to-day direction of technological development in the USSR is centralized in more than a dozen specialized state committees, each concerned with a major industry or a group of industries. All scientific research institutes and establishments in the particular field, all local plant laboratories, design shops, experimental stations, and testing grounds of the particular industry are subordinated to the particular state committee and work according to its plan. These state committees are responsible for all major technical policy decisions: They decide on the allocation of funds and subsidies to individual enterprises and institutes charged with designing and

---

[52] In November 1962, for example, it decided that machinery that could produce various things from plastics was needed. Cf. V. Tikhomirov, "Nuzhny mashiny dlya pererabotki polimerov," *Pravda* (Moscow), January 5, 1963.

[53] Early in 1963 the Central Committee resolved that all nonferrous and rare metal-producing plants in the country must study and adopt new oxygen-enriched smelting technology, for example. Cf. *Spravochnik partiynogo rabotnika*, no. 4 (Moscow: Gospolitizdat, 1963), p. 513.

testing some new machine or new process of production; which types of machinery or technological processes are obsolete and must no longer be used; and which major new inventions or innovations must be adopted by the industry.

Highly centralized guidance of technology has been adopted in the Soviet Union mainly to standardize technology throughout each industry. They are anxious to eliminate technological competition among the enterprises that causes one plant to adopt one type of equipment while others adopt something entirely different. *They prefer to have fewer types of machines and equipment and fewer types of products in general, but more products of the same type, for such standardization makes them cheaper, they believe.* The centralization of technical decision making makes it possible to order designs of various different machines and products to be such that many of their components and spare parts are interchangeable. Bolts and nuts, gearwheels and crankshafts, motors and chassis are then assigned a specific standard number or code, and the designers of new equipment include them as they are in their designs. Furthermore, centralization of research eliminates wasteful duplication. It also permits concentration of large financial resources and top flight personnel on very promising projects.

Despite this centralization, plant managers are given opportunities to push their own technological innovations. These are not likely to be on a large scale because large funds are not provided for this in the enterprise's plans; nevertheless, certain innovations can be introduced by the enterprise out of its last year's profits, depreciation charges, and some bank credit permitted for such purposes.

In addition to the centralized facilities of the industrial state committees, important research and development work is conducted at the scientific and technical institutes of the academies of sciences of the USSR and of each of the republics, as well as in colleges and universities. More than three quarters of all scientific personnel of the Soviet Union are employed by academic institutions.

Furthermore, there is also the State Committee for Inventions and Innovations, which is equivalent to the U. S. Patent Office. It is authorized to issue to inventors documents of authorship and patents. Inventions adopted for use become government property, however. Also rewards for inventions and innovations are very modest; they never can be larger than 20,000 rubles ($22,200), payable in a lump sum.[54] Some Soviet writers consider such rewards as very low and unsatisfactory.[55]

---

[54] *Zakonodatel'nye akty po voprosam narodnogo khozyaystva SSSR* (Moscow: Gosyurizdat, 1961), vol. 1, p. 578.

[55] *Cf.,* e.g., Yu. S. Nekhoroshev, "Ekonomicheskaya priroda voznagrazhdeniya za izobreteniya," *Vestnik Leningradskogo Universiteta* (Leningrad), no. 17, series 3, 1960, p. 5. Also *Ekonomicheskaya Gazeta* (Moscow), August 15, 1964, p. 5.

AN EVALUATION OF SOVIET ECONOMY

Now that we have described the manner in which the Soviet economy operates, let us evaluate its over-all performance. Communists took control of the Russian economy in 1917. The present economic system however was not founded until about 1930. A sufficiently long period has elapsed since then to reveal the potentialities of the Communist system. Before the evidence describing what has happened under the Communists in the USSR can be interpreted, it is necessary to formulate criteria by which the economy is to be judged.

Criteria for Judgment

First, the Soviet economy can be judged either by the avowed goals of those who led the Revolution or by the ends people hope to achieve by capitalism. We should judge communism both by whether it has done what it claimed to do and by whether it is the type of economy we would like for ourselves. If the system gives the Russians what they desire, it cannot be considered a failure in the Soviet Union. If, however, it does not give what we would want, it must be adjudged a poor system for the United States, no matter how the Russians view its accomplishments.

Second, we must establish what could legitimately be expected if communism were successful. It must be recognized that the Russians were the first to attempt detailed and thorough economic planning. They had to blaze a trail in an uncharted field. It was to be expected that progress would be slow at best, for the job they tried to do was enormous and they attempted it under highly adverse circumstances.

A Review of Soviet Accomplishments

The accomplishments of the Soviet Union will be discussed with the Communist party's objectives as a backdrop. First, we shall investigate the extent to which the Soviet Union has progressed toward its economic goals; thereafter, we shall discuss its noneconomic achievements.

Economic Accomplishments

Soviet leaders, since their advent to power, have set three major economic objectives for themselves: (1) to industrialize rapidly; (2) to develop planning machinery, procedures, and principles; and (3) to increase output greatly. Progress made toward each of these objectives will be discussed in turn.

Degree of Industrialization.   Industrialization is best measured by the changing proportion of persons engaged in agriculture and in industry. The rapid industrialization of the Soviet Union can be seen in the increased number of workers in nonagricultural undertakings over a short period. Table 16 shows, for example, that the number of persons engaged in industry more than tripled during the nine years between 1928 and 1937 and more than doubled between 1937 and 1962. All the nonagricultural occupations increased substantially more than the total population; the proportion of the labor force engaged in agriculture declined correspondingly.

Roughly 85 percent of the population of tsarist Russia were engaged in agriculture before the Revolution; by 1940, this share declined to 54 percent of the total, and by 1962, to 35 percent.[56] *This shift of labor force unquestionably represents the most speedy industrialization of a major nation the world has known. It was also the most painful conversion expe-*

Table 16.   Occupational Distribution of Soviet Nonagricultural Labor Force, 1928, 1937, 1952, and 1962

(in millions)

Branch	1928	1937	1952	1962
Industry	3.1	10.1	15.5	24.3
Construction	0.7	2.0	2.8	5.1
Railways	1.0	1.5	2.2	2.3
Waterways	0.1	0.18	0.2	0.3
Other transport	0.2	1.1	2.1	4.0
Communications	0.1	0.38	0.6	0.8
Education	0.8	2.3	3.5	5.5
Health services	0.4	1.1	2.2	3.8
State, administrative, and other institutions	1.2	2.5	2.8	3.5
Banking institutions	0.1	0.19	0.2	0.3

SOURCES: For 1928 and 1937 H. Schwartz, *Russia's Soviet Economy* (New York: Prentice-Hall, Inc., 1950), p. 444. Data for 1952 and 1962 from *Narodnoe Khozyaystvo SSSR v 1962 godu* (Moscow), 1963, p. 453.

rienced by any country, for it took place when living levels were very low.

Development of Planning Machinery, Procedures, and Principles. Another major objective of the Soviet leaders was the creation of a planned economy. Despite many handicaps, to be mentioned presently, the Communists have had the long period since 1917 to experiment with planning procedures, establish planning machinery, and formulate principles and procedures. It seems legitimate to judge the Soviet Union to a large extent by the efficiency of its planning. Unfortunately, there is far from general agreement on this point. The Soviet Union unquestionably has demonstrated that

[56] *Narodnoe Khozyaystvo SSSR v 1962 godu*, p. 451.

planning can work well enough to "keep going"; however, the efficiency of their planning arrangements is still in dispute. As already noted, even the Communists themselves have been critical of them. Foreign observers reach widely different conclusions about the effectiveness of Soviet planning. We simply lack sufficient information to evaluate Soviet planning procedure with confidence. The authors would describe planning in the Soviet Union as still rough, though improving, especially as a result of the recent introduction of mathematical techniques and electronic computers.

Expansion of Output.   In assessing the accomplishments of the Soviet Union, and most especially in evaluating its output record, the conditions between 1917 and 1965 must be taken into account. The period of Communist rule has been among the most disturbed in all Soviet, and perhaps world, history.

The many disturbances during this period influenced what achievements we could legitimately expect from the Soviet economic system. Two kinds of disturbances must be distinguished: namely, those of foreign origin over which the Soviet Union had no control, and those generated by the peculiarities of the Soviet political system and for which the economic system was not responsible. For a large part of its life, the Soviet Union was denied diplomatic recognition and was subjected to hostile pressures by other nations. Moreover, between 1932 and 1941, because of the increased threat of war, the Soviet Union had to increase its military power, primarily at the expense of nonmilitary achievements. Between 1941 and 1945, the Soviet Union suffered enormous losses in lives and property as a result of Nazi Germany's attack. The war set the Soviet economy back for a whole decade, for only in 1950 did the Soviet Union regain the productivity level it had attained in 1940. Since V-E Day the Soviet Union has been engaged in a Cold War that has made it necessary—from the Soviet point of view—to maintain military forces of great strength and to engage in a costly arms race with the United States and other Western powers.

Disturbances originating in the Soviet political system included, among other, unnecessarily harsh methods used in the collectivization of agriculture (1929-1934) as a result of which agriculture's productivity declined sharply; and Stalin's bloody purges in the thirties and late forties in which many leading professional, scientific and technical personnel, planners, and managers perished. Thus, during a substantial part of the period since the founding of the present economic system, conditions for its normal functioning have been extremely difficult by any standard. One must not therefore assume that the Soviet Union achieved what could have been expected if the period had been one of uninterrupted international and domestic tranquility.

Errors in Evaluating Soviet Production

In assessing the performance of the Soviet Union we must rely almost exclusively upon statistical results reported by the Soviet authorities. We have ample evidence that they believe economic facts to have high military value to potential enemies; they have actually prohibited the publication of many such types of information.[57] *On the other hand, experts on the Soviet economy are almost all in full agreement that Soviet output information is not deliberately falsified by the government statistical agencies because it is known that they themselves use the same statistics they publish.* Information is suppressed, and some that is published is misleading, but direct falsification is probably not practiced.[58]

A few points should be made at the outset with reference to Soviet data. First, they are relatively scanty, so that on many points of deep interest there is no factual information that has been made public. Second, while not consciously falsified, in all probability, economic data are constantly being used for propaganda purposes; consequently, one must presume that the information released to the public is presented in a manner that will create the most favorable impression of the planners' achievements short of outright falsification. Third, students of the Soviet Union lack an invaluable protection against being misled by government statistics that exists in countries without a firm and sensitive dictatorship: that is the independent expert who is free to comment upon and criticize the statistical reports of the government and to indicate instances where the actual facts differ from the conclusions that would ordinarily be drawn. Consequently, the review of economic developments in the Soviet Union poses unusually great difficulties—though it is possible to obtain a fairly reliable picture of what has transpired if one exercises caution and a scientific approach.

Many of the errors made in assessing the results claimed by the Soviet Union result from studying "synthetic" statistics; synthetic statistics do not describe production of a product directly in terms of concrete units of output; instead, they are "indices" that combine in a single number the output of many products. In the preparation of an index, often more than one method of computation is possible. The major problem faced in the construction of an index is the selection of items to be included and the

---

[57] The State Secrets decree of June 9, 1947 imposes anything from 8 years in a labor camp to capital punishment for the unauthorized disclosure of economic information. *Cf. Vedomosti Verkhovnogo Soveta SSSR* (Moscow), No. 20, 1947.

[58] Information sent to the statistical agencies by the enterprises and farms is sometimes falsified, however. This fact is recognized and dealt with in the enactment of the USSR Council of Ministers and the Central Committee of the Communist party of May 19, 1961, entitled "Concerning the Measures to Avert the Facts of Deception and Fraud of the State and to Strengthen Control Over the Reliability of Reports on the Fulfillment of Plans and Obligations."

"weight" to be attached to each one. Many Soviet official indices are inflated by inappropriate "weights," while many Western indices of Soviet production are deflated because of insufficient coverage of items and lack of data on military production, which is included in Soviet official indices and in their rates of growth.

If we stick to specific products, preferably to those whose output is reported in physical terms, and if when dealing with products whose output is reported only in terms of percentage changes, we concern ourselves only with those whose output is substantial, we should not go far astray. Since the Cold War is partly a statistical war, we must beware of statistical indices unless we know precisely how they are constructed.

Another possible source of error is the exclusive reliance on measurements in terms of percentage increases from a preceding period. The Soviet authorities sometimes compare current output with that of years when the output of some products was virtually nil; these comparisons show huge percentage increases, to which it is easy to attach undue significance. On the other hand, in studying the output of products that have been made for a long time, or whose output we know to be large in absolute terms, percentage increases are a satisfactory source of information. Indeed, one's mind typically tries to change absolute numbers into percentage terms in assessing production information.

General Indicators of Change in Soviet Output

The Soviet Union and the United States use different concepts and methods in computing their indicators of total output—the gross national product (GNP) and national income (NI). Consequently, their published statistics are not directly comparable. (On the average, Soviet measures of NI are about 25 percent below those calculated by the American method.)

Numerous attempts have been made in the West to recalculate Soviet NI statistics according to Western methods to make them comparable to Western NI statistics. The results are not very reliable mainly because many ingredients of the Soviet NI have been unknown (the true value of defense output, for example) or questionable (data on prices, agricultural output, and so on).

The best known and relatively most reliable is an American study of the Soviet national income by Professor Abram Bergson of Harvard. His major conclusion is that the total Soviet output, as measured by national income in constant prices, expanded by from 5.0 to 5.5 percent a year in the 1928-1937 period and by 7.5 to 7.6 percent a year in the 1950-1955 period.[59] *The significance of this finding is that such a rate of growth of total*

---

[59] A. Bergson, *The Real National Income of Soviet Russia since 1928* (Cambridge, Mass.: Harvard U.P., 1961), p. 219.

output has been among the highest in the world, and especially from two to three times higher than the rate of growth of the American economy during the same years and after.

The main reason for such a fast expansion of production in the Soviet Union has also been established. As can be seen from Table 17, the Soviet Union allocates to private consumption a much smaller part of its total output than does the U.S. or France. It thus has saved resources from consumption and allocated them to capital investments. The USSR devotes a much larger portion of its total output to capital investments than do other countries. Such expansion of new investments means the construction of new factories and mines, new plant and equipment, which increase productivity and accelerate the growth of production.

Table 17.   Allocation of the Gross National Products of the Soviet Union, the United States, and France, Average for 1950-1960

(percent of the total)

	Private consumption	Government consumption	Gross domestic capital formation	Total GNP
Soviet Union	56.3	16.2	27.5	100.0
United States	64.0	18.0	18.0	100.0
France	66.8	14.4	18.8	100.0

SOURCE: A. Bergson and S. Kuznets (eds.), *Economic Trends in the Soviet Union* (Cambridge, Mass.: Harvard University Press, 1963), p. 360.

These findings are corroborated by most other Western studies as well as by the Soviet official estimates. According to the latter, 28.2 percent of the Soviet national income went into capital accumulation in 1962, for example.[60] Numerically, the figures in different estimates differ of course, but two facts have been established quite firmly:

1. *The Soviet Union has been able to expand its total output very fast, faster than most other countries in the world; and*
2. *This expansion has been made possible by relative curtailment of consumption and heavy emphasis on new investments.*

These two facts have been made possible by the unique organization of the Soviet economic system. How and why this is done has already been explained.

---

[60] *Narodnoe khozyaystvo SSSR v 1962 godu*, p. 483-484.

The rapid expansion of Soviet output has narrowed the great gap that once separated the Soviet and the U.S. economies. According to Soviet estimates, total industrial output of tsarist Russia was equal to only 12.5 percent of that of the United States in 1913; in 1950 it was about 30 percent of that of the United States, and in 1962, about 63 percent. On a per capita basis, Soviet industry produced about 53 percent as much as did American industry in 1962. The output of Soviet agriculture was about 75 to 80 percent of that in the United States (less than 70 percent on a per capita basis).[61]

Western estimates of Soviet output are somewhat lower. One U.S. government study estimated the 1960 Soviet GNP to be equal to about 46 percent of the American GNP, both computed by American method. Nevertheless, taking into account that the Soviet GNP had grown by 6.8 percent a year in the 1950-1960 period, while the American GNP grew by only 3.3 percent, the study suggested that if these rates of growth continued, the USSR would catch up with the United States in total output sometime around the year 1982.[62]

Specific Indicators of Output

Table 18 describes the output of individual goods in the Soviet Union for selected years in physical terms. It shows the same broad characteristics as the general indicators of total production discussed above. We note the following features in particular.

As a result of World War I and the 1917 Revolution and Civil War that followed, production declined considerably in the Soviet Union by 1921. In addition, there was a terrible famine in that year in which many people perished. Only by 1928 was the Soviet Union able to regain the economic position it held in 1913; this means that the war and the revolution cost fifteen years of economic development.

In 1928 the First Five-Year Plan of Industrialization was launched and in 1930 the present economic system came into being. Considerable expansion of output by heavy industry occurred by 1940, but agricultural and consumer goods production lagged. The collectivization of agriculture by forcible methods created a farm crisis and resulted in drastic decline in crops and a heavy slaughter of farm animals. In 1932-1933 there was another famine with heavy loss in human lives. It mainly hit the peasantry of the grain-producing regions of Ukraine and was not felt much in the cities because the government was able to secure grain supplies for the cities and for export. Agricultural production lagged throughout the period; partly be-

---

[61] Narodnoe . . . , p. 72.

[62] U. S. Department of Commerce, Business and Defense Services Administration, *The Gross National Product in the Soviet Union: Comparative Growth Rates* (Washington, D.C.: Government Printing Office, 1963), pp. 7-8.

Table 18. Production of Selected Goods in the USSR

Product and unit	1913	1921	1928	1933	1940	1945	1952	1963
Industrial								
Electric power, bill. kwh.	2.0	0.5	5.0	16.3	48.3	43.2	119.1	412.0
Crude oil, mill. tons	9.2	3.8	11.6	21.5	31.1	19.4	47.3	206.1
Coal, mill. tons	29.1	9.5	35.5	76.3	165.9	149.3	300.9	532.0
Steel, mill. tons	4.2	0.2	4.2	6.9	18.3	12.2	34.5	80.2
Machine tools, 1000 units	1.8	0.8	2.0	21.0	58.4	38.4	74.6	183.0
Turbines, mill. kw.	—	—	0.04	0.3	1.2	0.2	3.4	11.9
Locomotives, units	477	78	479	948	928	8	439	2162
Trucks, 1000 units	—	—	0.7	39.1	136.0	68.5	243.5	414.0
Tractors, 1000 units	—	—	1.3	73.7	31.6	7.7	98.7	325.0
Grain harvesters, 1000 units	—	—	—	8.6	12.8	0.3	42.2	82.9
Escavators, 1000 units	—	—	0.1	0.1	0.3	—	3.7	17.9
Fertilizers, mill. tons	0.09	—	0.1	1.0	3.2	1.1	6.4	19.9
Timber, mill. cu. meters	67.0	6.5	61.7	173.3	246.1	168.4	291.4	352.7[a]
Cement, mill. tons	1.8	0.06	1.8	2.7	5.7	1.8	13.9	61.0
Consumer								
Automobiles, 1000 units	—	—	0.1	10.3	5.5	5.0	59.7	173.0
Washing machines, 1000 units	—	—	—	—	—	—	4.3	2282.0
Bicycles, 1000 units	4.9	7.7	10.8	125.6	255.0	23.8	1650.4	3352.0
Cameras, 1000 units	—	—	—	29.6	355.2	0.01	459.1	1432.0
Radio sets, 1000 units	—	—	—	29.0	160.5	13.8	1294.5	4802.0
Television sets, 1000 units	—	—	—	—	0.3	—	37.4	2474.0

Product and unit	1913	1921	1928	1933	1940	1945	1952	1963
Cotton fabrics, bill. meters	2.7	1.5	2.7	2.7	3.9	1.6	5.0	6.6
Leather shoes, mill. pairs^e	60.0	28.0	58.0	90.3	211.0	63.1	237.7	463.0
Sugar, mill. tons	2.2	0.06	1.9	1.4	2.8	0.5	4.1	6.2
Canned food, billion cans	0.1	0.1	0.1	0.7	1.1	0.6	2.1	6.4
Alcohol, mill. decaliters	55.2	10.2	23.3	38.8	89.9	26.5	89.1	184.0^b
Agricultural								
Grain, mill. tons	86.0	36.2	73.3	69.1	95.5	75.0^d	82.5^c	138.0^b
Cows, mill.	28.8	24.8	29.2	19.0	27.8	22.9	24.3	38.3
Hogs, mill.	23.0	13.1	19.4	9.9	27.5	10.6	28.5	40.8
Vegetable oil, mill. tons	0.5	0.03	0.5	0.3	0.8	0.3	1.0	2.2
Fish caught, mill. tons	1.0	0.3	0.8	1.3	1.4	1.1	2.1	4.7
Freight transport, bill. t/km	126.0	42.3	119.5	218.3	487.4	374.6	877.6	2300.0

a 1962   b 1961   c 1953   d Approximately   e Factory production only.

NOTE: Data for 1921, 1928, and 1933 refer to the USSR in pre-World War II frontiers, which enclosed a territory about 3 percent smaller than that in 1913, 1940, and the remaining years.

SOURCES: *Narodnoe khozyaystvo SSSR v 1958 godu* (Moscow, 1959); *Narodnoe khozyaystvo SSSR v 1962 godu* (Moscow, 1963); SSSR *v tsifrakh v 1963 godu* (Moscow, 1964).

cause of this, consumer goods output lagged also. In addition, deliberate government policy checked consumption and devoted resources predominantly to the heavy and defense industries.

The 1945 data in Table 18 reflect the great devastation due to the invasion and occupation of large portions of the Soviet Union. In 1946 unprecedented drought destroyed the harvest, and there was another famine. Only in 1952 did the Soviet economy surpass its pre-World War II levels. The year 1952 was also the last full year of Stalin's life. After his death major reforms in the management and planning of the Soviet economy have unleashed new productive vigor.

The decade between 1952 and 1963 is reflected in Table 18 by very substantial increases in all lines of production. Notice in particular the growth of agriculture and of consumer goods production; in this period they became quite large for the first time in Soviet history.

If we compare 1963 with 1928, the following facts emerge: the output of capital goods and heavy industry has grown very fast. In thiry-five years (in fact twenty-five, since the war decade must be excluded), the output of machine tools increased 96.5 times and their quality undoubtedly improved; the output of electric power increased more than 82 times; that of cement, 34 times; steel, 19 times; petroleum, almost 18 times; coal, 15 times. Freight transport increased more than 19 times during this period. The growth of consumer goods production lagged far behind, however. The output of cotton fabric increased but 2.4 times, and this is not because the Soviet citizens had enough of it (see Table 19). Likewise, sugar production increased only 3.3 times and canned goods, 6.4 times. There was considerable expansion in the production of bicycles, however; and especially since 1952, such new consumer goods as TV sets and washing machines were produced in rapidly growing amounts.

The growth of farm production has lagged behind that of consumer goods, however. Compared to 1913 (with the same national frontiers as in 1961), the output of grain increased by only little more than 60 percent and the herds of livestock less than doubled.

In assessing the foregoing statistics describing Soviet output, the growth of Soviet population from 159.2 million in 1913 to 224.8 in 1963 (within the same frontiers), or by 41 percent, must be kept in mind.

Levels of Living in the Soviet Union

In 1965 the average Soviet family still was poor by American and European standards. By saying this, one is making explicit what was implied in the foregoing review of consumer goods output and agricultural production.

Two questions about the level of living in the USSR are raised frequently: How much has it improved since the Revolution? How high is it at present? Answers to both questions are extremely difficult because the available information about Soviet consumption is spotty and bedeviled by omissions and by changes in definition and in geographic area. However, it is possible to discern broad patterns of change, even though their precise dimensions are obscure.

Changes in Living Standards since the Revolution.   When the Communists took power, about 85 percent of the population was engaged in agriculture; half of these persons were tenantlike farmers whose condition was one of extreme impoverishment and ignorance. The other half were small-scale farmers almost equally poor and in debt. Contrary to a popular notion, most of Russia is not well adapted to agriculture by rainfall, climate, and soil fertility. Moreover, farming methods were about as primitive as those employed at present in the underdeveloped countries. The farmer's income was kept very low by the heavy taxes and rents he had to pay for his land. Farm workers were far poorer than the workers in the expanding industry in the cities.

Before the Revolution the Russian industrial worker was poorer than his counterpart in the United States and Western Europe by a wide, though unmeasured, margin. There was no strong demand for his services, he was uneducated and unorganized; moreover, because of lack of training and skill, his low productivity kept his income below that of his counterparts in Western countries.

Thus, both in industry and agriculture, Russia was an extremely backward and poor country on the eve of the Revolution. In methods of production and levels of skill and education, it had more in common with the Balkan countries and such countries as Turkey, Iran, and India than it did with, say, Austria-Hungary.

Today, Soviet living standards are much higher than those in Turkey, Iran, and India, and possibly are above those in Austria.

There is little question that Soviet levels of living have improved—even relative to conditions in many other countries—since the Revolution. However, this improvement did not take place at a steady rate; indeed, there were periods when the level of living declined, apart from the drop due to World War II.

According to the best available study of Soviet costs of living and wages and salaries of the nonagricultural employees, real wages in the Soviet Union in 1940 were only 57 percent of what they were in 1928; by 1948 they declined to 45 percent of the 1928 level. They have risen steadily since then. However, even in 1954, the last year covered by this study, they were still 12 percent below the 1928 level.[63] Peasants' real income undoubtedly

---

[63] Janet G. Chapman, *Real Wages in Soviet Russia Since 1928* (Cambridge, Mass.: Harvard University Press, 1963), p. 145. In 1928 real wages were considerably higher than in 1913, by the way.

fared even worse, although data on this subject are scattered and less reliable.[64]

During the period 1921 to 1940 (and even to the present) there was a steady movement of population from the farms to the cities. As a result, the need for urban housing grew steadily—at times the increased need greatly outran the ability or willingness of the authorities to provide it. As a result, housing conditions in towns and cities have deteriorated. According to Soviet estimates, urban housing space per capita was 7.3 square meters in 1913 and 8.2 in 1926, but by 1940 it declined to 6.9 square meters; in 1950 it was still only 7.2, and by 1957 it rose to 7.7 square meters, which amounts to about three people per room.[65]

The foregoing account—taken against the backdrop of a steady and steep rise in the output of producers goods—shows that the wishes of the Soviet consumer were not considered to be on a par with the desire of the Communist party to industrialize. Compared with consumers in the United States and other non-Communist industrialized countries, the Soviet consumer did very poorly under the Soviet economic system up to 1953. However, it would be inaccurate to say that his wishes were ignored altogether. He was given evidence from the very start—apart from statistical reports of expanding capital goods production and some visible grandiose projects— that his personal lot was in a way improving. Perhaps the most visible signs to him of the government's concern took the form of greatly improved educational facilities for his children, free medical care, and other social services.

In recent years, living levels of the Soviet population have been rising faster than ever before. According to Soviet official statistics, between 1954 and 1959, real wages of the nonagricultural workers and employees increased 16 percent, and between 1959 and 1962, by another 18 percent.[66] Real incomes of the collective farmers increased at a similar rate, if not faster, due to a number of major increases of the government procurement prices for agricultural produce. Urban housing construction was brisk, although the Seven-Year Plan was underfulfilled in this respect.

Current Levels of Living in the Soviet Union. Despite the improvement in the lot of the average Soviet citizen since 1953, he was poor in 1965 by American standards. As his condition had improved, so too had that of consumers in all industrialized nations.

The typical level of living of the Soviet worker is not only different from that of workers in other industrialized countries in absolute level, its com-

---

[64] *Cf.* Naum Jasny, *Essays on the Soviet Economy* (Munich: Institute for the Study of the USSR, 1962), pp. 93ff.

[65] S. P. Figurnov, p. 109.

[66] Figurnov, p. 136, and *Narodnoe Khozyaystvo SSSR v 1962 godu*, p. 487.

position is quite different also. In some respects, it is shockingly low; in others it is surprisingly high.

The poverty of the average urban Soviet family is most acute in the matter of housing which, while it costs but a trifle, nevertheless is insufferable by American standards. (Of course, our slums are worse than their average level of housing, but not by very much.) The rate and volume of new housing construction in the USSR has been larger than in the U.S. recently.

The average Soviet citizen has been compelled to rely heavily upon a diet composed of grains, potatoes, and cabbage. His consumption of meat, dairy products, and fruits is low, though it has risen rapidly of late. However, if he is prepared to forego meat and dairy products, the Russian can live on very little, for potatoes, bread, and other cereal products are extremely inexpensive.

Clothing is plain and of comparatively poor quality in the Soviet Union, though important strides have been made toward improving the quality of consumer goods in recent years. Selection is limited and, to the typical American tourist, the population's dress appears drab. Only a very exceptional Russian owns a car, a television set, washing machine, vacuum cleaner, or an electric shaver. All these facts can be seen from Tables 19 and 20. Since 1958-1960 Soviet situation has improved but only slightly.

Table 19.   Per Capita Consumption in the Soviet Union and the United States, 1958

	USSR	United States
Meat, poultry, bacon and lard (lbs.)	83.6	200.2
Milk and milk products (quarts)	224.0	314.0
Eggs (units)	105.0	358.0
Fish (lbs.)	30.8	26.4
Sugar (lbs.)	57.2	96.8
Flour (lbs.)	349.8	127.6
Potatoes (lbs.)	330.0	105.6
Cotton fabrics (yards)	30.5	51.2
Wool fabrics (yards)	1.6	1.5
Shoes (pairs)	1.7	3.3

SOURCE: A. Bergson and S. Kuznetz (eds.), *Economic Trends in the Soviet Union*, p. 252.

A few respects in which the level of living of the average Soviet family is relatively high are in the fields of education, medical care, and cultural services. Education is free for all who meet prevailing academic standards; medical services are free; the theater, ballet, concerts, and the like are heavily subsidized by the government and performances are inexpensive. In these spheres the Soviet citizen may be as well off as his American counterpart, on balance, or better. Soviet sources claim that the Soviet Union has almost 20 percent more doctors for the same number of hospital beds than does the United States; almost 40 percent more teachers for the same number of high school students; and about 20 percent more college and university graduates of equal educational standing.[67]

Thus, the Soviet consumer's desire for more goods was not given first priority. Even though the average level of living was very low, the Communists called for large increases in the output of capital goods; as a result, the supply of goods for consumer use could not be expanded rapidly. The Soviet consumer paid a heavy price for industrialization. However, it seems that the time has come when he is to be repaid for his sacrifices. The enormous increase in the Soviet industrial capacity contains the potential of steady growth in future levels of living. *Nothing about the Soviet economic system requires the curtailment of consumption to be a permanent feature. The economic system made possible curtailment of consumption and the*

Table 20. Stocks of Consumer Durables per 100 Families in the USSR and the United States, 1960

	USSR	United States
Radio sets	48	94
Television sets	10	89
Refrigerators	3.5	98
Washing machines	5	95

SOURCE: *Dimensions of Soviet Power*, p. 364.

relocation of resources into the expansion of capital accumulation; it is capable as well of securing the rapid flow of resources into consumption, if desired. Decisions to allocate resources to one sector or another are made by political authorities in the Soviet Union, not dictated by its economic system. Hence, if these authorities decide to emphasize consumption, the latter can be expanded rapidly.

In recent years Soviet leaders have modulated their previous one-sided emphasis on the expansion of capital goods production. They have held to the principle that the output of capital goods must grow faster than the output of consumer goods, but they agree now that this difference can be reduced. New investments in consumer goods production and housing construction have increased at a slightly faster rate during the last decade than have new investments in capital goods production; new investments in agri-

---

[67] *SSSR-SShA* (*Tsifry i fakty*), pp. 108, 119, 122.

culture have increased even faster. This undoubtedly indicates a significant shift of economic policy.

Noneconomic Accomplishments of the Soviet Union

Noneconomic goals have always figured prominently in Communist thinking. Accordingly, Soviet leaders have pursued many ends in addition to economic goals, sometimes at the sacrifice of economic achievements.

Major Noneconomic Achievements. The following achievements are relatively noncontroversial, though they are not universally acknowledged.

1. The Soviet Union has become a first-rate military power with an influence in the world never enjoyed before in its history and extending far beyond its frontiers.
2. It has made notable advances in pure and applied sciences, as shown in the exploration of outer space and of Arctica and Antarctica. It has made important discoveries in the fields of nuclear physics and in taming thermonuclear energy for peaceful purposes.
3. The traditional social conditions in agriculture and in rural ways of life have been changed in the USSR. Rural society has become modernized socially, technically, and culturally. Previously overpopulated rural communities and small semirural towns have become more closely linked with the new industrial centers. There has been an enormous increase in mobility of people from villages to cities.
4. One of the foremost social results of the Soviet Union's industrialization has been the general increase in the number of social positions of relatively high rank open to those from the lower classes. The great rise in social mobility in the country as a whole literally turned the traditional social structure upside down. The traditionally sharp differences in the ways of life of the different social classes, previously isolated from each other, have been eliminated to a noticeable extent.
5. Literacy has expanded enormously in the Soviet Union, from some 20 percent of the total school-age population before the Revolution to 98.6 percent in 1959. Educational and cultural levels have been raised greatly. Education has become the chief ladder between social classes and the most important tool of individual achievement and advancement.
6. Interest in political and public affairs has become extremely keen among the great majority of the Soviet population. Even peasants regularly subscribe to national newspapers and are aware of political developments in the Soviet Union and abroad.

The Political System of the Soviet Union.   Since the Soviet Union's political arrangements determine who will set the directives for its economic plans and be entrusted with carrying them out, they are an intrinsic part of its economic structure.

Of all its features, the Soviet Union's political system is the object of greatest criticism—except possibly for the "methods" used by its leaders to attain their ends and to take over the state power.[68] In form the Soviet Union is a constitutional democracy in which, however, only one single political party has the right to offer slates of candidates to the general electorate and thus to govern the country. The Soviet Constitution does not foresee the functioning of any political parties in the USSR except the existing Communist party (Article 126). Furthermore, since only one candidate runs for each elective office, the electorate has really no choice of candidates. The unique and most puzzling feature of these political arrangements is the nature and functions of the Communist party.

The Communist party of the Soviet Union has a membership that has varied considerably from time to time, but is counted in the millions. By the end of 1961 it had 9,800,000 members, or about 7.5 percent of the total adult population. The social composition of its membership (by origin, not by actual present status or job) was as follows: workers, 34.5 percent; peasants, 17.5 percent; white-collar employees and others, 48.0 percent.[69] Membership in the Communist party bears practically no semblance to party membership in any non-Communist country. The Communists claim that failure of foreigners to understand the high degree of democracy that exists in the USSR results mainly from failure to appreciate the meaning of party membership.

Membership in the Communist party, at least in theory, involves very substantial sacrifices. If there is any analogy that might be familiar to Americans, it would be to membership in a devout religious order which imposes fairly strict rules of personal conduct and whose main rewards are psychic and spiritual rather than material.

Tasks calling for great personal sacrifice—like the opening up of new regions, taking employment at a great distance from one's family, participa-

---

[68] The brutal, terrifying, and strange methods sometimes used by Communist leaders are suggested by a non-Russian case; however, it falls so neatly into the apparent Soviet pattern that it may help to explain some puzzling events in Soviet history. That is the case of Rajk, former Foreign Minister of Hungary, who was hanged in 1949 and exonerated in 1956.

Innocent men have been executed in all countries, but what is singular about this case is the behavior of the defendant. Rajk confessed fully, openly, and with apparent willingness to all of the crimes of which he was accused in 1949. Moreover, he virtually demanded that he be given the death penalty. Yet in 1956 it was announced that he was innocent and the victim of a frame-up.

[69] *Partiynaya Zhizn* (Moscow), no. 1, January 15, 1962.

tion in adult education programs, the conduct of propaganda meetings—fall to the lot of the Communist party member. Unless he does his share of these chores, he is likely to be dropped from party membership. In recent years the annual rate of expulsion was about 0.5 percent of the total membership, or about 50,000 a year. To be dropped from the party is a personal blow which few people would willingly endure. Conversely, to be elected to party membership is an honor to which many people aspire in the USSR.

Since every Communist must accept assignments made by party leaders, the leadership has at its complete disposal a reservoir of manpower which undoubtedly includes a very high proportion of the most energetic and talented Soviet citizens that can be assigned to difficult tasks in a crisis. This is of special significance for the smooth functioning of the Soviet economic system.

Full-time party workers and officials (or the members of the party "apparatus," as they are known) must be distinguished from other party members. It is these members who work full time *for the party,* carry on the bulk of party functions, and are required to be especially exemplary Communists. Of course, party members working full-time in the usual jobs—plant managers, engineers, collective farm chairmen, writers, university professors, or ballet dancers—all must from time to time, fulfill some temporary duty for the party that may involve a sacrifice on their part. Scientists, for example, are required to deliver at least a few public lectures a year in some workers' clubs; ballerinas may be sent to perform before the collective farmers during the harvest. On the other hand, the members of the party "apparatus" do all the "dirty work" all the time. They are the "organizers" of everything in the USSR and it is on them that the party's power rests. They may be said to run the country as well as the party. (They comprise from 20 to 25 percent of the total party membership.)

Thus, *in theory,* the Communist party of the Soviet Union represents a dedicated minority whose duty it is to devote a major share of their thinking and time to the country's welfare by studying and participating in economic and political affairs. Its members are expected to be vigilant for errors or shortcomings on the part of others. In their decisions within party circles and their criticisms of individuals, they are expected to be motivated by the "good of the masses."

Also *in theory,* the Communist party is internally democratic. The top leaders—the Presidium—are elected by the Central Committee of the Communist party, which in turn is elected by representatives of republic, regional, and industrial Communist party units. Thus, Communist party officials theoretically represent all members of the party. Practically, however, it is the party "apparatus" that runs the party, organizes internal party elections, and names the slates of candidates to party committees. Since the members of the "apparatus" are not elected but appointed to their positions by the top party secretaries, it is not surprising that there is mutual rapport, unity of interest, and complete interdependence between the leaders of the party and the "apparatus." It is on this rapport that the dictatorship of the Communist party's leaders over the party and the whole country rests for the most part.

It shocks many Americans to find that the Russians claim their country to be more democratic than ours. Americans are certain that the truth is quite the other way around; indeed, they regard the Soviet Union as one of the clearest examples of dictatorship. So sharp a difference of opinion is unusual and is to be explained in several ways. First, and most important, Americans use the term "democracy" differently from the Russians. Second, no matter how the term "democracy" is defined, it is difficult to assess the degree of democarcy that exists in any country.

Americans tend to think that democracy exists if everyone can vote and that it is imperfect to the degree that the right to vote is restricted. By this test, the Soviet Union is quite democratic. Indeed, a far larger proportion of the adult population votes in the Soviet Union than in the United States. Moreover, to judge by many of the provisions of its Constitution, the Soviet Union would *seem to be* democratic. In addition to "guarantees" of freedom of speech and press, freedom of assembly, freedom of street processions and demonstrations, and the like, the Soviet Constitution provides for "placing at the disposal of the working people and their organizations printing presses, stocks of paper, public buildings, the streets, communications facilities, and other material requisites for the exercise of these rights." (Article 125.) In addition, it outlaws infringements of personal liberty by restrictions of the rights of individuals on account of race or nationality, and punishes "advocacy of racial or national exclusiveness or hatred and contempt" (Article 123).

However, one must always distinguish carefully between appearances and reality in the Soviet Union; especially is this true with respect to its Constitution. In the first place, it is doubtful how much the Constitution has influenced what was actually done—at least until fairly recently. In the second place, even if one takes the Constitution at face value, it contains some verbal booby traps that obscure and could nullify its apparent meaning. For example, Article 126 sanctions the one-party system which, almost by definition, would make the political system considerably less than highly democratic. Weaknesses of the Constitution from the standpoint of protecting civil liberties and other liberties covered in our Constitution and Bill of Rights include the following: Article 111 specifies public trials "unless otherwise provided for by the law"; Article 127 provides for arrest "by decision of a court or with the sanction of a procurator" but without the right of *habeas corpus,* nonassumption of guilt before proven guilty, or assurance of a fair trial; Article 133 provides no safeguards against false accusations of treason. Furthermore, the Constitution does not establish any body that is empowered to interpret its meaning.

To define democracy in terms of form has little meaning, of course. We know, and from few cases better than the Russians, that a Constitution may have little bearing upon events. Accordingly, our interest centers on the substance of democracy.

Whereas Americans define democracy in terms of political procedures and rights, Communists ordinarily define democracy in social and economic terms. They consider equality of social advancement and of economic opportunity the major elements of democracy. To the extent that they attach importance to the average person's exerting an influence over government officials, they emphasize that the influence shall be exerted in matters that concern the individual directly—as in matters affecting his living, rest, and his general working conditions. They belittle the value of obtaining the general electorate's views on more remote matters, such as foreign policy and basic economic philosophy.

As far as freedom of thought and expression is concerned, the Communists point proudly at their peculiar institution of "criticism and self-criticism." Soviet newspapers are literally full of complaints and critical comments written by leaders as well as ordinary citizens about all sorts of very concrete shortcomings, mistakes, and failures in Soviet daily life. Soviet Communists cherish this "freedom to complain if you are unhappy" as a vital and unique liberty in their kind of democracy. Under capitalism, they say, if your boss has fired you, you have no one to complain to, except God in Heaven; if the farmer's cow dies or if a housewife buys a dress that shrinks after the first washing, they have no one to blame but their "luck." In the Soviet Union, on the other hand, they have the right to actually blame people who were directly responsible for their misfortunes, and the law provides that the government agencies and newspapers receiving complaints from the public must investigate them, publish the facts, and thus criticize those responsible in public. Those criticized are then obliged to reform and perhaps apologize in public. Public criticism, however, must be accurate, concrete, and limited to specific facts. A Soviet citizen can complain, for example, that there are no shoes of his particular size in the neighborhood stores, and he can name the manager of that store as responsible for this; but he would be unwise to criticize the top leadership or the Communist party as a whole for not supplying enough shoes of all sizes all over the country. Such a letter to the newspaper will not be published, of course, while the writer will be investigated as disloyal.

It must be stressed that this Soviet institution of public criticism and self-criticism is sometimes misinterpreted in the West. The true significance of Soviet criticism of failures and shortcomings is sometimes exaggerated. For example, a worker might write a letter to his newspaper denouncing the fact that a few lathes in the backyard of his plant stand unused and even uncovered. He would probably write this because he knows that he would be praised by the party for having been vigilant and careful with "people's" property; he might even be promoted for this. On the other hand, it is obviously unlikely that an American worker would write anything of the sort or that a newspaper would publish it, even if some lathes did indeed rot in a backyard of some American plant. Thus, the Soviet worker's criticism does not necessarily mean that lathes are wasted more in the Soviet Union than they are in the United States. Similarly, when a high official denounces the fact that at some state farms in Kazakhstan thousands of sheep died during a severe winter, this does not *necessarily* mean that Soviet farming is inefficient or that meat and wool crisis is imminent in the USSR. If the President of the United States suddenly were to speak publicly about sheep dying on some rancher's farm in Texas, this would undoubtedly happen only in case of a major disaster, perhaps a plague endangering all sheep in the United States. Otherwise no President would consider it his business to criticize some rancher's ways of caring for his sheep. And neither would that rancher inform the President or the public of what is happening to his sheep; they are his private property. The USSR, however, is a *public* economy; ultimately, the top officialdom is responsible for those sheep and must speak up. The institution of "criticism and self-criticism" simply means that if the Soviet Union existed one thousand years, all this time Soviet newspapers and public meetings would inevitably be filled with criticism and complaints, for such is the compelling nature of the openness of the "people's" economy.

Attitudes and Personal Security under the Communists.   In our discussion of the noneconomic effects of capitalism, we noted primarily the creation of a materialistic outlook that contributes to personal unhappiness and feelings of personal insecurity. Does the Soviet economy directly or indirectly create similar conditions?

In the basic philosophical sense of the term, Communists accept the materialism espoused by Karl Marx. In the popular sense in which the term is used here, the Communists are opposed to materialism. Public statements by the Soviet leaders, teachings in the schools, literature, arts, and other public media try to influence individuals to serve the country and the general ideals of communism. They clearly try to minimize the importance of worldly possessions. Indeed, many speak of communism as a form of religion because, among other things, it calls for selfless devotion to a "cause." The Communists claim that Soviet citizens regard themselves as builders of a new and superior society. To the extent that this is true, and it is impossible to tell how true it is, communism would give a satisfying purpose to life.

Personal insecurity in the United States is fundamentally economic. The danger of losing one's job or one's accumulated wealth due to an adverse turn in general business conditions or to a single error of one's own is the major cause of a feeling of insecurity. In the Soviet Union, unemployment —that is, the inability to obtain a job—is absent. On the other hand, other types of insecurity have been created by the Communists (or have been carried over from the tsarist regime). It has been argued that no Soviet citizen feels politically secure because he would be ruthlessly deprived of his personal freedom if he were charged with opposition to the regime.

Soviet citizens who strongly oppose the existing system or the individuals in power doubtless feel very insecure. Perhaps all Russians who are prominently engaged in political activity recognize that they run a risk of pushing minority views too strongly and might come to be regarded as politically unreliable and receive harsh punishment as a result. There is no objective way of telling, however, whether an average Russian, who, according to many reports, is loyal and behaves much as the party's leaders would have him do, feels insecure. We simply do not know what percentage of Russians fear that they will be unjustly accused and punished.

One aspect deserves special mention in this connection. Much of political insecurity of Soviet citizens seems to stem from their dissatisfaction with the Communist party's interference with such nonpolitical aspects of their lives and views as, for example, their attitude towards abstract painting, or Western music, or the preservation of some old cultural customs, including religious beliefs. For some strange reason, the Communist party suspects that all attitudes that are not shared by it are necessarily a threat to its security and power. It is obvious, however, that not all Soviet citizens can or want to be convinced and active Communists; the whole population of the USSR cannot one day belong to the Communist party and espouse its principles and philosophy of life. Hence, for example, if the Communists stopped interfering with the beliefs, views, desires, and feelings of those people who are not *anti*-Communists or who do not want to be active politicians at all, and who, therefore, do not constitute any political threat to the regime and do not want to trespass the existing laws, a lot of unnecessary pressures could disappear in the Soviet society and more peace and tranquility could ensue.

Forced Labor in the Soviet Union.   One of the most criticized features of the Soviet Union was its use of forced labor. In Stalin's time, millions of prisoners were interned in forced labor camps. They worked in mines, as lumberjacks, and construction workers; they built many railroads, canals, and hydroelectric stations. They worked under extremely adverse conditions and many of them either died or became crippled for the rest of their lives. Some critics of the Soviet Union contended that as much as 9 percent of the Soviet GNP had been produced by forced labor before World War II.

Since 1954 most of the concentration camps have been closed, however.

Some of them still presumably exist, but not on any scale comparable to Stalin's time. Their economic contribution seems to be negligible today.

It has been charged that the Soviet Union must depend heavily on this source of manpower for its success. This charge will not bear close examination, however. One wonders why the Soviet Union would favor forced labor over free labor. Forced labor generally is inefficient and wasteful. That is, a given group of workers will ordinarily produce more if they are working freely in response to positive incentives that elicit their voluntary efforts than if they work under threats and coercion. Consequently, one would expect the use of forced labor to lower output rather than to increase it. Although it would be necessary to pay free labor more than forced labor to perform unpleasant tasks, that fact is surely no obstacle to the Soviet authorities. They do not hesitate to pay large wage differentials to those who do skilled work or who work in remote areas of the country. The use of free labor instead of forced labor to do unpleasant and dangerous jobs thus would both increase national output and redistribute it somewhat. The argument that the Soviet authorities prefer to use forced labor rather than free labor implies that they willingly forego increased output in order to save themselves the need of paying high wages to those who do dangerous and unpleasant work. This contention is not particularly persuasive.

CONCLUSIONS

Clearly the Soviet Union is unique and complex. It has undergone radical change under a Communist regime that has shown a readiness to experiment; it may still develop along unexpected lines.

The Soviet Union has demonstrated that a detailed planned economy can work under Communist leadership. Moreover, it was transformed from a state that had been a third-rate power into a great world power.

As yet, the achievements of the Soviet Union leave in much doubt the suitability of detailed planning in kind for nations that already have high living levels. Moreover, the issue of whether detailed economic planning requires dictatorship is at best unsettled.

Most striking about the Soviet Union is its detailed economic planning. It seems that the planners decide vital matters quite arbitrarily and accordingly are in danger of making important mistakes. However, the means for correcting errors also exist. While planning procedures have improved since the Communists took power, existing procedures seem to be still imperfect.

In the mid-sixties the Soviet political and economic systems are both in transition. Major political changes appear to be under way, and one can only guess how they will eventuate. As they have unfolded thus far, they appear to be in the direction of greater democracy and lessened brutality, lawlessness, and terror. Accompanying these developments has been an energetic bid for the support of uncommitted nations and for the support of "independent thinkers" in all countries. By a combination of offers of foreign aid to developing countries and "sweet-talk" the present Soviet leaders are helping to erase the forbidding countenance the USSR previously assumed toward the rest of the world. All present signs point to the fact that they have achieved a measure of success in these efforts.

One fatal flaw which afflicts all phases of the Soviet Union could undermine the Communist party in time. One cannot easily characterize it with a brief phrase, unfortunately; if one must be brief, he might call it self-righteous conceit and intolerance of heresy. Russian Communists combine conceit with the more self-destructive quality of self-righteousness. They are certain that they alone are correct on most matters and that they, almost alone, are moved by moral motives. In their view, those who disagree with them are vicious and evil persons seeking their own enrichment at the cost of untold misery for the masses. The orthodox Communist outlook has no place for men who are honestly led to some contrary conclusions and who are no less virtuous than they themselves. With this outlook, it is not surprising that Russian Communists do not shrink from cruel actions—and even justify them. This self-righteousness threatens Russian Communists themselves. In their self-righteousness, they have destroyed some of the finest minds and leaders in their midst and thereby lowered their chances for success.

Changes in the Soviet economic sphere are almost as significant as those in the political. Clearly, the Soviet economy has reached a new stage. It can now provide substantial improvements in consumer living levels even while concentrating primarily upon the output of producers goods. By virtue of its acquisition of the most modern weapons, it can place relatively smaller emphasis on national defense and thereby free resources for its many other pressing needs.

As its industrial base becomes broader and the national income increases to levels near those now attained by the United States, the Soviet Union's problems will change. Planning in kind will become far more complex while its procedures will have to be simplified as the needs to be served become more subtle and controversial. Also, as rates of improvement in output and productivity slow down, some of the enthusiasm for highly centralized planning is likely to wane. Perhaps in time, Russian leaders (and the populace, which may come to exert greater influence over the policies adopted) will be more ready to retreat from many of their present doctrinaire positions. In the long run, the Soviet Union can be expected to decentralize its planning and government to transfer more and more decision-making powers to the republics, economic councils, and individual enterprises, and to bring in a broader representation of various management, labor union, and consumers' interests on the planning councils, perhaps, much as it is done in France or Yugoslavia today.

It is always hazardous to speculate about the future, but the available evidence leads the authors to conclude that the expectations sometimes expressed in the West that the Soviet Union will one day return to capitalism or even adopt a system of "market socialism" are wrong. "Revisionism" in the Soviet Union is unlikely to develop any further than it has in Yugoslavia. In the economic sphere, output goals stated in kind are only likely to be further and further decentralized in details, rather than suddenly abolished. The people in power will undoubtedly prefer to determine the basic contours of the economy in accordance with their preferences, rather than leave it to "market forces."

Some expect that as the Soviet economy grows richer, Soviet people would become more "bourgeois" in their moral values and outlook, and that ultimately they will cease to be anticapitalist-minded, and the Communist Revolution will be over once and for all. Although this hypothesis is worth contemplating, one is not justified in considering it a certainty. The Soviet Union will almost certainly develop along unexpected lines. We must be prepared for many, some surprising, possibilities.

CHAPTER 4

THE FRENCH ECONOMY: THE NEWEST "MIDDLE WAY"

WHAT IS A MIDDLE-WAY ECONOMY?

In economic organization, most nations do not follow the example of either the United States or the Soviet Union. They believe that neither free enterprise nor the minute government control of individual enterprises offers the best solution for their economic problems. Between the U.S. and Soviet economies lies a wide gap which offers opportunities for other solutions to national economic problems. Most nations of the world operate within this gap and have developed economic institutions and policies to blend with their particular traditions and goals. One must not assume, however, that a compromise—something midway between two extremes—necessarily represents an improvement over either one of them.

As stated at various points, an economic system ordinarily can be understood only if viewed as a whole. Its parts must fit together much as do the components of any mechanism. Individual parts of different economies cannot be considered independent and interchangeable, for the history, traditions, values, levels of public understanding, technical skills, caliber of public service, all vary widely from country to country.

This chapter describes the French economy, a "middle-way" economy. France has undoubtedly gone farther today than any other middle-way capitalist economy toward developing novel arrangements and methods for the solution of basic economic problems.

The purpose of the following review should not be misunderstood. It is, above all, to stress *the possibility and the great value of economic inventions,* to illustrate the form they might take, and to provide specific examples. Certainly man can improve his economic and social environment as

167

much as he can alter his physical environment. He has devoted relatively little effort to economic invention; indeed, in some quarters attempts to develop new forms of social control are considered immoral per se. This view is rejected here. Even in the United States most businessmen accept the inevitability of a large number of government regulations of one form or another.

The general plan of this chapter differs slightly from the two that precede it. Since in this country the French economy is not widely understood, the chapter presents a broad description of the economic, political, historical, and cultural setting of modern France so that the reader may see the French economy as "one piece." These introductory sections provide a general background that should help to understand the French nation's approach to its economic problems. The section that follows will then discuss French economic planning in about the same way as the Soviet planning was discussed. The following section will summarize the answers to the same five questions about the French economy that were asked about the United States and the USSR: Who determines what shall be produced? How it shall be produced? In what occupations shall factors of production be employed? How is income distributed? How is technical progress achieved? The final section will discuss France's achievements under its economic system.

A broad comparison of the U.S., Soviet, and French economies will help the reader to fit together the individual parts of the French economy that are described in this chapter. On one hand, the U.S. economy is basically a price and profit system in which individuals (businessmen, laborers, investors, and consumers) are essentially free to use their funds, facilities, and skills as they wish. The U.S. economy is not simply based upon economic liberty; instead, it relies upon "natural" forces of competition; legislation enacted to increase economic efficiency; output that responds to and reflects customer desires; and income distribution strongly influenced by effort and initiative. The USSR, on the other hand, has a sort of "command economy" in which those located at and near the top of the power pyramid tell what each plant is to produce. The USSR does not rely upon market competition; it seeks to attain the same results by conscious decision, calculation, coordination, and direction.

No similar single principle can explain the French economy, however. (That is not to say that the foregoing principles underlying the U.S. and Soviet economies are sufficiently comprehensive.) The French economy represents a complex blend—some would call it a hodgepodge—of dissimilar, if not contradictory, arrangements and principles. This blend has not been consciously developed; rather, economic institutions, procedures, and practices have evolved in response to a host of political, social, economic, technical, cultural, and even military forces.

Four major elements compose the French economy. Each either represents a sector of the economy that is unique in some regard, or represents a control mechanism that touches all sectors of the economy. A separate examination of these elements should illuminate the nature of the French economy. They are,

1. The free enterprise sector, characterized by a blend of market competition and cooperation among rivals.
2. The state-owned sector, including wholly nationalized and partly owned firms.
3. Economic planning, which represents the most unusual feature of the French economy and which touches virtually every element of it, but which is yet distinctly different from what prevails in the USSR.
4. Government regulations, including here only those that vitally affect almost all firms.

Most of the following discussion is concerned with these elements. However, to understand how the French economy works and how it came to be what it is, it is necessary to understand the unique features of the French way of life. These will be sketched briefly to establish the essential fact that the French economy reflects a set of values, intellectual convictions, and prevailing institutions different from those of the United States, and the USSR. The effects of cultural tradition, social values, intellectual convictions, and established institutions demonstrate why no economic system can be fully explained or understood simply by describing "the letter of the law" or the broad economic principles comprising its "model."

THE FRENCH BACKGROUND

France is about as big as the northeastern quarter of the United States. Its population in 1964 was over 47 million. It has a fairly highly developed industry and agriculture, centered around well-balanced natural resources and numerous outlets for overland and overseas trade. Not so long ago France possessed the second largest empire in the world, and still today a large number of African states maintain close economic, military, and cultural relations with it.

In terms of the level of economic development, France stands more on par with the USSR than with the United States. The structure of the French GNP also displays a marked difference from that of the United States as Table 21 indicates:

Table 21.   Industrial Composition of French, U.S. and Soviet Economies, 1960

(percent of GNP)

	France	United States	USSR
Agriculture	10%	4%	30%
Mining, manufacturing and construction	54	39	43
Trade, transportation, and services	36	57	27

SOURCES: *Annuaire Statistique de la France 1962*, p. 435; *Statistical Abstract of the United States 1962*, p. 915.

Recent Influences

Although largely established through reforms introduced by Socialist administrations before and immediately after World War II, the present French economic system is mainly an outgrowth of economic conditions that existed long prior to World War II and of long-standing French traditions.

When the economic depression of 1929 hit the world, France with its self-sufficient agriculture, small-scale industries, and relatively small dependence on foreign trade proved able to withstand the shock better than most other nations. However, subsequent financial mismanagement, inflation, and massive strikes undermined the nation's stability at a time when other countries were recovering from the depression. The Popular Front government was voted into power in 1936, when the economic crisis became most acute. Premier Leon Blum's program included state control of the *Banque de France,* nationalization of armaments industries and railroads, as well as increased unemployment relief and a broad scheme of public works. Within two years, the government carried out its program, and none of its major reforms was subsequently undone. However, Blum's Socialist government lacked a clear and long-range economic program, and most of its policies were piece-meal. Inflation, foreign trade deficits, and a decline in industrial production brought about another financial crisis by 1938, and the Popular Front disintegrated.

German occupation and Allied bombardments in World War II devastated the French economy. At the time of the liberation in 1944, industrial production had fallen to 20 percent, and agricultural production to 70 percent, of the 1938 level.[1]

The Provisional Government of General De Gaulle, consisting of the Socialists, Communists, and Christian Democrats (Catholics), the three parties that had headed the anti-German resistance, emerged victorious in the elections of October 1945. It embarked on a new program of wide social

---

[1] Warren C. Baum, *The French Economy and the State* (Princeton: Princeton University Press, 1958), p. 17.

and economic reforms, which included extensive welfare and rehabilitation measures, and the nationalization of the coal industry, gas, electricity, and petroleum refining, the *Banque de France,* and four other major credit establishments, as well as most of the insurance business. These nationalizations were carried out in 1944-1946. Some industrial establishments owned by German collaborators, particularly the Renault automotive works, were also nationalized at this time. The promotion of industrial recovery was facilitated by a comprehensive national economic plan, the so-called Monnet Plan of 1946-1950.

De Gaulle resigned suddenly in 1946 and started a new nationalistic political movement. This action had no economic impact, however. The government continued to shift among the Socialists, radicals, and/or moderate Catholics, but no new major reforms were introduced. (The Communists were in the government from November 1945 until May 1947, when they were expelled largely for using their ministerial powers to staff the administration and the boards of the nationalized enterprises with their own men.) The left-of-the-center coalitions lasted until 1951. Since then the political pendulum in France has moved to the right of center.

France was in deep financial difficulties, mainly as a result of overexpansion and partly due to the cost of its colonial wars, when General De Gaulle was returned to power in 1958. He changed the constitution and the electoral law and made the French government system more stable, but tipped the balance of political power even more to the right. Today, political France is nationalistic and right-of-center, if old terms and designations still fit it.

Traditions and National Values

What is interesting and, for some observers, surprising, is the fact that modern French nationalism is evidently not oriented to the past and is conservative only with respect to French national values and interests. For one thing, De Gaulle's government has not only retained all past social and economic reforms, but has embraced them, it seems, earnestly; moreover, it has repeatedly urged its countrymen to continue experimenting with new reforms and institutions so as to give full play to French intellectual creativity and to develop elements of an indigenously French system and way of life.

To some Americans, French desire to retain and develop their own peculiar way of life and independent domestic and international policies may appear "reactionary";[2] but possibly this is because we, much like the French themselves, believe that our way of life and our economic and polit-

---

[2] For critical analysis of the French society, economy, and politics from the American point of view, see Edward M. Earle (ed.), *Modern France: Problems of the Third and Fourth Republics* (Princeton: Princeton University Press, 1951).

ical system are the "best" in the world. All nations differ in some of their subjective values. Modern French nationalism assuredly is not General De Gaulle's creation; the French would have pursued their own ways and their own interests under any government, even under the Communist.

Attitude toward Competition

The ideal of vigorous business competition, which we in the United States have inherited from late eighteenth-century England, has never been shared by France or most of Europe. Even the Common Market countries do not completely prohibit such monopolistic practices as cartels; the Treaty of Rome which established the European Common Market, too, permits "concerted practices or groups of practices among firms which contribute toward improving the production and distribution of goods or promoting technical or economic progress while reserving the users a fair share in the benefit." [3]

For many decades prior to World War II, French participation in international cartels has been a matter of public record. Also the existence of many effective price- and market-sharing agreements among members of a trade has been known to and accepted by the government authorities and the public alike.

One of the top French authorities on monopoly and competition made the following paradoxical observations:

> It has often been maintained [in France] that, prior to the last war, competition was more widespread in France than . . . in the United States. . . . Since 1945, public opinion has . . . lost interest in the issue of combination and monopoly. . . . All proposed measures concerning agreements (among the firms) have met with opposition from Trade Organizations, and indifference on the part of the public. . . . Hostility and indifference have been such that all proposals aiming to impose some measure of control over agreements have remained projects of legislation and have failed to come before Parliament for discussion.[4]

How does one explain this peculiar French belief that, despite trusts and cartels, their economy was more competitive than ours? And how can they be indifferent to monopolies and combinations? Yet, in terms of the French environment and traditions, these seeming inconsistencies do make sense. Like most other Europeans, including the Russian Communists,[5] the

---

[3] The quotation is from the Treaty's text and taken from PEP, "Cartel Policy and the Common Market," *Planning*, vol. XXVIII, no. 464, August 27, 1962, p. 281.

[4] Robert Goetz-Girey, "Monopoly and Competition in France," in E. H. Chamberlin (ed.), *Monopoly and Competition and Their Regulation* (London: The Macmillan Company, Ltd., 1954), pp. 21, 40-41.

[5] See, for example, a recent study of the French industrial combinations by A. Goncharov, "Growth of the Power of Monopolies in France," *Ekonomicheskaya Gazeta* (Moscow), no. 10, March 9, 1963, supplement, p. 10. Goncharov says ex-

French associate monopoly and competition mainly with the size of the firm. Accordingly, the colossal American corporations appear to them as monopolies because the small-scale firms allegedly cannot compete with them successfully. They regard the survival of their small-size enterprises as strong evidence of competition. The French have never experienced vigorous competition among their few big businesses. They have never seen advertising and sales-promotion battles like those among American corporate giants. French economic thought as well as legislation on problems of monopoly and competition "has always been dominated by the price concept" and the price concept alone.[6]

Due to the deep mistrust of big business by the French, one can understand the following appraisal by Professor Goetz-Girey:

> In France the solution of the problem of monopoly and monopolistic competition will manifest inself in a different form: a large section of public opinion remains convinced that only the development of medium-sized and small firms is compatible with French traditions and with the conditions of economic progress.[7]

Traditionally most firms in France have belonged to powerful industrial and trade associations, which are discussed below. The latter, among other functions, have had "a natural goal to defend their corporative interests, notably against the ruinous competition." [8] French firms form such associations precisely to minimize competition among themselves. (American trade associations are far less effective than these associations.) This attitude can hardly be understood without reference to the values of French businessmen, to their socioeconomic ethics, their goals in life and in business which can, perhaps, be summarized as follows: Every man is entitled to a place in society and no one has the moral right to push him out of it if he makes an honest effort to meet his responsibilities. This attitude is not merely one of "live and let live," nor entirely noncompetitive. Indeed, Frenchmen do encourage competition in certain forms; they are acknowledged to be enterprising and innovating, and take considerable pride in such qualities. Their actions are subject to one unwritten and tacit condition, namely in their competitiveness they must not *intentionally* upset the applecart of their neighbor.[9]

---

plicitly that because French industrial establishments are of comparatively small size, he believes that "in terms of the level of monopolization France continues to lag behind . . . the United States, Federal Republic of Germany, England, and—as some bourgeois economists believe—also of Italy."

[6] PEP, *Planning*, August 27, 1962, p. 221.

[7] Goetz-Girey, p. 42.

[8] André Bisson, *Institutions financières et économiques en France* (Paris, 1960), p. 119.

[9] See D. S. Landes, "French Business and the Businessmen: A Social and Cultural Analysis," in Earle, *Modern France*, p. 348ff. See also David Granick, *The European Executive* (New York: Doubleday & Co., 1962).

The attitudes of Frenchmen toward competition can be summarized best in a set of general propositions:

1. The French businessman's attitude toward competition is very different from what one finds in the United States. He and most of his countrymen do not regard it as socially beneficial; rather they consider it wasteful and destructive—and quite amoral.

2. The desire of French businessmen to gain ever-higher incomes or to have their enterprises grow is comparatively weak from the American viewpoint.

3. Frenchmen treat competitors as neighbors and friends rather than enemies. In part this feeling seems to come from a nationalistic feeling that Frenchmen should not injure other Frenchmen; it possibly results also from a Catholic view about the brotherhood of man—even in business matters.

4. Large French businesses apparently prefer to cooperate rather than to compete with their rivals. They go to considerable lengths to avoid direct market competition and to cooperate with other large firms in the same trade.

5. The behavior of French businessmen is strongly conditioned by the trade associations to which most of them belong. It is often in the decisions of these associations and their rules that competition expresses itself. In an important sense, competition works itself out in the conversations and bargaining inside the associations among their members rather than in the market place.

6. French businessmen cooperate freely with one another within their trade associations; however, they exercise great restraint in the use of their associations' power to abuse customers. Although they do not usually engage in vigorous price competition, they also refrain from charging what the market would bear. They seem to have some notion for "just price."

7. Rivalry among French enterprises ordinarily takes the form of trying to develop distinctive and superior product features and ingenious personal sales efforts; it usually does not consist of price competition or intensive sales promotion rivalry.

8. When one firm has substantially improved its offerings and is drawing many customers from a rival who is threatened with serious losses and even bankruptcy, it might offer to join forces with the injured firm or permit it to adopt the product improvement. It would rarely take, or even be permitted by the trade association to take action that would hasten the threatened firm's end.

9. Whenever the associations practice legal or concealed price agreements among their members, they usually fix the price slightly above the costs of the least efficient firms and thus permit them to survive, while the more efficient firms reap a higher rate of profit. Similar aims are pursued whenever they practice sharing of the market by sales quotas.

1**. Since the end of World War II, French businessmen have been very mindful of the nation's interest in developing export markets and in modernization, rationalization, and expansion. As a result of national interest in these goals, it appears that they temper their profit objectives on occasion to serve the nation's interests—possibly on the assumption that they will benefit in the long-run.[10]

Class Structure

French society has long been characterized by sharp class distinctions, inherited class ideologies, and traditions of both class solidarity and class struggle.[11] Yet, the class structure in France never, in modern times, became so concentrated and polarized that it produced a full-scale revolution. In 1964, the working class constituted about one third of French society; the peasants, some 25 percent, and the small and big bourgeoisie, about one eighth. The middle class, consisting of the richer part of peasantry, the relatively small-scale proprietors and petty bourgeoisie, has been almost predominant in France. Strangely, at least from the U.S. standpoint, this class apparently has *not* strived hard to get richer and richer, as it does, for example, in the United States. On the contrary, it has tended to be satisfied with its socioeconomic status. However, it has seldom been satisfied with its political status and with the political conditions *of the country in general*. Being very active in politics, the French middle class has created a great number of political parties and movements. Its vigorous activity has preserved a high degree of democracy in France, contrary to the situation in prewar Germany or Italy.

The continuous social and political strife which has characterized French democracy has given the nation an aspect of anarchy and caused it to be criticized by many foreigners. The latter have found it difficult to grasp the passionate devotion of the average Frenchman to political activism, freedom, and independence—at least most of the time. Yet it is from this perennial strife, on the one hand, and from the Frenchman's political self-consciousness, on the other, that a peculiar attitude toward the state has arisen in France. None of the existing parties and classes alone could dominate the nation, for they all have been minorities of roughly equal strength. Hence, the state has come to be seen as playing the role of an arbiter and a conciliator of opposing interests. This is not to say that the government in

---

[10] These statements no doubt apply much more accurately to certain trades than to others. Also, it should be recognized that it would be virtually impossible to establish such generalizations on a solid factual basis without extensive field research. They nevertheless summarize the essence of what the authors have learned from many original sources. These statements have been reviewed by a large number of persons who are very familiar with the French economy and most agree that they are essentially valid—though not for all French industries during the entire recent period.

[11] John E. Sawyer, "Strains in the Social Structure of Modern France," in Earle, *Modern France*, pp. 293-312.

France has often taken positions that are independent of voter sentiment. Any such tendency is continuously checked by the French political consciousness and activity. What has developed, however, is a special form of *social* democracy in the organization and manning of the organs of government. In France there are many national and local government advisory councils manned proportionally by appointed or elected representatives of different but specific social and professional groups and organizations. It has become an unwritten custom in France that whenever any government embarks on some major new social, economic, or cultural policy—be it old-age pensions, school construction, general economic planning, or even fire insurance—it first of all establishes, in one form or another, an appropriate specialized advisory council with at least the right to criticize the government policy and to air its views in public.

As a result, an average Frenchman views the state differently from an average American. The French are much less prejudiced than Americans against the government, they do not oppose government intervention in economic, social, or cultural life *a priori* or as a matter of principle, as most Americans do.

MAIN SECTORS OF THE FRENCH ECONOMY

As indicated earlier, the French economy is a unique blend of four dissimilar subeconomies and measures for economic direction and control. One of these subeconomies resembles free enterprise in the American style. The firms operating within this sector are essentially outside the direct influence of French planning. They are mainly "disciplined by the market"—that is, their operations are largely governed by the forces of competition. Even as in the United States, competition is far from pure and perfect in most industries. French industries governed by competition also depart very substantially from idealized descriptions of competitive arrangements. Moreover, French markets differ in many cases from those in the United States, and competition is dissimilar both in form and degree from what characterizes U.S. industry.

The Free Enterprise Sector: A Blend of Market Competition and Cooperation

No less than 85 percent of all output of French industries is presently produced by privately owned firms,[12] while commerce and agriculture are almost 100 percent privately owned. However, private banks transact less

---

[12] See Henry W. Ehrmann, *Organized Business in France* (Princeton: Princeton University Press, 1957), p. 346f.

than one half of all banking activities, and private transportation handles no more than one third of all freight shipments in France. These privately owned firms are partly governed by market competition, partly, too, their behavior reflects active cooperation among rivals and the influence of economic planning arrangements, and finally they are subject to many government regulations.

Big Business

French private enterprises are relatively small in size and are family-owned. Some large, impersonal, joint-stock companies and corporations do exist, notably in heavy industries and public utilities, but even in these industries the role of unincorporated family-controlled firms remains important. Thus, the largest steel company of all, Les Petit-Fils de François de Wendel; the big automobile maker, Peugeot; a leading specialist in metal alloys, Holtzer, are all closed family enterprises.[13]

Industrial concentration does exist in France although it is not as great as in most other industrialized countries. The fifty largest French industrial enterprises produced 16.3 percent of the gross national product of France in 1961, while 500 largest enterprises, including the preceding fifty, produced only 34 percent of GNP and employed but 15 percent of the labor force.[14] In the United States, on the other hand, the 500 largest industrial firms produced 41 percent of a far larger GNP in 1959.[15] A number of French industries have considerably more firms than have the same industries in the United States, even though their output is far smaller. For instance, their iron and steel industry has fifty-nine enterprises, of which twenty-one are large-scale; in the U.S. there are but sixteen big companies in this industry. Although there are not many big businesses in France that could compare in size to the American colossi, some French industries are almost completely dominated by a few large firms. Thus for example, Pechiney controls some 80 percent of capacity in the aluminum industry, while the Société d'Ugine accounts for the remainder. At the same time, these two companies hold stock in a number of the aluminum-consuming companies. The automobile industry is dominated by four companies: the government-owned Renault and the privately owned Simca, Citroen, and Peugeot.

An American student of the French automobile industry recently concluded that it was not less competitive than the automobile industry in the

---

[13] Landes, "French Business . . . ," p. 337.

[14] "Les 500 premières sociétés françaises," *Entreprise* (Paris), no. 367, September 22, 1962, pp. 37ff.

[15] *Statistical Abstract of the United States 1962,* pp. 312 and 489.

United States. The main promoter of competition happens to be the government-owned Renault, however.[16]

The electrical engineering industry is also largely under the control of four big businesses: Jeumont, Alsthom, Cie Electro-Mecanique, and Schneider-Westinghouse. The glass industry is dominated by two producers, St.-Gobain and Boussois; in addition, their policies are said to be closely coordinated, the first specializes in large and the second in small articles.[17]

One of the peculiarities of French big businesses is that a considerable portion of their stock is held, not by the investing public, but rather by other big companies. Thus, leading steel manufacturers own blocs of stocks in a number of iron ore mines, collieries, various consumers of their steel, as well as within the industry, that is, one steel company in another steel company. Such interlocking stock ownership is commonplace in many other industries and is not prohibited by French law. Interlocking directorates and other forms of management cooperation are commonplace phenomena among French big businesses, as in many other nations.[18]

Agreements are said to be common among ostensible competitors. Citing a number of official documents, Professor Goetz-Girey classifies the known agreements into four types: (1) General agreements with selling agencies. In this case producers do not enter into direct contact with customers, but establish a joint agency which allocates orders to member concerns and fixes supply prices to the public. Such arrangements are found in iron and steel industry, chemical and nonferrous metals industries, for example. (2) General agreements without selling agencies. In this case, members undertake not to sell below certain prices or to sell only at prices calculated on the basis of the agreed formulas. Each member is then assigned a quota of production generally computed as a percentage of the industry's total output. (3) Price rings. Their members agree to observe some minimum price but do not limit themselves in any other respect. (4) *Ad hoc* agreements for the purpose of bidding on government contracts, for example.[19]

Most of these monopolistic arrangements are officially permitted and even initiated by the government. In view of this fact, they must first of all be understood in terms of the peculiarities of the French economic system and traditions and only then judged according to other, including theoretical, standards. Let us, therefore, take a look first of all at the French anti-

---

[16] See John Sheahan, "Government Competition and the Performance of the French Automobile Industry," *The Journal of Industrial Economics* (Oxford), vol. VIII, no. 3, June 1960, pp. 197-215.

[17] Goetz-Girey, pp. 32-33.

[18] *Cf.* Goetz-Girey, p. 34.

[19] Similar practices have existed from time to time in various parts of the U.S. economy and some no doubt exist still. However, they are illegal and usually short-lived, though hardly to be ignored.

monopoly laws, for they embody the basic French attitudes in this respect.

The French *do* have antimonopoly legislation drafted as far back as 1810, but it is not as sweeping as ours. The French Penal Code prohibits all amalgamations and coalitions among the principal dealers in the product concerned, if their object is to raise or lower prices above or below the truly competitive level. Being of such broad definition and quite unspecific, these laws were difficult to apply in practice, albeit reference to them is known to have been made in some court verdicts as recently as 1950.[20]

More specific antimonopoly legislation was adopted after World War II. A 1945 ordinance forbade four specific monopolistic practices: (1) refusing to sell; (2) increasing prices without increases in cost; (3) making the sale conditional upon the purchase of other goods or of a stipulated quantity of the given good; and (4) fixing minimum prices.[21] This last point is even more sweeping than corresponding legislation in the United States. It applies not only to resale price maintenance, even for branded goods, but also to horizontal price maintenance of the sort usually enforced by cartels. Another ordinance enacted originally in 1945 prohibits

> every concerted action, convention, combine, express or implicit, or trade coalition in any form and upon any grants whatsoever, which has the object or may have the effect of interfering with full competition by hindering the reduction of the costs of production or of selling prices, or by encouraging the artificial increase of prices.[22]

Next, however, the decree makes two decisive exceptions from this prohibition, and they make all the difference. It states that the prohibition

> shall not apply to any concerted action, convention or combine: (1) arising out of the application of a legislative provision or regulation; (2) whose promoters are able to prove that its effect is to improve and extend the market for their product or to ensure further economic progress by means of rationalization and specialization.[23]

In other words, monopolistic agreements and cartels established or agreed upon by the government are legal in France, particularly because they are thought to be economically rational, progressive, and in the national interest.

According to a British study of French cartel practices based on the cases argued in courts, the French government's approach in each particular anti-

---

[20] Goetz-Girey, p. 38.

[21] "Ordonnance no. 45-1438 du 30 juin 1945 relative aux prix," *Journal Officiel de la République Française*, no. 160, July 8, 1945, p. 4153.

[22] "Decret no. 53-704 du 9 août 1953 relatif au maintien ou au rétablissement de la libre concurrence industrielle et commerciale," *Journal Officiel de la R.F.*, no. 187, August 10, 1953, p. 7046.

[23] Decret no. 53-704.

monopoly case "is economic rather than legal"; the government's prosecutors weigh each case in the light of its economic advantages or disadvantages and openly encourage reorganizations and mergers of firms that entered into illegal agreements, rather than disband and punish them. Such policies are deemed necessary because the government believes that French private enterprises are too small in size to be able to compete with foreign, particularly American and British big businesses.[24] The French business community shares this attitude wholeheartedly.[25]

The notion that cartels are progressive is also incorporated in the Treaty of Rome. Similar legally permitted cartel arrangements and other restrictive practices also exist in the other countries of the European Common Market.[26] There is also a considerable body of modern theoretical literature in Europe which defends and justifies such restrictions of competition on purely economic grounds, stressing the economies of scale in large enterprises, availability of capital for technological improvements in them, and so forth, and criticizing such wastes of competition as expenditures on advertising and so forth.[27]

Against this legislative background the actual French practices now become clearer. According to the government decree of July 4, 1947, for example, the joint selling agency of all the firms comprising the iron and steel industry, called the *Comptoir Français des Industries Sidérurgiques,* has the exclusive right to apportion the orders and sell the output of its members. This cartel, however, has not only been created by the government, but it is also partially controlled by the government. The prices of all steel products, in particular, are directly fixed by the government. The cartel is responsible before the *Chambre Syndicale de la Sidérurgie,* which is an industrial association. The *Sidérurgie* has its own board, where decisions on the allocation of orders and other matters are reached by a majority vote. However, its decisions become effective only on ratification by the Ministry of Economic Affairs.[28] Another well-known and government-sponsored cartel is the *Comptoir Français de l'Azote,* which markets about 65 percent of the total output of nitrogenous chemicals in France. Less directly controlled by the government are such private cartels as the *Comptoir des Glaces,* which unites the glass-making enterprises. *L'Éntente Éco-*

---

[24] See PEP, *Planning,* "Cartel Policy and the Common Market."

[25] See "La menace anglaise," *Entreprise* (Paris), no. 370, October 13, 1962, pp. 55ff.

[26] See PEP, *Planning.*

[27] See, for example, Edgar Salan, "Antitrust and Concentration," *The Journal of Economic Abstracts* (Cambridge, Mass.), vol. I, no. 3, July 1963, p. 326. The complete article is in German, in *Kyklos* (Basel), vol. XVI, no. 3, 1963. See also *Les cartels et les associations professionnelles de nos jours* (Rueschlikon: Fondation «Le Prêt Vert», 1956), vol. 2.

[28] This and the following information is borrowed from Goetz-Girey, pp. 31-32.

nomique du Cycle unites most bicycle manufacturers, component makers, and wholesalers and plans their purchases and sales according to an agreement. Some mergers, such as the *Union Sidérurgique Lorraine* (*Sidélor*), have taken place with the purpose of unifying the management of mines and steel mills on a regional basis. None of these nor many other cartels and mergers have ever been prosecuted by the government for any unfair practices, however.

From this we must conclude that the government is satisfied that these combinations do not harm the French economy and are, perhaps, advantageous to it. These arrangements cannot be evaluated from a simple theoretical point of view because in all of these cases it is the government rather than the cartels that fixes prices. In the French view, if these organizations are properly controlled, they serve a useful purpose. (On price practices in France see more below.) However, it is true that there is little, if any, competition among the firms belonging to cartels.

Small Business and Farming

To return to a description of the free enterprise sector of the economy, one must recognize that a large proportion of the French population consists of farmers and shopkeepers. French commercial establishments are especially characterized by small size. By far more than one half of all stores do not employ hired labor. Firms owning more than one store accounted for but 13 percent of total retail turnover in 1961; chain and department stores sold but 5.5 percent of all merchandise. Consumer cooperatives, with 3 million members, accounted for 7 percent of all sales of main foodstuffs, which also is not much.

As noted earlier, the overwhelming majority of French firms are relatively small, family-managed businesses. (This fact may result from the desire of French consumers for highly individualistic, custom-made, artisanlike products in contrast to mass-produced standardized goods.) One might suppose that competition would therefore be fierce—at least most English-speaking economic theorists might assume that to be the case. The facts seem to be very much to the contrary. Due to the individuality of their output, variations in quality, and emphasis on personal service, individual firms—especially those in the retail trades—serve a narrow circle of customers. Within these circles, price competition operates, but not fiercely. A survey among nonfood shopkeepers in France asked how they compete among themselves. All answered that they compete in quality; almost three quarters replied that they do not compete by means of advertising; about 40 percent replied that they do not compete in price.[29]

---

[29] J. Aubert-Krier, "Monopolistic and Imperfect Competition in Retail Trade," in Chamberlin, *Monopoly and Competition* . . . , p. 289.
The same study has also found that "the chain store—however paradoxical this may

Over 21 percent of the French population still makes its living from the land. Although larger than in some parts of Europe, French farms are quite small: 79 percent of its 2,100,000 commercial farms are under fifty acres; 56 percent are even less than twenty-five acres, compared to over 300 acres for the average farm in the United States.[30] Despite their small size, however, French farms are among the most productive in Europe. Of late, French agriculture seems to have produced a surplus of crops. Government farm policies in France have aimed at continuous expansion rather than contraction of agricultural output.

The small size of most French farms raises costs and reduces efficiency. Farms of such size are better suited to hand-and-horse tillage than to modern agricultural techniques. Since World War II, French farming sustained massive introduction of modern equipment, however. The number of tractors in use rose from 35,000 in 1938 to more than 800,000 in 1962. Fertilizer consumption trebled in the same period.[31] But farm machinery lies idle much of the time, and contributes to high costs. French farmers are also heavily in debt.

A solution of France's agricultural problems will require the formation of larger units of production and a reduction in farm acreage and population. But such a change is painful for farmers. In recent years, about 100,000 people have left the land for the cities every year, and the farm population has declined from 27 percent of the total in 1955 to 21 percent in 1963. This process probably would continue even if there were unemployment in the cities. With the strong demand for labor prevailing in recent years, the movement to the cities is large.

Thus, in certain ways French agriculture appears to face problems similar to those in the United States—and very different from those of the Soviet Union.

Industrial and Trade Associations (Syndicats)

Another essential feature of French private enterprise is the strong influence of industrial and trade associations similar to the *Chambre Syndicale de la Sidérurgie* mentioned above. These associations are not exactly comparable to those found in the United States. It is estimated that in commerce and industry combined there exist close to 5000 regional and more

---

appear—seems to have more of the competitive spirit than the small firm. . . . The results drawn from a study of the various sales conditions indicate that it is often the large-scale firm which, in commerce, has a competitive nature."—pp. 295-296. The fact that this finding appeared "paradoxical" to the researcher illustrates typical French presumptions.

[30] E. Higbee, "The French Paysan Is Angry," *The New York Times Magazine,* October 27, 1963, p. 20.

[31] *The Economist,* Sept. 1, 1962, p. 774.

than 800 national industrial and trade associations; in turn, these belong to over 200 national federations, confederations, and businessmen's unions. Membership in them is voluntary and not all small firms belong; but in terms of capital, almost 90 percent of French private enterprise is united in these associations.[32]

Before World War II, these associations developed as the businessmen's unions, employers' organizations counterbalancing labor unions and promoting their own members' interests economically and in politics. Full and direct participation of employers' and employees' organizations in politics, including lobbying, has always been legal in France.

Industrial and trade associations have long been an accepted part of the French economic system—even as are labor unions in most industrialized nations. These organizations openly hampered certain kinds of competition. Indeed it was because they did precisely this, among other reasons, that they have been thought to be necessary and justifiable. In current French thinking, these associations are still regarded by most people both as an instrument for the democratic self-government of private business firms and vehicles for the social and political representation of the business class interests, as well as purely economic institutions, fulfilling many organizational, distributive, and control functions thought to benefit the national economy as a whole. Some critical writers like Goetz-Girey, quoted above, express strong suspicions that the industrial and trade associations often act as unauthorized cartels. Some evidence brought up in courts has, indeed, implicated a number of *syndicats* in illegal price increases, for which they were punished. In principle, however, and as long as not proven guilty, of course, the industrial and trade associations are quite legal and respected French economic institutions.

The main purpose and function of the vertically arranged, specialized industrial associations are, at the present time, the collection and dissemination of all sorts of professional information, statistics, data on new markets, new technologies, government policies and legal decisions. Territorial suborgans of these associations represent local firms, on the other hand, in communal, national, and political life. Since a substantial part of collective bargaining with labor unions in France is territorial rather than national, local *syndicats* also take active part in representing their member firms in negotiating and signing contracts with the local unions.

Associations of the particular branches of business as well as the territorial associations form in their turn national associations of their kind, and these, in the last instance, form a single confederation of almost all employers' organizations in France, the *Conseil National du Patronat Français,* popularly known as the *Patronat.* The *Patronat* as an organization is similar

---

[32] Ehrmann, *Organized Business in France,* pp. 151-152.

to the National Association of Manufacturers in the United States; but actually it has a much broader representation than has the NAM. Even more important, it fulfills many economic functions, which the NAM is neither legally permitted nor willing to fulfill: it takes an active part in national economic planning, negotiates general agreements with the labor unions concerning some basic problems, such as social insurance, for example, takes active part in parliamentary politics, and so forth. The *Patronat* is officially recognized in France to be the "voice of business." When the government wants to call in someone to talk for business interests, it summons the representatives of the *Patronat,* for they claim they speak for 900,000 French companies. In fact, a *Patronat* decision on a question—such as the perils of too much competition from U. S. companies—becomes something akin to national policy.

The State-owned Sector

We have just reviewed that vast sector of the French economy that is privately owned and is, in most respects, a system of "free enterprise," even though it operates quite differently from the United States economy. At the opposite pole from the free-enterprise sector of the French economy is the state-owned sector—including those enterprises that are partly owned by the state.

The French government owns a large number of enterprises and banks as well as some entire industries. In fact, the state-owned sector of the French economy is larger than in any other capitalist country, with sole exception of Italy. The extent of the government's influence over the economy in France is vastly larger than its ownership of property, of course, but we shall first discuss state ownership per se.

Government-owned Industries and Transportation

Estimates of the size of France's nationalized sector vary considerably in accordance with the yardstick used. In 1959 the Economic Council stated officially that the available basic documents do not permit a precise calculation of the government-owned portfolios.[33] One rough estimate by the Ministry of Finance suggested that nationalized enterprises account for 20 percent of French industrial capacity, but what was included is unclear.[34] Another source has estimated that nationalized industries and mixed companies in which the state holds a majority share, account for 20 percent of the employed persons in the fields of industry and transportation combined.[35] As far as the industry alone is concerned, this share was once put only at 13 percent, though it is again not certain whether mixed companies were in-

---

[33] Bisson, *Institutions financières et économiques en France,* p. 63.
[34] Baum, *The French Economy* . . . , p. 170.
[35] Baum.

cluded.[36] Another authority has calculated that all public enterprises in France absorb about one fourth of all capital investments in the economy.[37] Whatever figure we accept, however, it is obvious that the state-owned sector of the French economy is substantial on all counts.

The totally or predominantly (more than 50 percent) government-owned industries in France include the following among others: (1) coal; (2) electricity; (3) gas; (4) petroleum; (5) nonferrous ores mining; (6) armaments and munitions; (7) aircraft production; (8) railroads; (9) canals; (10) ocean passenger shipping; (11) airlines; (12) telephone and telegraph; (13) radio and television; (14) motion picture production; (15) newspaper publishing.

State-owned enterprises can be classified into five groups: (1) establishments directly attached to the state budget and managed by a ministry; (2) quasi-independent enterprises of monopolistic nature; (3) independent public corporations that are exposed to competition; (4) mixed state-private enterprises; and (5) municipal enterprises.

The first and second groups are similar to nationalized enterprises in Soviet-type economies. In France there are few enterprises of the first class, but they do exist; among them are the postal, and telecommunication services, the munitions industry, and such establishments as the National Industrial Office of Nitrogen and the Potash Mines of Alsace. These enterprises have no business accounts of their own and pay no taxes; they are financed directly from the state treasury.

The second group of nationalized enterprises is much larger. To it belong such monopolistic "sociétés nationales" as *Électricité de France, Gaz de France,* and *Charbonnages de France,* which include all enterprises in the given industry and thus know no private domestic competitors. These enterprises are run as financially independent public corporations, in which all capital is owned by the state. Their boards of directors consist, in equal parts, of the appointees of the government, of the trade unions, and of consumers. Theoretically these boards possess considerable decision-making powers, including decisions on prices and wages, volume of production, and enterprise budget. In practice, however, most of these decisions are made and enforced by the ministry under whose authority the particular industry operates. Output planning, price fixing, and cost calculation in these enterprises is similar to what one finds in the Soviet Union,[38] as is explained below.

The third group of state-owned enterprises differs from the second only in minor detail, for its ownership and the organization of its management

---

[36] Ehrmann, *Organized Business in France,* p. 346.

[37] François Perroux, *L'Économie des jeunes nations,* Paris, 1962, p. 27.

[38] M. Maillet-Chassagne, *Influence de la nationalisation sur la gestion des entreprises publiques.* (Paris, 1956) pp. 203ff.

are more or less identical with the second group. This group includes such enterprises as the *Regie Nationale des Usines Renault, Regie Autonome des Pétroles, Société Nationale des Entreprises de Presse,* and many more. These are wholly state-owned enterprises amid a number of private firms in their respective industries. Sometimes they dominate the private firms in their industries by the volume of their sales, but this is not always the rule. Renault is the largest producer of cars in France, but its share in the total market is less than 40 percent. Enterprises in this group must compete with private firms, and therefore their costs, prices, and output are determined more by demand and current market conditions than occurs in the nationalized enterprises belonging to the first two groups. In most cases enterprises in this group belong together with private firms to their common industrial or trade associations. In the associations they share equally with private firms in the internal market regulations and policy agreements. This condition partly explains why the French left-wing maintains that French nationalized enterprises are under the control of private "monopolies" and in their business activities are hardly distinguishable from privately owned firms.

The enterprises of the fourth group are seminationalized: the state owns only a portion of their capital stock while the rest is owned by private investors.[39] Among them, for example, in railroads the government owns 51 percent of stock in the *Société Nationale des Chemins de Fer Français,* while 49 percent is owned by private concerns; ocean shipping and airlines (government's share in brackets): *Compagnie Générale Transatlantique* (66 percent), *Air France* (96 percent); oil companies: *Compagnie Française des Pétroles* (31 percent), *Société Française des Transports Pétrolièrs* (28 percent); aircraft manufacturing: *SNCAN* (95 percent), *SFENA* (80 percent); chemicals: *Compagnie Française des Matières Colorants* (10 percent); movie making: *Société Cinématographique Méditerranéene d'Exploitation* (60 percent); even investment in foreign securities: *Société Nationale d'Investissement* (0.005 percent); and many more.

The fifth group of public enterprises consists of city-owned transportation systems, water works, housing projects, and various utilities. Funeral establishments are also community-owned in France, though some private undertakers also exist. These public enterprises are traditional in France rather than recent developments.

Government-owned Banks and Financial Institutions

The French banking system in 1963 consisted of 349 banks. Of these, 344 are privately owned, but their combined capital accounted for only 35 percent of the total banking capital in the country. The rest, 65 percent,

---

[39] Bisson, *Institutions financières* . . . , pp. 240, 299-301. At least one of these, SFENA, was absorbed by a private group since this book was published.

belong to the state-owned *Banque de France,* which is France's central bank and four other big nationalized banks.[40] These banks though owned by the government are conducted very much like private concerns.

In addition to the usual banks, France has a considerable number of specialized credit-extending establishments, which are not called banks in France, but would be in the United States. They all are public institutions— most of them government-owned, while a few are cooperatives. In this group are such institutions as *Crédit National, Crédit Foncier, Caisses de Crédit Agricole, Caisses de Crédit Coopératif, and Crédit Muncipal de Paris.* In legal terms they are independent public corporations, but their operations are strictly controlled by the government, and a sizable portion —from 20 to 30 percent—of their reserve capital used for the expansion of credit is supplied every year from the state budget.[41]

Combined with the banks proper, the state-owned credit establishments increase even more the state-owned share in France's total banking capital. In fact the state's share is 76 percent, while private banking capital accounts for only 24 percent. *This furnishes the French government with a massive tool of financial control and influence over the whole national economy,* which is particularly important, as will be shown shortly, for France's national economic planning.

Life and property insurance business is also predominantly nationalized and municipalized in France. The proportion of total insurance activity of the thirty-four state-owned insurance companies has been variously estimated to account for from 50 to 62 percent of the total market.[42] However, since private insurance business is also considerable, the public insurance companies have to compete for their share.

The Planned Sector

In a very important sense, the total French economy is planned; every firm is therefore affected by the plan, although some enterprises and industries are far more directly affected than others. Most affected are capital goods production and virtually all phases of the construction industry. Firms producing consumers goods primarily for domestic consumption are practically unaffected by the plan. Even though affected—sometimes very directly and strongly—by planning arrangements, *the French economy is basically a market economy.*

It is perhaps misleading and even confusing to speak of a particular sector of the economy that is planned. Actually all sectors are at least indirectly affected by the plan and none are totally determined by the plan. If the reader would find it more congenial to do so, he might think of this

---

40 *Annuaire statistique de la France 1962,* pp. 418-419.
41 *Annuaire statistique.*
42 Baum, *The French Economy* . . . , p. 179.

section as explaining one set of powerful forces operating on the French economy—rather than a separate sector of the economy.

FRENCH PLANNING

To understand what is unique about the French economy, we must learn how French planning and French markets *actually work*. (Similarly, to understand the U.S. economy, we must truly understand the nature of market competition and how it operates.) That is not easy to do, however, for planning is complex in both structure and underlying concept. Moreover, the way that French planning actually operates is subtle and reflects many intangibles; it differs substantially from one sector of the economy to another. Certainly, it is not to be understood simply by learning the formal regulations and procedures that exist; it is necessary to know what actually happens, how often, under what circumstances, and why.

Before describing French planning in detail, it will be characterized in general terms. *French planning is totally different from planning in the Soviet Union.* First, it is essentially "indicative"—it indicates what would be desirable rather than dictates what should be done.[43] Second, French plans are not highly detailed; plans are drawn for between 100 and 150 specific industries out of the many tens of thousands that exist in France. Third, plans are drawn for four-year periods and only establish goals for the final fourth year of the period; they do *not* set down goals for intermediate years. Fourth, many persons who participate in planning are business owners and executives. With them, though in smaller number, are labor unionists and technicians. The number of full-time government planners is extremely small.[44] However, many regular civil servants from other branches of the government also participate, though not full-time.

The Goals of French Plans

The goals of French planning are political and social as well as economic. On one hand, the nation resorts to planning partly because it wishes to "be able to make France's presence felt and her voice heard whether on the European or the world scene." It seeks to "prevent the society of tomorrow—once expansion is achieved and self-sustained—from being

---

[43] Its present head prefers to call it active planning, for the planners do have and use some direct and indirect powers that permit them to affect the action of businessmen significantly.

[44] See Pierre Massé, "Why France Adopted National Planning After the War, and the Advantages She Sees in Retaining It," *French and Other National Economic Plans for Growth,* published by Committee for Economic Development, New York, June 1963, p. 7.

merely a consumer society or an unjust society." [45] The long-term objectives of French planning, "still small in terms of a single plan, may, in terms of a whole generation, transform living conditions. The problem thus emerging is none other than that of the basic orientation of a modern society." [46]

Economic expansion is clearly the primary aim of French planning. Another important goal, especially as French businessmen view it, is "rationalization" of industry. Although this goal is somewhat vague, it mainly expresses opposition to a waste of resources because of redundancy—excessive productive facilities. In the name of rationalization, industrial associations make organized efforts to scrap obsolete equipment, and the French antitrust laws are often set aside. The appeal of this goal and its link to planning goes far to explain business support for planning in France.

The French plan is far more than an economic plan. It deals directly with social and cultural matters as well as with economic issues. (At the beginning, however, the plan was almost entirely economic.) For example, the latest plan (the fourth) includes policies governing education, medical care, the absorption of Algerian refugees, university expansion, labor retraining, redistribution of income, urban renewal, and many other matters not strictly concerned with production.

The purely economic goals of the Fourth French Plan can be summed up as follows:

1. To expand total output as rapidly as possible.
2. To maintain full employment subject to the constraint of minimizing inflation, and increase France's opportunities to trade with other nations.
3. To reduce regional imbalances in the levels of economic development to the greatest possible extent and, in particular, minimize expansion of the Paris area. (The regional aspects of the plan received attention as an important problem starting about 1955.)

Genesis of French Planning

French planning arrangements developed out of the need to organize and expedite postwar reconstruction. This need was combined with a determination to modernize the economy and speed economic growth. These arrangements partly grew out of the controls used to regulate the French economy before the end of World War II and in the immediate postwar period. French planning is being revised constantly in important details; very likely it will develop currently unknown measures and will pursue more ambitious goals in the future. Judged by what they are now, the plan-

---

[45] From statements of the Premier and Finance Minister to the National Assembly, May 22 and 29, 1962.

[46] Massé, "French Economic Planning," p. 19.

ning arrangements in France are novel and impressive. They are, however, likely to puzzle those not familiar with the traditions, culture, and balance of political power in France.

The nature of economic arrangements in any nation necessarily reflects the nature and balance of political power and its history, traditions, and values. France's planning methods can only be understood against the background of military defeat and physical damage in World War II and the revival of French nationalism with the end of the war. France has since been swept by national determination to regain her position as a world power and to achieve a high level of economic prosperity.

> It may be said that the reconstruction period ended, in France, with the year 1949. At the moment, the facts of having explicitly fixed growth objectives and of having conceived the great basic programs, especially those of the nationalized industries, so as to make the basic programs compatible with the growth objectives, did indeed play a great part in the psychological reactions of an economy which . . . did not know before the war even what the idea of economic growth meant. But at that time the objectives of growth could be formulated very simply. The living standard of the French was still relatively low. Consumption and investment could still set their sights on objectives that, in detail, could rather easily be defined intuitively. Under these conditions, it was sufficient, as experience has shown, to formulate in a global way, a growth target, and to take a certain number of fundamental decisions leading towards that target, in order, without great difficulty, to set the whole mechanism going.[47]

France has had four national economic plans since the end of World War II and in 1965 the fifth was being prepared. At the time of liberation popular sentiment strongly favored government planning of the war-torn economy. While in North Africa and England, the National Resistance Council had worked out a state plan for the postwar "intensification of national production." The Ministry of National Economy began elaborating some piece-meal plans in 1944. The nationalizations of 1944-1946 were doubtless supported by some ministers out of a desire to establish a planned economy in France.[48] Also, the American Marshall Plan negotiations in 1947-1948 helped to encourage the French planning efforts that had already begun by "pressing the French representatives for a more systematic presentation of the economic objectives toward which the aid funds would be utilized." [49]

In January 1946 the General Commissariat of the Plan of Moderniza-

---

[47] Massé, p. 37.

[48] See, for example, the speech of André Philip, the Socialist minister of national economy and finance, in the parliament during the debate on one of the nationalization bills: *Journal Officiel de la République Française: Débats de l'Assemblée Nationale Constituante,* no. 54, April 24, 1946, p. 2144.

[49] Baum, *The French Economy* . . . , pp. 21-22.

tion (*Commissariat Général du Plan de Modernisation et d'Équipement*) was established and headed by Jean Monnet. It became an autonomous agency, first under the Premier, and then under the Ministry of Finance, but administratively independent of the Cabinet, so much so that Cabinet changes did not affect the planning agency's work. By the end of 1946 the new agency proposed and attained the Cabinet's approval of its first plan for the years 1947-1950, which in 1948 was extended to 1952 to make it fit with the Marshall Plan term. The first plan was known as the Monnet Plan or, officially, the Plan of Modernization and Equipment, 1947-1952. The work on a second plan began in 1952, but it was not ready for the Cabinet's approval until April 1954. In 1948 a law was passed requiring parliamentary approval of the plan; the second plan passed the parliament only in May 1955. The year 1953 was subsequently labeled the year of transition. State investments were approved in these years on an annual basis. The second plan was elaborated for the years 1954-1957 under the direction of Étienne Hirsch, who headed the General Commissariat of Plan after J. Monnet. The third plan ran from 1958 until 1961, but in 1959 it was substantially altered on account of the franc's devaluation, acute balance of payments deficits, and other troubles in the economy. An "interim plan" was prepared for an eighteen-month period in 1960 and 1961. Then the fourth plan, for the years 1962-1965, was elaborated under Pierre Massé, new head of the planning agency.

It must also be mentioned that in addition to the four-year plans, the French have recently prepared special plans of different duration, designed for specific industries and purposes. An example is the current five-year plan for the nationalized coal industry. The crisis in the coal industry in 1959-1960, that affected most European coal industries disrupted the coal industry's plan for 1958-1961, which was part of the third French economic plan. Consequently, the Ministry of Industry and the *Charbonnages de France* prepared a new five-year plan for 1961-1965, which reduced the previous coal output targets by almost 20 percent. This plan was immediately put into effect, even without waiting for the approval of the General Commissariat of the Plan and its incorporation into the fourth national plan then being prepared, because the crisis and the miners' plight were pressing.[50]

Planning Organs

Responsibility for the French plan's elaboration and for the supervision of its implementation is lodged in three domains:

1. Administrative authorities, consisting of the General Commissariat of the Plan, which works in close conjunction with the Ministry of

---

[50] *Journal Officiel: Débats Parlementaires, Sénat*, June 22, 1960, pp. 443-444.

Finance and Economic Affairs, under the supervision of an inter-ministerial committee.

2. Organs on which are represented the country's economic and social interest groups: the modernization committees and their working subcommittees, the Economic and Social Council, and several similar representative councils.

3. Political authorities, that is, the government and the parliament.

Placed under the authority of the Minister of Finance, the General Commissariat of the Plan is an administrative agency that possesses almost no power of its own, but enjoys a form of intellectual autonomy. It is responsible, under the Commissary-General, for preparing the plan, submitting it to the approval of the government authorities, then seeing to its implementation and assessing the results obtained. It assigns to various public and private research bodies a large part of the preliminary work aimed at clarifying the long-term perspective and at establishing the targets of each plan. Furthermore, it sketches the general framework for the detailed studies of the modernization committees' working groups, which represent the main socio-occupational interests, and then establishes a synthesis of their studies for each plan. Possessing an over-all view of the problems of national growth, the General Commissariat is the permanent adviser to the government in the area of economic policy.

Since its function is to work in cooperation with the various government bodies concerned, the General Commissariat's staff is quite small: it comprises about forty planning specialists and fifty executive personnel. The staff members come from highly varied fields, both administrative and technical, and are divided into general divisions—economic, financial, regional planning—and specialized sections—industry, agriculture, energy, transportation, education, urban development. The Commissary-General is responsible for his activities directly to the Premier. He works in direct liaison with the other ministers, particularly at the time of the drafting of the budget and the preparation of the plan, participates in or is represented on numerous interministerial committees and commissions; speaks before the parliamentary committees or even before the National Assembly and the Senate when the plan comes up for a vote; is a member of the directorate of the Economic and Social Development Fund (FDES).

The Ministry of Finance and Economic Affairs has a twofold role in the organization of the plan. It participates closely in the preparation of the plan through its statistical and research services: (a) the National Institute of Statistics and Economic Studies (INSEE) is responsible since 1962 for drafting medium and long-term forecasts, for preliminary sketches for the plan, and checking on the coherence of the studies of the modernization committees; and (b) the Economic and Financial Research Service

(SEEP) is responsible for short-term economic programs connected with drawing up the annual state budgets, as well as for reports on the nation's past, present, and proposed economic accounts. The latter are submitted to the National Commission for Economic Accounts and Budgets, which meets only once a year and is responsible for analyzing the disparities between short-term developments and long-term goals in order to propose corrective measures.

The modernization committees are each composed of thirty to fifty persons, who all provide their services without pay and are selected by the government on the proposal of the Commissary-General from three major groups: (a) heads of enterprises selected individually and leaders of industrial and trade associations; (b) workers represented by the major labor union confederations;[51] and (c) government officials and experts from the various Ministries concerned. The number of the modernization committees has been increasing: there were eight of them for the first plan, twelve for the second, nineteen for the third, and twenty-five for the fourth. Members of the modernization committee are appointed by the government on the basis of socio-occupational categories, and they not only act as representatives in the strict sense of the term, but also serve as expert advisers in the field of economic planning. On the basis of the preliminary sketches and in agreement with the government's directives, they study in detail the production possibilities and targets for their respective sectors.

Pierre Massé has stated several times that approximately 3500 persons are engaged in the work of the modernization committees and their work groups. De Clinchamps, a paper manufacturer and the president of the Modernization Committee on General Manufacturing Industries, states:

> For the manufacturing industries alone there have been 2,000 of us taking part, in a very cooperative manner—going to meetings, bringing in figures, criticizing others. We have sent to all heads of business concerns a relatively detailed questionnaire . . . Therefore, all the business managers have had the questionnaire in hand, have asked themselves questions, have

---

[51] It is important to keep in mind, however, that not all unions were equally represented on the planning committees for various reasons, some of which are not clear.

For example, the Communist-oriented CGT, numerically the largest, did not take part in the work on the second and third plans, presumably, for political reasons; it participated in the elaboration of the fourth. The Socialist-oriented CGT-FO is known to have been consistently enthusiastic about French planning, but it also complained that it was not always invited to sit on the planning committees. M. F. Légéndre of the Economic and Social Council has reported to the authors that one half of the unionists who actively participated in the drawing of the fourth plan were members of the Catholic unions. M. B. Cazes of the General Commissariat of Plan informed the authors in a private letter that there is a standing offer of more than one thousand seats on the planning committees open to the unionists, but their absenteeism is still very great.

answered us. We, in turn, have sent them the report, and they were able to form an idea of the growth estimates for our sector, what the importance of investment would be, and perhaps to derive from it the feeling that they would have to act with a certain care.[52]

An analysis has been published of the composition of 3137 persons who worked full or part-time on the fourth plan in 1962. The results are shown in Table 22.

Table 22.

Heads of enterprises	715	23%
Other businessmen	562	18
Farmers	107	3
Trade unionists	281	9
Government officials	781	25
Experts, professors, etc.	691	22

SOURCE: Pierre Bauchet, *La Planification française: Quinze ans d'expérience* (Paris, 1962), p. 48.

The Construction of a French Plan

As suggested before, French planning has changed substantially over the years and now is far more sophisticated than ever before. The French employ some advanced techniques that permit them to achieve—at least on paper—a "coherent plan." This means a plan that achieves crosswise and backward balances. But the French plan, like its structure, is characterized by a "lightness." It does not go into great detail; it rarely deals with individual firms. Specifically, it is oriented around product groups, rather than single products or industries. However, more and more the French are developing measures to ensure the cohesion and consistency of the individual subplans drawn up for industry groups and for particular geographic regions; for labor and some basic materials; for imports and exports; for money supply, and similar categories.

Nature of the French Plans

Physically, the French plan is a book about 500 pages long;[53] legally it is an annex to a law signed by the President and ministers and is designated as "a guide for the economy to follow and as a framework for all investment programs." It thus may be called a "document approbated by a law." [54]

---

[52] *French and Other National Economic Plans for Growth,* p. 62.

[53] See *Quatrième plan de développement économique et social (1962-1965), annexe à la Loi No. 62-900 du 4 août 1962 (Journal officiel* August 7, 1962), 493 + IV pages.

[54] This and the following description of the French plan is based upon a statement by Pierre Massé; see his, "The economic planning experience of France," *Looking Ahead* (New York) January 1963, pp. 1-2.

The contents of the document are divided into the following sections: A general assessment of the problems and potentialities of the French economy—past achievements, rate of growth of national output; level of employment in agriculture, industry, rate of capital formation, imports and exports, and the like. Then come statements of government policy intentions and objectives—amount of military expenditures, foreign aid, scientific research, allocation of remaining resources among private disposable income, nonwage benefits, public investment, fiscal provisions, incentives, and the means that the state will use to help the economy reach the goals set. Third, statement of the requirements to be met in order to achieve these national objectives—training and allocation of manpower, technological research, balance of foreign trade and payments, savings, tax structure, countercyclical provisions, and the like. Finally, and the largest part of the plan, discussions of individual sectors of the economy and of the economic and social activities of the government—the contemplated growth process for each sector.

Several characteristics of the French plan already were touched on briefly but warrant repetition, for they help to understand the procedure by which it is prepared. The French plan is made for a four-year period; it sets down output and growth targets for the final year of the planning period—and not for any of the intermediate years; it establishes targets for between 100 and 150 industry groupings rather than for each product and each firm; (there are a few exceptions to this statement for nationalized firms and cartels such as steel and electricity); almost all of its targets are in value terms, not in physical measures; and, finally, it deals with the regional implications of growth and investment.

Now that we know the nature of the final document that constitutes the French plan, we can describe the procedure employed in its preparation.

Planning Procedure

The French planning procedure is divided into the following stages:

1. Determination of alternative schemes of development, suggesting future possibilities of the economy and several possible courses to follow during the plan period.
2. The selection of a planning strategy by the Cabinet upon the recommendation of the General Commissioner Plan.
3. Preparation of preliminary targets for output, manpower, productivity, investment and foreign trade for individual sectors of the economy by modernization committees and their subcommittees.
4. Review of the detailed targets for individual sectors to insure consistency by committees with this function and the staff of the General Commissariat of Plan.

5. After revision of the targets, modernization committees draw up a set of recommendations as to how the plan might be carried out.
6. Submission of the plan to the government and parliament.
7. Revision of the plan after its adoption as conditions warrant.

Determination of Alternative Planning Strategies. This stage might also be described as establishing the framework of the plan. The preparation of a plan begins with the selection of an over-all rate of growth for the economy. Those engaged in this process describe it as examining reasonable possibilities and selecting the highest reasonable rate of growth. The selection is made only after consideration is given to the implications of the various rates of growth in some detail.

In preparing the fourth plan, for example, two basic steps were taken by the planners before the modernization committees were set to work. First, a long-range forecast was made for the years 1965 and 1975 to indicate probable changes resulting from technological advance, thus providing a framework for the current four-year plan. Three drafts were then prepared by specialists for the final year of the four-year plan, 1965, from basic statistics of the French national accounts—net national product and national income—subdivided into twenty-eight economic sectors according to origin of income. Each of the three drafts projected a model of final demand and supply structure in the economy for the year 1965, all in terms of constant prices, not in kind. Each one assumed a different rate of growth of the total production; 3 percent, 4.5 percent, and 6 percent per year. Each draft presented tables showing what the French economy could be like in 1965, if it developed according to the assumed rate, and at the same time preserved the following four basic balances: full employment, equality of saving and investments, balanced public finances, and balanced foreign payments.[55]

Starting with estimates of final demand in terms of assumed prices,[56] and assuming that demand must be equal to supply, French planners must determine what resources are required to produce that combination of goods and services. In effect, any output of finished products requires an output of raw materials components, power, transportation, labor, and investment funds to make its production possible. The planners must, accordingly, ascertain whether the economy is capable of turning out the output of specific product categories entailed in each "strategy." To do so, they use a powerful technique largely developed by Vassily Leontief of Harvard University,

---

[55] The conclusion was reached that the 6 per cent annual increase would probably lead to inflation.

[56] These are based upon market studies, plus estimates of the effects of changes in national income on purchases of major classes of product, including imports and exports and forecasts of government spending, as well as possible price changes.

which is known as input-output analysis. This tool organizes information about final output and the things necessary to produce it that proves out the crosswise and backward balances that must be maintained if planning is to be effective. (See Ch. 3 which discusses similar balances.) This tool is, fortunately, comparatively simple to use, involving only routine mathematical work once the information that it requires has been assembled. This point is important, for it explains that French planners can try out, on paper, a large number of different possibilities before settling on the one they consider best. Thus, they do a kind of laboratory experiment (called simulation) that should indicate what would happen in the real world without actually trying it.

Input-output analysis starts with information about the amounts of labor, raw materials, and capital required to produce a given bundle of items. For example, a thorough investigation of the facts might show that the coal industry uses 0.3 tons of steel, 0.003 man-years of labor, 0.02 tons of coal itself, and 74 ton-miles of transportation to produce a ton of coal. Such data are termed technical coefficients and are quite difficult to derive accurately; moreover, the coefficients change as methods of production are altered.

What is interesting, to remain with our example of coal, is that coal both uses other factors of production and itself represents a factor of production for other items. Even as the coal industry uses steel and transportation, the steel and transportation industries are major users of coal. Clearly, the interrelations between the output of individual products is highly intricate and calls for careful study to keep them properly sorted out. That is the function of the "input-output" table. A simple and hypothetical example is presented in Table 23.

The totals of the columns and rows in this table are of crucial importance; they represent the point at which one can determine whether "balance" has been achieved. One would want the amount of coal consumed (and steel and transportation) to be equal to the amount produced—no more and no less. That is, planners would want the output of any item to be equal to the demand for it (output should equal consumption, plus desired changes in inventory reserves). In our table we have selected figures that show such a balance.

Up to this point we have considered only a highly simplified hypothetical economy. The French economy includes literally millions of different commodities—if one defines them narrowly. Even if products are classified very broadly, their numbers are surely to be measured in the hundreds. To treat each and every end-product as a separate unit for purposes of input-output analysis would involve an incredible amount of information, expense, and time. The French planners have effected a compromise between precision and expense. They divide the French economy into only twenty-eight sec-

**Table 23.   Simulated Intersectoral Input-Output Matrix
Used in the Preparation of French
Economic Plans**

(hypothetical figures, billions of francs)

	Sector 1	Sector 2	Sector 3	Sector 4	Sector 5	etc. Sector 28	Total supply (output)
Sector 1	20	50	40	10	10	80	210
Sector 2	60	80	50	10	20	90	310
Sector 3	30	50	20	20	10	120	250
Sector 4	10	10	20	20	10	90	160
Sector 5	10	20	0	10	10	20	60
Sector 28	80	100	120	90	0	20	410
Total demand (input)	210	310	250	160	60	410	820

SOURCE: Adapted from Pierre Bauchet, *La Planification française: Quinze ans d'expérience* (Paris, Seuil, 1962), p. 151.

tors, meaning that they lump together some things that are quite dissimilar. Even though they are "adding peaches and pears," they can crudely determine the productive factors (technical coefficients) required to produce bundles of dissimilar products added together in terms of their assumed prices.

That is, the French planners start by computing technical coefficients for twenty-eight broad product groupings *in value terms.* They then set this information down in a table (better termed a *matrix*) similar to the simplified Table 23. From this table, they can determine what output is required from each of the major sectors of industry to accomplish different rates of growth for the entire economy. Interestingly, modest increases in total output for the entire economy might involve very large increases in the output of individual products. (It would be very simple if, say, a 6 percent increase in total output would require only a 6 percent increase in output of each product. The reader might ask himself why disproportionate increases in output of individual products are required.) Thus, by input-output analysis, the French planners can determine what output expansion is required in individual product sectors to accomplish different strategies of growth.

Their next problem is to pass on the feasibility and desirability of these rates of growth. For example, the input-output analysis might reveal that a 6 percent increase in GNP would require a 37 percent increase in the output of such chemicals as sulfur and potash. The planners would possess information (technical coefficients) that indicates the quantity of resources required to expand existing production facilities in order to increase the output of those items by different amounts. With this information before them, the planners are equipped to pass on the feasibility and desirability of different planning strategies. They know what output of the major product categories (the twenty-eight sectors) is needed; they know what those increases entail in supplies of components, raw materials, power, labor, and capital; and they know what resources would be required to expand productive facilities, where needed, to attain those levels of output. And, they know what must be done to achieve such production increases *in balance*.

Now they face the task of making decisions—selecting among alternative methods of expanding the economy. (There might well be dozens of reasonable ways of employing the nation's resources to attain any desired rate of growth.) At this point, their decisions are not mathematical but subjective evaluations of the costs and sacrifices involved in alternative planning strategies. The input-output tables simply permit them to understand what is entailed in different strategies and in different rates of growth.

The foregoing description of the use of input-output analysis has been somewhat long, but is nevertheless an oversimplification of the highly complex and painstaking efforts that the French planners make. Hopefully, it does explain, in principle, that such a balancing process—on paper—is altogether possible. And, it should therefore make clear that techniques of planning could permit gross errors to be detected *in advance* and make it possible to uncover in advance what must be done to make a plan succeed. We must therefore expect substantial progress in the development of techniques of planning with increased planning experience and the development of electronic devices for the collection, storage, and processing of information. In the near future, French planners expect to rely more and more on mathematical methods of planning (linear programming and the theory of games) and electronic computers.[57]

Apart from taking account of the interrelations among various industries to determine what rate of growth is needed and is possible (by means of input-output analysis), other interdependencies are examined by French planners in assessing alternative strategies and in deciding what they imply. These are mainly: (1) The interdependence of production and distribution

---

[57] Pierre Massé, "Une approche de l'idée de plan," *Encyclopédie française,* vol. IX (1960), p. 9.24-1.

of income; (personal income is derived primarily in the production process; changes in the amount of output and the mix of goods and services produced will alter personal income distribution and geographic patterns of income distribution). (2) Income distribution is then directly related to the level and composition of consumer demand; (what consumers buy depends largely on the size, distribution and geographic characteristics of income distribution). (3) Investment and potential rates of growth; (mainly expansions in output are related to increases in physical facilities and their technical efficiency).

The planners, working with broad relationships among these interdependent factors, can forecast consumer spending for various sectors of the economy, increases in productivity and output, and changes in the size and distribution of personal income. These forecasts enable them to develop a comprehensive picture of the economy under different planning strategies. (This picture is developed for the final year of the planning period only, though some committees "look at" intermediate years.) Thus, in selecting one of the alternative strategies considered, those responsible are given a fairly clear picture of what each one involves.

The planning activities described up to this point are essentially technical and involve the analysis and processing of broad statistical information. They do not involve the modernization committees; rather these activities provide a framework and background information upon which the modernization committees build.

It is obvious from the preceding discussion that the technique used by French planning in construction of their plans is entirely different from that used by the planners in the Soviet Union. In strict accordance with the nonobligatory nature of their planning, French planners rely heavily on estimates of probable demand and supply, which imply that all producers and consumers are free to spend their funds as they wish. They also use data mostly in value (money) terms, rather than in physical units. (In most cases they are compelled to use value data, for otherwise "peaches and pears" cannot be added together. The twenty-eight final product sectors used in the input-output calculations are themselves so broad that only a few of them—such as steel, electricity, and transporation—can use data in physical measures.) As a result of the use of data in value terms, the French are able to sum up and balance out their matrix tables not only by row (which also can be done in physical units), but also by column (which cannot be done in physical units because tons cannot be added to boxes or kilowatt-hours). Thus, they can arrive at an internally consistent, optimum structure of all inputs and outputs considered. However, all French calculations are vulnerable to sudden price changes, especially to inflation.

In practice, as mentioned above, French planners have not yet arrived at complete optimization of their twenty-eight-sector matrix because they still lack reliable statistics.[58] Besides, they also refuse to be dogmatic about the methods and techniques they use.

> We have been averse to any complete formalization of the models on which our plans are based . . . (because) in short, we have here to resolve a conflict between rationality and realism, to find what Ragnar Frisch has called "the art of making realistic models" . . . I myself think that it would be desirable, in practice, to substitute for the Leontief model a frame of thought that would take into account the multiplicity of techniques.[59]

Another essential difference between the French and the Soviet planning techniques consists in the fact that the French plan only twenty-eight broad sectors of their economy, rather than every commodity and every enterprise. On this account Pierre Massé made the following observations:

> We do not think that we would be making any real progress by increasing the number of sectors of activity for which targets would be defined.
>
> While the attainment of specific targets is indeed essential for the plan's success where the major basic investments like steel and electricity are concerned, it is different when we come to deal with the immense diversity of consumer goods. Although changes in cost prices and variations in consumers' tastes may cause more refrigerators to be bought and fewer washing machines, or more belts and fewer suspenders, it cannot be said that the success of the plan is impaired.
>
> Conversely, the more detailed a plan, the greater the danger of its being belied by circumstances. The planner's task would be complicated by the size of the initial program and by the frequency of revisions that would be necessary. He would need to have a much larger staff to achieve results that would be much more dubious.
>
> Lastly—and most important, perhaps, being the human aspect of the matter —the whole body of economic agents would be deprived of the powerful inducement provided by the decentralization of decisions.[60]

Selection of a Planning Strategy. When the planning technicians have worked out alternative growth strategies and their implications, these are

---

[58] P. Massé says: "We are already carrying out a preliminary global optimization, selecting the highest growth rate that seems reasonably compatible with the fundamental balances of the economy. *Some may wonder whether by doing this we have not achieved the essential, in other words, whether the full employment of the factors of production is not relatively far more important than their optimum employment. My own tendency would be to think that both are of great consequence,* and that is why I attach extreme importance to the research I have just mentioned." Pierre Massé, "French Economic Planning," pp. 17-18.

[59] Massé, pp. 16-17.

[60] Speech before the National Assembly, on May 29, 1962, *French Affairs* (New York) no. 139, June 1962, pp. 38-39.

submitted to the Cabinet by the General Commissioner of Plan together with his recommendations. The Cabinet selects the strategy to be implemented after a discussion of the matter in which the General Commissioner participates. Generally the rule of selection is that the best draft is the one that maximizes the rate of growth of the economy while preserving its fundamental balances.

Preparation of Targets for Individual Sectors of the Economy. Twenty-five modernization committees have the job of translating next the selected planning strategy into specific output, manpower, productivity and export targets for fairly narrow product groups. These include twenty-one "vertical" (industry) committees—one for steel, another for chemicals, a third for transportation, still another for agriculture and so on—plus one called a Committee on General Manufacturing Industries, which is divided into broad groups and subgroups. In addition, there are four "horizontal" committees which cut through the vertical committees; these are responsible for ensuring that fundamental balances are maintained: the Committees for Manpower, for Investment, on General Equilibrium, and for Regional Development. These try to ensure that investment does not exceed saving; that the total of exports plus consumption equals production plus imports—in total and by individual sectors of the economy.

As stated, most French planning revolves around economic sectors and product groups, and geographic regions rather than individual firms or single products. At prior stages in the planning process, the plan has only been concerned with twenty-eight broad industrial sectors. Many of these include dozens of major product groups. In this stage of plan preparation, planning becomes relatively specific and detailed.

The preparation of detailed targets for output, manpower, productivity, and exports is entrusted to modernization committees. (Their name suggests their emphasis.) These carry out their assignments through large numbers of working groups—subcommittees. One can understand this process best if he considers the work of a specific committee. The president of the Committee On General Manufacturing Industries, Felix de Clinchamps, describes its work thus:

> My Committee consists of about 60 members, of whom eight are trade unionists, some ten or twelve civil servants representing the pertinent departments of the Ministry of Industry and of Finance, with, possibly, representatives of the Ministry of Town-Planning, and of other interested Ministries; and some forty representatives from industry (delegates from organizations of industrial managers and heads of business concerns). . . . Clearly, this Committee of 40 [sic] members, however competent its members may be, cannot tackle all of the problems involved. It therefore delegates its powers to work groups which are formed at the request of the President and of the Committee members. In each work group are present

all members of the Committee concerned with the particular activity under discussion.

My Committee has 70 work groups which cover 240 basic industries. . . . We will, therefore, have to use the figures which have been given us by officials who have studied the problem, but who have studied it in broad outline. [He is referring here to the data assembled by the technicians and in the input-output tables.] Each of these work groups, then, takes up these general figures and tries to see how, basing its projection on these overall figures, it can establish, for its own sector, targets for production, manpower, productivity and foreign trade for the last year of the Plan, so that the figure of 5.5 per cent growth, the basic parameter for the four years, becomes for the general manufacturing industries, the figure of 7 per cent, and for each of our sectors, a figure that is extraordinarily different and where the accuracy of a moment ago disappears, diluted into a kind of estimate, to something vague, dim, but a dim image which has this characteristic: it is worked out and established by competent people who know their business.[61]

What might be added to this vivid description is the fact that the twenty-one vertical committees should arrive at a total for all of the individual sectors under their jurisdiction that gives the result set down in the original planning strategy. Although, as de Clinchamps observed, the individual sectors behave very differently, an effort is made to keep the total in line with the targets for the entire sector. Otherwise, the planning strategy must be revised, however slightly.

As indicated, French planning varies from industry to industry in its effects and its objectives. The methods employed by the planners and the amount of conflict engendered in pursuit of their objectives vary considerably. One reason for this situation is that French planning is highly eclectic; it provides opportunities for the planners, professionals, businessmen, and laborers who are engaged in the process to pursue almost any goal and to use a variety of means to attain it. Since little compulsion, if any, is used to achieve the plan's objectives, no one tries to limit the suggestions made by these participants in planning. Specifically, no restrictions are placed on the subjects that modernization committees can consider. Their meetings have been likened by one close student and writer about French planning (Hackett) to "brainstorming sessions." As a result, these committees come forward with many and diverse suggestions intended to strengthen French industries in competition with foreign sources, to lower costs, to widen distribution, to improve product quality, and the like.[62]

The following ends are pursued by planners and, to a large extent, businessmen also.

---

61 *French and Other National Economic Plans*, pp. 59-60.

62 Hackett, J. and A.-M., *Economic Planning in France* (London: Allen & Unwin, 1963).

1. Reduce costs of production:
    a. Concentration of output in fewer and larger plants.
    b. Increased scale of operations, even where some firms are very large, to achieve economies of operation.
2. Modernize production facilities:
    a. Encourage increased investment in modern plant and equipment.
    b. Expose nonmodern industries to foreign competition.
3. Increase research and development effort—to revitalize industries as well as to reduce payment abroad in the form of license fees.
4. Relocate industries—or direct new investment into selected areas.
5. Increase total output—by indicating expected levels of demand.
6. Prevent overinvestment—by providing realistic demand information and coordinating investment plans for entire industries.

Review of Detailed Targets to Ensure Consistency.   The first rough drafts of reports prepared by the modernization committees are sent to the horizontal committees. Perhaps the most important of these is the Committee on General Equilibrium. This committee may find, for example, that the sum of the individual industries output does not coincide with the estimates laid down in the input-output analysis. At that point, a process of adjustment starts between the vertical and horizontal committees.

It is not clear how far these horizontal committees go in reviewing the reports of the modernization committees. They could, and there is some evidence that they do, go beyond the mere totaling of the individual parts of the plan to ensure consistency. They occasionally make suggestions about content and lines of approach that help to improve the plans prepared by the modernization committees.

Preparation of Recommendations on Carrying Out the Plan.   When the revised and agreed-upon targets for individual sectors have been completed, the reports are returned to the modernization committees and to their work groups. Their next assignment is to draw up recommendations that will bring about the attainment of the plan. These recommendations can encompass almost anything. They vary from recommendations to governmental authorities regarding fiscal policy, labor regulation, the financing of investments by public or semipublic institutions to recommendations addressed to trade associations and organizations of wage earners—these may have to do with making available more accurate statistical information, training of personnel, or standardizing of product. Finally, they may make recommendations to individual firms dealing with such matters as research, mergers, specialization, and increases in productivity.

When these recommendations have been completed, they are collected by the general rapporteur who draws up a single report for the entire modernization committee. It is likely to be a booklet on the order of 150 or 200 pages.

Submission of the Plan to the Government and Parliament.   The individual targets and recommendations of the modernization committees are combined into a single document by the General Commissioner of Plan. This represents his recommended plan, which he submits to the Cabinet, the Economic and Social Council, and subsequently, on behalf of the government, to parliament for approval. When approved by parliament, it becomes what de Gaulle has called an "ardent obligation"—since no one is forced to follow the plan by law.

Revision of the Plan After Its Adoption.   The modernization committees meet periodically—in principle, every year, to determine whether the plan requires amendment. If the committees believe that amendment is required, they recommend one. In 1960, an *ad interim* plan representing a very substantial change was inserted to correct the original version of the third plan, for example.

The process of the formulation of a French plan is summarized for the reader's convenience in the diagram.

The Implementation of French Plans

The government by approving the plan assumes the moral, and therefore also political (in the face of the electorate) obligation of directing its economic policies accordingly. Its budgetary, fiscal, credit, price, and wage policies are expected to have as their chief goal the attainment of the economic development traced out by the plan.

Under the system of French planning, unlike the Soviet type, the powers of the state under the plan are *not* lodged directly with the planners. *French planners have no direct economic power whatsoever.* Generally, actions taken to further the fulfillment of the plans in France are by regular governmental ministries and agencies, though often on the advice and at the suggestion of the planners. Every plan specifies the proposed means of its fulfillment in addition to or from among those usually resorted to by the government in its everyday controls and regulation of the nation's economy; but these are only recommendations of the planners, not their commands.

The chief question that puzzles most persons who study French planning is, How can everyone be free to do as he likes under the plan and still have the plan mean anything? Or, without the power to direct the actions of businessmen or workers how can the planners bring about the attainment of their plans? Or, don't businessmen do under the plan what they would do anyhow? Or, what powers are possessed by the government or the planners whose use can bring about the attainment of the plan's goals?

A nation might employ several approaches that provide complete freedom to businessmen, consumers, and labor and yet alter their behavior to

FORMULATION OF THE FOURTH FRENCH PLAN

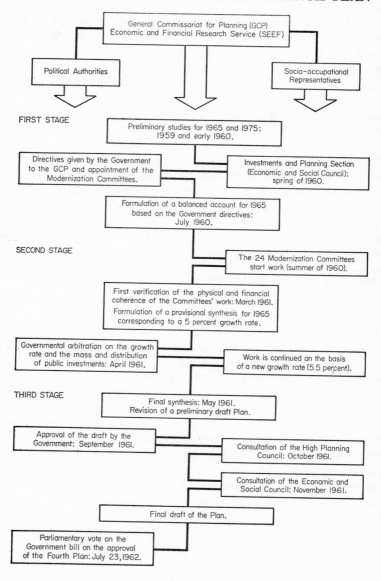

comply with a plan. The first, as already explained, is by making information available to them that causes them to alter their actions voluntarily; that is, they achieve a better understanding of what would serve their own interest when provided information about demand and supplies—and foreign competition—so that they do what need be done.

Second, persons may feel that they have a moral obligation to conform to the plan, where the penalties for so doing are not great. That is, the owner of a business may consider it his civic duty to take actions that foster achievement of the plan if he cannot see strong reasons for doing otherwise. On the other hand, one would not expect him to knowingly take a large loss or lose market position to comply with the plan on the basis of his patriotic duty.

Third, and most important, the planners could give individuals or businesses a sufficient financial inducement to persuade them to comply with the plan. They would not be coerced or required to do something but "enticed" to do so. More simply stated, they would be paid to do so.

Fourth, the government and planners could contribute to the attainment of the plan by their own decisions—in those spheres where the government is already engaged in economic activity. For example, the investments of nationalized enterprises could be adjusted to the needs of the plan; the prices that the government pays for its purchases for defense purposes—or for its nationalized industries—could also foster compliance with the plan. And, of course, the tax and monetary policies of the nation could be adjusted to the plan's requirements. In other words, in France—as in most modern industrial nations—the government is already and inescapably the largest single economic factor as a producer and as a purchaser. In its fulfillment of those roles, it can assist in the attainment of the plan.

Finally, and close to the borderline of interfering with personal freedom but still on the freedom side of that line, the government can require permission for certain actions by private business. The government does not, when it uses its power in this way, actually require businessmen to do what they do not want to do. It simply refuses them permission to do things they want to do in order to facilitate the execution of the plan.

There should be no doubt that the far-flung powers to control and regulate many aspects of the economic activity can be and are used by the French government to carry out the plans. We shall now see how some of these major means are put into practice.

Authoritarian Regulations

Let us first discuss the semicompulsory methods by which the French government assists the economy in the attainment of plans, while preserving individual freedoms for businessmen, labor, and consumers to do what they wish. These may be considered authoritarian controls arising from three main powers invoked by the French government at the present time: (1) requiring building and financing permits; (2) requiring permits to establish a business above a certain size in the Paris area; and (3) requiring permits to establish a refining and distillation plant in the petroleum and industrial alcohol industries.[63]

Almost all private and business construction in France must be authorized by the government. By regulating the number and type of permits granted, the government influences the volume of construction, the demand for investment capital by the building industry, and the demand for building materials and labor. Partly these regulations reflect urban planning and involve local authorities. Since construction is a major activity in France at present, these controls represent an important lever by which the government can help to fulfill the nation's economic plan. Moreover, many demands—as for machinery, furniture, home-furnishings and consumers durable goods—are largely derived from the level of construction.

Authoritarian controls also exist over bank borrowings and capital security issues.[64] The French government essentially controls borrowing by private business. By determining which firms can and cannot borrow from the banks and which may issue securities, the government exerts very great power over the level of private investment. Almost all bank credit facilities are nationalized or are under the centralized control of the *Banque de France* through the national Council of Credit. Access of private firms to credit is, therefore, basically controlled by the state. The *Credit National* is, in particular, the state-owned bank which grants more than 90 percent of all loans made to private firms for capital construction and equipment. This bank may not grant credit beyond a certain figure unless the borrower can prove that his use of the funds will conform with the national plan. All long-term credits in excess of $500,000 must be submitted to the Commissariat General du Plan for its written opinion. Middle-term loans in excess of $200,000 need not be submitted to the planning agency, but the borrower must convince the bank that his business is in line with the plan. Only short-term credit is unrestricted; however, since it is extended by the nationalized banks, its total amount and the areas where loans are made are under direct government control.

Private firms' stock and bond issues must be authorized by the Treasury. If the amount to be floated exceeds $200,000, the issuing firm is required to obtain approval from the Ministry of Finance. The Ministry will not authorize such security issues unless the firm can prove that its activities contribute to the achievement of the plan's objectives.

---

[63] *Cf.* Pierre Bauchet, *La Planification française: Quinze ans d'expérience.* p. 89.
[64] Bauchet, pp. 99-100.

Financial Incentives and Inducements

The line between authoritarian controls and inducements to take action is not always sharp and clear. When the government allows a business to borrow and urges the bank to make it a loan, is it exercising its authoritarian power by requiring permission to get a loan? Or, is it allowing a firm to borrow that might otherwise not have been able to persuade the bank to make a loan? It could be either.

It is generally agreed that the French government does more to implement its plans through financial incentives and inducements than by its authoritarian controls. Financial enticements that the government can offer take a variety of forms, but they can all be translated into a form of subsidy. That is, the government actually gives the firm something or exempts it from some obligation that is the equivalent.

For example, if the plan calls for certain industries to modernize their equipment, the government could provide for rapid amortization of the investment (to reduce the firm's tax obligations); or, it might actually exempt the firm from any of the many taxes a firm must pay; or it might underwrite part of the interest cost on its borrowings. If, to carry out the plan, the government wished to entice a firm to locate a plant in a particular area it might do any or all of the following: It could grant a financial subsidy—an outright gift. It could place orders in advance for the merchandise produced by that plant, if the government is a customer for the things it makes. It could offer a partial or total exemption from taxes levied by the national government.

For certain selected private borrowings in the capital market the state may undertake to guarantee the payment of interest (on bonds), or may grant a 50 percent tax exemption for dividends (in case of stocks), if the firm issues its securities for specific purpose mentioned in the plan as having top priority. The government purchasing agency, the *Caisse Nationale des Marchés de l'État,* may also be instructed to purchase a certain amount of newly issued stocks of a firm that is of particular interest to the plan.

Finally, the 1960-1961 intermediate plan suggested for the first time that the government experiment with the so-called quasi-contracts with the manufacturers of capital equipment. The *quasi-contracts* has been described as follows: "The firm undertakes, in exchange for certain financial support by a public authority, to carry out a program of investment, of research, or of production of specified goods, which is of particular interest to the national economy." [65] The current Fourth Plan recommends that the government should further this experiment,[66] but there are indications that it is not very successful.

---

[65] Bauchet, p. 99.
[66] *Quatrième Plan de développement économique et social,* pp. 37-38.

It has been said that "the control of prices also plays an important role" in the French government's steering of private enterprise towards national plan's targets.[67] The significance of price controls in French planning should not be exaggerated, however. The government has fixed high prices on a few final products in order to attract private investment in such industries by the prospects of above-average profit margins. However, not many products have been involved in such practices, and most of them were in the export industries only. Similarly, and for the same reasons, wage controls have not been widely used in France to help reach the goals established by the plan. Increased wage rates have been used to attract labor into certain underdeveloped regions in accordance with the plan, however. Attempts have been made at "income planning," consisting mainly of reducing income inequalities, but these have been frustrated in various ways.

To sum up what has been said about the extent and form of governmental intervention, a private businessman must come to a government agency to obtain permission or a license to do a number of things: to borrow, to build a plant; sometimes he must obtain approval of the price he wishes to set for his new product. To obtain what he wishes, he ordinarily will be required to submit evidence that his actions are consistent with the plan and will contribute to the realization of its goals. In this sense, the French government obviously possesses powerful means of influencing the activities of the private sector of the economy in the plan's direction.

However, the extent of state controls should also not be exaggerated. We must remember that the French plan is *not* drawn in such detail that the government could tell each firm what to produce, how much, or by what means and methods. Since there are no such details in the plan, it probably is not very difficult for a private firm to convince the government that its activity conforms to the plan in general.

French government officials explicitly declare that they neither favor nor believe in the use of compulsion to realize the plan. For instance, D'Estaing, Minister of Finance and Economic affairs, said:

> I readily pledge that all the resources of persuasion shall be exhausted before such a decision (to use government pressure) will be taken. . . . If recourse to public resources should prove necessary in exceptional circumstances, the State would withdraw its participation as soon as the desired end were reached, in order to put this enterprise back into the framework of the market economy.
>
> Imposing by their number and their variety, the means of intervention at the State's disposal will certainly be employed in an even more effective way for the realization of the Fourth Plan. But as *improved* as these means might be, when used by themselves they will continue to be inadequate to assure the correct execution of the Plan. We should not be surprised by this,

---

[67] Bauchet, p. 100.

nor should we deplore this. If this were otherwise, it would mean that all the freedom of action of economic agents and individuals would have disappeared. It is therefore necessary that, in the absence of constraint, the French people give their freely granted and freely considered support to the realization of the Plan.

The State should not expect the country's support, it should deserve it. If the Plan is drawn up well, if it is coherent, if the options have been reasonably and democratically decided upon, the State will more easily obtain the consent of all.[68]

The spirit in which French planners use their limited power of coercion and the behavior expected of them even by businessmen highly sympathetic to economic planning, is revealed strikingly in the following statement by Jean-Paul Delcourt. The president of the *Société Nationale des Pétroles d'Aquitaine,* a privately-owned oil company with some stock owned by the state, Delcourt is an outspoken supporter of French planning.

> I would draw attention to the spirit in which these powers should be used, because I believe—and I think the French Administration has always so understood it—the primary object of possessing them (powers to intervene in the investment programs and the development of business firms) to be that of permitting the State to engage the enterprise in discussion.
>
> It would be a disaster—I use the term advisedly—if the State wanted to use its power as an expression of bureaucratic authoritarianism, and did not take, in practice, the largest possible account of the cares, interest, ambitions and natural aspirations of the enterprise.
>
> In other words, the only justification for these controls is to engage business management, at the point where it is constrained to seek authorizations, in discussion with the Public Authorities. This discussion must not have as its primary aim the possibility of permitting a civil servant to force a decision upon management.—And it is quite possible that management, after a personal study of the market, might arrive at a solution different from one decided by the Committees of the Plan. It might be that it is the head of the company who is right, and it might become necessary to adjust the Plan accordingly. . . .
>
> But of course there may also be cases—and this whole system of regulation is based on this assumption—where the State can actually impose and enforce the solution or investment it prefers. At that moment, one can still expect that the discussion held between the government representative and the representative of the producer will make the company better understand the reasons for what the public powers want. It is only in extreme cases that this fulfillment can and must be forced by the State in a given industrial sector.
>
> In practice it rarely happens that discussions between the State and an industry do not lead to an agreement. . . . The very fact that these conflicts

---

[68] Speech in the National Assembly, May 29, 1962 in *French affairs* (New York), no. 139, June 1962, p. 17.

are limited is proof, in my opinion, of the ultimately satisfactory character of French planning, because the absence of conflict clearly means that the companies, precisely because they have taken part in the drawing up of the Plan and because they know the objectives of the Plan are reasonable, spontaneously modify their programs within the objectives of the Plan.

A review of the powers exercised by the French government to carry out its plan shows they are mainly carrots and to a small extent a stick. When one understands their nature, however, another big question arises about the nature of French planning. One wants to know whether government officials are not put in a very difficult position in dispensing favors or in exercising the so-called authoritarian controls. If someone in the planning authority can recommend that a firm be given a subsidy, a tax abatement, or a reduced interest cost, will not strong pressures be brought to bear to influence his decision? Is not such power exercised by government officials susceptible to corruption?

Frenchmen have little anxiety on this score, it seems. They have a high regard for members of the civil service, even though they do not pay them well. Many civil servants engaged in planning are young and will later move to private business, where they will be well paid. Moreover, civil servants and businessmen come from the same social classes; they attend the same schools and often meet socially, despite their income differences. Consequently, French businessmen do not regard government officials as personally hostile or unsympathetic or without understanding of their problems.

In addition, the actions taken by the government are matters of public record, and the government officials must feel that competitors are watching them carefully lest they give special favors to one firm. Moreover, it appears that the trade associations and other business groups really do screen applications for most favors and most awards of special benefits have been cleared by members of the trade.

General public interest in planning is still small, however. A public opinion poll on the question, "Have you heard of the Fourth Plan?" showed in April 1963 that 66 percent of those questioned still said that they had heard nothing of it whatsoever, though such answers were 11 percent less than the number of negative responses to this question a year before.[69] Even some relatively well-informed and highly educated Frenchmen only know that there is some form of planning, but know almost nothing about its nature.

General Observations about French Planning

We have just examined, in some detail, the rationale underlying French planning, the institutions involved in the process, and the procedures by which it is developed and carried out. Now that we have discussed what it does, let us consider what it does not do and examine the major prob-

---

[69] *Sondages* (Paris), vol. 25, no. 3, 1963, p. 80.

lems, criticisms, potential weaknesses and dangers that some observers have seen in it. As is usually the case, French planning is criticized by some for doing too much and by others for doing too little.[70] In the views of some, French planning up to the drafting of the fifth plan, really was concerned primarily with obvious problems. Almost all of the aims and techniques employed were quite apparent to any careful analyst of the economy. In particular, they maintain that there was virtually no connection between such concepts and findings derived from computations such as input-output analysis.

The French plans drawn to date have not incorporated any policy governing incomes. That is, no statements are made regarding legitimate levels of profits or permissible rates of wage increases, defensible increases in rents and the like. Only a pledge to minimize the threat of inflation is included in the plan, but not kept—though efforts surely are made to do so.

On the subject of inflation, the French planners meet their most serious opposition within the government. Almost everyone associated with French planning judges its success largely by the rate of growth achieved by the economy. Accordingly, they press for high rates of growth, which tends to intensify the drain on the nation's resources, with a consequent increase in inflationary pressure. Rapid growth is a threat to financial stability, however. As a consequence, the planners and the Ministry of Finance are at odds, the first favoring, if anything, overfull employment, the latter preferring for a modest amount of temporary unemployment to relieve the threat of inflation.

One possible error should be avoided. It has been suggested that French businessmen support French planning partly because of the absence of many labor representatives on the planning committees. This would not seem to be the case. It appears to the authors that a large increase in labor representation on the planning bodies would not affect the attitudes of businessmen toward planning—if it continued to employ its present procedures. French businessmen associated with planning believe that labor representatives might only alter the result by providing some information and constructive suggestions that might possibly improve planning—and make it even more acceptable to them. (It should not be forgotten that virtually nothing about French planning is settled by a vote.) The chief fear expressed by businessmen is that the sphere of French planning will be expanded from essentially economic areas to social issues. They approve of measures that quicken growth, strengthen France against foreign competition, modernize production methods, lower costs, and the like; but they do not want the planners to alter the French social structure.

French industries differ not only on the objectives sought by the planners,

[70] This discussion of reactions to French planning is based upon conversations held by the senior author in September 1964 with approximately ten persons directly associated with French planning or who had studied it in some depth.

but also in their responsiveness to and cooperativeness with planners. One finds virtually all gradations of attitude toward existing planning arrangements among French industrialists. At one extreme, some owners of large French enterprises object strongly to planning, both in principle and to specific things that planners are trying to achieve in their industry. These men essentially ignore planning and the planners; some do not participate at all in discussions, will not provide data requested, and often take special efforts to oppose the programs undertaken by those engaged in planning. This is a tiny group, according to all reports. At the opposite extreme is another small group of young and progressive French business owners and executives who are highly sympathetic to the French style of planning. They identify themselves with it; they know personally and well many of the planners and consider them personal friends; many are actively engaged in the planning activities and may hold some position of responsibility—if not authority—in planning committees. These men consider French planning arrangements quite helpful to French economic growth and to French revival as an economic and political power, as well as helpful to their own industry and firms.

One point often overlooked in assessing French planning is that it has *not* been accompanied by a substantial growth in the rate of investment. As of 1965, the planners have not forced French consumers to give up current purchase of goods in order to increase greatly the number of new plants and the output of equipment for farm and factory. That is what makes France's substantial achievements all the more remarkable. Let us now turn to a review of what was achieved under the four plans in effect between 1946 and 1965.

Performance under the Four Plans

The goals of the first plan (1946-1952/1953) were to set France's productive machinery in motion again, to fill the technological gaps caused by four years of occupation and to reduce the economy from possible post-war depression or stagnation. The individual basic goals of this plan were achieved by just over or under 100 percent. France's industrial production increased 71 percent in this period, agricultural production, 21 percent, and the level of living, 30 percent. The keynote of the second plan (1954-1957) was no longer merely to produce more; it was also to produce better, to meet severe international competition. On the whole, the targets of the second plan were exceeded. In 1957 the national production index reached 130 (target 125) and the industrial production index, excluding construction, rose to 146 (target 130). Electricity production and the automobile and chemical industries made unexpectedly large strides forward.

The third plan (1958-1961) sought, under conditions of monetary stability and balanced international payments, to increase national output by 20

Table 24.   Objectives and Realization of the Three French Plans

Production	Actual output 1952	First plan goal 1952	Percent realization of the first plan 1952	Actual output 1957	Second plan goal 1957	Percent realization of the second plan 1957	Actual output 1961	Third plan goal 1961	Interim plan goal 1961	Percent realization of the interim plan 1961
Coal, mill. t.	57	60	96	59	61	97	56	62	56	100
Electric power, bill. kilowatt	41	43	95	57	55	105	76	76	76	100
Steel, mill. t.	11	12	87	14	14	100	18	17	17	103
Aluminum, 1000 t.	—	—	—	—	—	—	280	230	260	108
Cement, mill. t.	9	8	105	12	—	—	15	15	15	99
Grain, mill. quintals	84	95	88	110	95	116	96	110	—	88
Meat, 1000 t.	2065	2200	94	2500	2500	100	3000	3100	—	97
Sugar, 1000 t.	900	1300	70	1350	1500	90	1810	1550	—	118
Housing, 1000 dwelling units	75	—	—	270	240	111	320	300	—	106

NOTE:—indicates that the target was not planned.
SOURCE: Pierre Bauchet, *La Planification française*, pp. 192-193.

percent in four years. However, the disruptions and economic drains caused by the war in Algeria among other things, made it impossible to fulfill this plan. National production increased by only 2.5 percent in both 1958 and 1959. The original plan was modified, and in 1960 a new interim plan for the years 1960 and 1961 was worked out. It provided for an 11 percent increase in national production, and this target was reached on time. Some details on the fulfillment of the three plans in Table 24 indicate a *mixed* performance. The agricultural sectors of the French economy have departed most from the planned targets. The French economy clearly increased rapidly. The average rate of growth of France's national output was almost 1½ times higher than that of the United States (though it was lower than in West Germany, which used no planning). The informed French public seems to be almost unanimous in its opinion that the French planning is a success.[71]

Returns of the fourth plan (1962-1965) were not complete at the time of this writing, but they probably will be similar to those of the past. The fifth plan (1966-1970) came under public discussion at the end of 1964. It calls for an increase of 27 percent in over-all production, 24 percent in private consumption, and 39 percent in public consumption during the period. The draft plan acknowledges that this means "a slight sacrifice" on the part of private consumers in favor of over-all social needs. Public consumption foresees increases of 34 percent in expenditures on government-subsidized housing, 54 percent for schools, hospitals, roads, and tele-communications, and 34 percent for military equipment (atomic and hydrogen weapons). Against the opposition of Socialists and Communists, the draft plan was adopted by the Parliament with more than a two-thirds majority.[72]

GENERAL GOVERNMENT REGULATION OF BUSINESS

The foregoing pages described the chief regulations and controls whereby the French government seeks to carry out its economic plans. These regulations, however important, represent only a part of the regulations that affect French business. Like all other governments, the French

---

[71] Even French Communists recently started to admit that the planning in France makes sense and works, despite France being not a Socialist country. On the other hand, they complain, of course, that planning is conducted in the interest of monopolies. *Cf.* A. Plassèqués, "A propos de la planification capitaliste," *Économie et politique* (Paris), nos. 118-119, May–June 1964, pp. 25ff. The Russians, however, are not yet reconciled to the idea that economic planning can also work under capitalism; they sharply criticize French planning and insist that it is not planning at all. *Cf.* A. Vernovskiy, *Ch'i eto 'plany'?* (Moscow: Znanie, 1964). In private conversations with these authors, however, some Russian planners and economists have expressed admiration for the decentralized and democratic nature of French planning processes.

[72] *The New York Times,* November 25, 27, and 28, 1964.

has enacted many regulations to improve specific business situations and to correct particular abuses. Such regulations probably are numbered in the thousands and concern such things as sanitation in barber shops and bakeries, hours of operation of retail shops, and the procedures to be followed by undertakers. We shall not consider such detailed regulations but will concentrate on two central regulations that are conducted differently in France than in most nations of the world. These two are price and wage controls.

Price Controls

The French government has traditionally dominated and controlled industrial and farm prices. Although it does not possess *absolute* power over prices, except in the nationalized sector, it possesses—and occasionally uses—its great power over prices *especially to combat inflationary and deflationary pressures*. It has rarely used these powers to influence the allocation of resources, to redistribute or to help carry out its economic plans.

Industrial Price Regulation

The actual application of price controls in France since the thirties has alternated between vigorous supervision of prices in most industries and almost complete freedom for private sellers and producers. Rigid wartime price controls were largely abolished in the summer of 1949, but no free price mechanism took their place. In effect, the government passed over part of its price-fixing authority to industrial and trade associations and official cartels. By 1952, under the impact of the wars in Korea and Indo-China, rigid government control of prices was restored in the form of price "freezes." (That is, businessmen were compelled to maintain then existing prices, though they could lower them.) Following the franc devaluation and subsequent financial reforms, price controls began to be gradually withdrawn starting in 1958. In the face of strong inflationary pressures in the fall of 1963, the General Directorate of Prices established ceilings for most food prices, while prices of meat were ordered to be reduced.[73]

The French government has legal stand-by powers to establish ceiling prices, price formulas, or to directly fix prices for the products of any industry or individual firm.[74] These stand-by powers were initially granted to the Ministry of Economic Affairs by the government ordinance of June 30, 1945, which granted the ministry's central committee for prices power "to proceed with fixing prices on all products and services." [75] This law is still in effect today. *Although the Ministry of Economic Affairs has the right to*

---

[73] See *Le Monde*, October 9, 1963.

[74] See John Sheahan, "Problems and Possibilities of Industrial Price Control: Post War French Experience," *The American Economic Review*, vol. LI, no. 3, June 1961, p. 346. See also Bisson, *Institutions financières*, pp. 110ff.

[75] "Ordonnance No. 45-1483 du 30 juin 1945 relative aux prix," *Journal Officiel de la R.F.*, no. 160, July 8, 1945, p. 4150.

fix all prices, it rarely has exercised this right. In practice, a complex but flexible system of price setting allows most industries and firms a high degree of freedom most of the time. Nevertheless, the principle of state sovereignty over prices prevails in France and is embodied in law.

The system of government price controls in France is administered by a special agency, which was established within the Ministry of Economic Affairs in 1945, and exists today under the name of the National Committee on Prices; it is attached to the Ministry of Finance. It is a twenty-seven-man advisory board, which includes representatives of business, labor, agricultural, and consumers' organizations as well as of governmental economic agencies. Similar price committees exist also on the regional level. They have the power to investigate and debate any price issue. However, the actual price control powers are vested in the General Directorate of Prices, an executive agency within the Ministry of Finance. This directorate has its own staff of price inspectors, attached to the organs of the Ministry of Finance in the local governments. Price inspectors continuously check on all prices in their localities, in accordance with current government regulations.

Government price regulations divide all French industries into three main groups: (1) those subject to direct price fixing by the government, (2) those exercising the so-called controlled liberty in price fixing, and (3) those allowed complete freedom.[76] Since the end of World War II, the French government has fixed prices directly for steel, aluminum, sulfuric acid, fertilizers, coal, wood pulp, newsprint and a number of products in the machine-building industries. Industries subject to "controlled liberty" have included agricultural equipment, combustion motors, tires and other rubber products, oils and paints, most pharmaceuticals, and electrical household appliances. Prices have been "free" for automobiles, cement, textiles, porcelain, watches, toys, and most foods. *No explicit and rigorous economic doctrine underlies this system.* Administrative convenience, concern with inflation due to price changes that would become widely diffused, and the relative weight of particular products in the major official price indices seem to determine the classification of products among these three price groups. The government has the stand-by authority to alter the classification of any industry by decree. All such decrees and all current price regulations are published in the *Bulletin Officiel des Prix,* while major decisions involving parliamentary and Cabinet action are published in the *Journal Officiel.*

Of particular interest is the controlled liberty class of commodities, which is only second in scope to the free class. Firms in this class are obliged to submit to the General Directorate of Prices both (1) explanations of any intended price increases and (2) complete formulas by which prices are computed. They must then delay application of the new prices for

---

76 Sheahan, p. 346.

a fifteen-day examination period, during which the government can reject or order a change in the proposals, or do nothing and thus allow them to go into effect at the end of the waiting period. The General Directorate of Prices can carry out a thorough study of costs in the given firm or industry, if it is dissatisfied with the submitted explanations. It may also compel the firm to accept its own formula or instructions as to how to calculate the price.[77]

Most French prices are now officially "free," but by American standards they can hardly be called such. Actually, they are free only in the sense that the government passed its authority to control them to the Patronat and its affiliated industrial and trade *syndicats*. The latter are obliged, however, to report to the government any changes in their prices. Many French and American students of French prices agree with the conclusion that "whenever prices were 'freed,' the trade associations were unhampered in their own price-fixing and attempted to enforce the prices stipulated in cartel and similar agreements." [78] The members of the associations usually agree among themselves to charge such prices which would "correspond to the average necessary for all enterprises to live." [79] This means that the prices are fixed at the level of the highest-cost and least efficient enterprises. As a result, the best-equipped firms enjoy high profit margins, while the marginal firms merely survive.

The rationale underlying French prices is most unclear. A high government official once stated quite explicitly that the price of a commodity in France "has nothing to do any more with economic laws. It can be justified only by a monographic study which would take into account not only the technical structure of the given industry but also the number of producers, their political influence, their sociological solidarity." [80] Different kinds and degrees of price controls, on the one hand, and naturally different increments in productivity and innovations in different industries, on the other, produce changes in the relative structure of French prices in uncontrolled directions. In the long run, agricultural prices increased on the average

---

[77] For example, while officially permitting the manufacturers of rubber-and-cotton transmission belts belonging to the *Union Professionnelle du Caoutchouc* to form a cartel "in order to put an end to competition which led the producers to sell below costs," the State Secretary for Economic Affairs ordered, however, that the cartel should report to the government, at the beginning of every year, all costs and prices of its member firms, in accordance with a particular questionnaire.

The official also requested that prices charged of state-owned enterprises, which consume the belts, be listed separately, implying, perhaps, in this way that these prices must be more favorable. *Cf.* "Rapport de la Commission Technique des Ententes," *Journal Officiel (Documents Administratifs),* no. 12, June 15, 1961, p. 314.

[78] Ehrmann, *Organized Business in France,* p. 302; *cf.* also John Sheahan, *The American Economic Review,* June 1961, and the French authors he quotes on pp. 352ff.

[79] Ehrmann, p. 303.

[80] Quoted by Ehrmann, p. 301.

much less than industrial prices, and the prices of non-durable consumer goods increased less than those of durable goods.[81] Many prices have been subsidized by the government so as to keep them low. Subsidies have been used in agriculture, foreign trade, numerous raw materials industries, particularly coal, as well as in transportation and construction. In 1959 alone the government "price subsidies" were estimated to be 463 billion francs.[82] This is equivalent to almost $1 billion.

The extent of irrationality of French prices should not be exaggerated, however. The most rigid price regulations in France apply to noncompetitive and highly concentrated industries. At least one researcher has concluded that French government controls "may well have held prices and wages in a pattern more nearly consistent with efficient resource allocation than would have resulted in the absence of controls," for where an economy is split into competitive and noncompetitive sectors, both prices and wages in the latter move usually much too high relative to their levels in the competitive sectors.[83] This same researcher made an interesting comparative study of changes in wholesale prices in some selected French and American industries; he concludes that the resulting French patterns "might well be judged to have come closer to a competitive structure than in the United States." [84]

Farm Price Regulation

The French government establishes "guaranteed" wholesale prices for farm products that are designed to furnish farmers with a fair return from their sales and which distributors of farm produce are obliged to pay. Under the existing arrangements,[85] the guaranteed price does not necessarily apply to the entire output of a given commodity; its application may be restricted to a certain volume, called the quantum. Beyond the quantum, farmers

---

[81] See Bisson, *Institutions financières,* pp. 136-137; also Alfred Marc, *L'Evolution des prix depuis cent ans* (Paris), 1958.

[82] Bisson, p. 54.

[83] Sheahan, p. 356.

[84] Sheahan, p. 358. Sheahan's findings for the period 1952-1957 were these:

| | Percent change in price index | |
Industries	United States	France
Primary metals	+30	+9
Electrical machinery	+19	−6
Motor vehicles	+13	+3
All manufacturing	+9	+0.4
Chemicals	+5	−8
Leather products	+4	+7
Textiles	−7	−3

At the same time hourly wages in French manufacturing rose 36 percent as against 24 percent in the United States.

[85] See "France's Farming Explosion," *The Economist* (London), September 1, 1962, p. 774.

must accept the prevailing (lower) market price. Quantum regulations have been introduced only recently and the quantities of farm products sold below the guaranteed price supports have rarely exceeded 10 percent of total expected output. Thus, support prices are used to stimulate larger production.

In addition to guaranteed prices, the government also pursues policies aimed at securing domestic and expanding export markets for France's agriculture. Imports of meats, poultry, fruits, and vegetables are restricted to leave the domestic markets for French producers (though whenever prices soar too high, import quotas are temporarily lifted). Subsidies are paid on certain farm exports, including wine.

Although most of these policies penalize consumers, and are beginning to yield unsalable surpluses, the French can do little to change them. Farmers play an important role in French politics as voters, and cities are filled with people whose roots are still in the countryside. Hence, "in France, most people are in sympathy with the farmer anyway." [86] Although surplus production is certainly the outgrowth of the high guaranteed prices, the government is reluctant to lower prices, for such a move would destroy a large number of small and inefficient farmers and would arouse sharp reaction on the part of the electorate. To most Frenchmen, the chief villains are the food distributors who control the pipelines from the country to the urban centers and who benefit from the existence of surpluses on the farms. The surpluses enable them to buy cheaply, but their resale prices do not go down. As a result, though the average city wage in France is less than half that in the United States, retail food prices are about on the same level as in the United States.

Wage Controls

To understand the nature of the French government's involvement in wage determination, we will briefly review the history of the French labor movement, its collective bargaining arrangements, the chief legislation affecting minimum wage rates, and the actions of the regulatory agencies.

French Labor Unions

About 50 percent of French labor force—workers and employees in industry, agriculture, trade, transportation, and government—belong to the labor unions. This percentage is more than twice as high as in the United States, where no more than 25 percent of the comparable workers belong to unions.

Most of the French unions are relatively small, closely specialized organizations that should properly be called craft unions. They are united in a number of industrial and territorial federations, and these, in turn, in one of

---

[86] Higbee, "The French Paysan Is Angry," p. 20.

the three major national confederations, distinguished mostly by political affiliation. The largest of these confederations is the General Confederation of Labor (CGT), with a membership of more than 2 million workers. Next in size is the French Confederation of the Christian Workers (CFTC), with about 600,000 members. The third is the General Confederation of Labor–Workers' Force (CGT-FO), which split from the CGT in 1948 and has a membership of about 500,000. There is also a fourth large national federation, but it is clearly specialized; it is the General Confederation of Agriculture, the chief national peasant organization. Of interest is also the fact that France's professional men, such as graduate engineers, scientists, laboratory technicians, medical workers, and teachers, also have unions of their own that are affiliated to either one of the three labor union confederations or to their own national confederation known as the *Confédération Générale des Cadres* (CGC).

The French labor union movement is sharply divided along political and ideological lines. For several decades the CGT was a more or less united organization. The Socialists finally split from it, forming their own confederation, the CGT-FO. Although the CGT denies its affiliation with the French Communist party, its top officials are for the most part Communists and in politics it usually follows the Communist line. It has consistently opposed most actions taken by the French government and has made little positive contribution to the construction and development of the postwar French economic and social system, save in the first two years after the war, when the Communist party participated in the French government. To be sure, the CGT has always been in the forefront of labor demands for higher wages and other benefits; its demands have often been the most radical and far-reaching, and a good many of them have been realized. In this respect, the CGT has undoubtedly contributed to the well-being of French workers. However, in many other respects it has frequently put itself into isolation. For example, it refused to participate in the work of the planning committees for the second and third national economic plans, considering them to be instruments of the "monopolists." It returned, however, to participate in the elaboration of the fourth plan.

The CGT-FO though on friendly terms with the Socialist party, has nevertheless pledged itself, and has kept the pledge, never to give its official support to any government whatever. It participates actively, though critically, in various socioeconomic arrangements and institutions, including some planning committees, seeking to promote various reforms and improvements.

It may be illuminating to compare the demands contained in the resolutions of the recent congresses of the CGT and the CGT-FO.[87] In addition to

---

[87] See *International Labour Review* (Geneva), vol. LXXXV, no. 3, March 1962, pp. 306-311.

a number of the purely political Communist slogans of the day, such as "ban atomic tests" or "liberation of the union leaders jailed in Greece," the CGT resolutions demand only (1) all-round increases in wages and pensions; (2) shorter hours of work; (3) four-week paid holiday; (5) retirement for men at the age of sixty and for women at fifty-five; and (6) equal pay for men and women for equal work. On the other hand, demands of the CGT-FO include (1) through (6), though stated in less aggressive terms, and in addition the following: (7) setting up of a unified state investment fund for the economy, financed by a tax on capital and with union participation in management; (8) democratization of the planning machinery, more equitable union representation in the planning committees; (9) reform of the administration of the nationalized enterprises aimed at return to the tripartite system of representation on the boards of directors (unions, government, and consumers); and (10) making state-subsidized housing a national social service.

The Catholic Workers' Confederation, the CFTC, has been more pro-government in recent times than any other major labor organization. It has been more active than any other labor group in the work of the national planning agencies, although like all other unions it has been dissatisfied with the small number of votes allocated to labor in these agencies. In its economic demands, the CFTC has especially concentrated on various social welfare pensions, family allowances, and the like, proposing and pushing through a number of particular schemes.

Collective Bargaining

Despite existing legislation, collective bargaining in postwar France was in complete disuse because wages were under strict government control. Only since the decree of April 2, 1955, which permitted greater regional differentiation of the minimum guaranteed wage (wage regulations are discussed below), did collective bargaining start to gain momentum.

The French collective bargaining system has a number of peculiarities.[88] First of all, the law places it strictly under government auspices and control. Collective agreements are concluded between the labor unions and employers' *syndicats* but the initiative for their conclusion may come from the Minister of Labor. He has the right to convene a joint labor-management committee for the purpose of concluding a *national* collective agreement to regulate the relations between employers and employees in a given industry. Supplementary agreements then may be concluded for each of the principal occupations and/or regional locations of that industry, based on the national agreement. Since 1955 about forty national collective agreements

---

[88] See "Act No. 50-205, of February 11, 1950, respecting collective agreements and proceedings for the settlement of collective labour disputes," International Labour Office, *Legislative Series*, July–August 1951 (Code: 1950-France-6A).

have come into existence in such industries as chemicals, textiles, printing, glass-blowing, wood-working, and merchant marine.[89] When an employer becomes a party to a collective agreement, all of his employees, even if they are not trade union members, are governed by its provisions.

The law also provides that at the request of one of the parties to the national agreement or on the labor minister's own initiative, the national collective agreements may be extended by force both to continue beyond their date of expiration and to apply to every employer and employee within the territorial or occupational scope of the agreement, whether or not he is a party to the agreement. In case of such a compulsory extension, the minister is only obliged to publish his reasons for the decision. In practice, this great power has not been used frequently, but among the national collective agreements now in operation in France several have been extended under this power. Decisions to extend them were made after prolonged strikes and disturbances. Obviously, the unions dislike national agreements under such circumstances.

The fulfillment of collective agreements is supervised by a staff of labor inspectors, employed by the Ministry of Labor and its agencies in the local governments. Infringement is punished by the courts. On major collective bargaining policies, the Minister of Labor is advised by the Superior Collective Agreements Board, which consists of fifteen representatives each of the workers and the employers and is chaired by the minister himself. Among other functions, this board is charged also with the task of studying the cost of living which is the basis for determining the guaranteed national minimum wage. The latter is then recommended to the Council of Ministers and after some bargaining among the ministries is published as an official decree and sets a floor under wages.

---

[89] According to the law, every national collective agreement must contain at least the following provisions: (1) guarantee of freedom of association for the employees; (2) elements of the wage agreement, based on the pertinent national minimum wage, the scale of its differentials that applies for the given locality, additional pay provisions for dangerous work, etc.; (3) conditions of hiring and dismissal of employees; (4) the terms of notice; (5) holidays with pay; (6) representation of employees on the works committees; (7) procedure for the revision and termination of collective agreements; (8) procedure for conciliation of disputes; (9) organization of apprenticeship; and (10) special provisions on working conditions for women and young persons. In addition, national agreements may likewise contain provisions concerning (11) overtime and night work; (12) conditions for remuneration by piecework; (13) payment of bonuses; (14) repayment of expenses arising from work and from traveling to work; (15) provisions for the reduction of the working hours; (16) agreement on the arbitration procedure; (17) supplementary superannuation pensions, and so forth.

Arbitration and Settlement of Disputes

According to the law of February 11, 1950, cited above, every collective labor dispute must be immediately submitted to conciliation. Conciliation proceedings can be instituted either by one of the parties involved or by the Minister of Labor or the local governments.

The National Conciliation Board, headed by the Minister of Labor, meets at the ministry. It is competent to hear disputes that affect the entire national territory or several regions.[90] If the conciliators fail to reconcile the parties involved in the dispute, the law says that the parties are then "entitled" to submit their case to arbitration. The arbitrator is either chosen by the parties together (some collective agreements provide for such a procedure), or is appointed by the government. The arbitrator submits his findings and recommendations to both the government and the parties concerned. His ruling can be appealed by any one of the parties, but only on the ground that the ruling is contrary to the existing laws. The Superior Court of Arbitration is established to hear such appeals. Otherwise, the ruling of the arbitrator is binding on both parties. His findings and proposals are immediately published in the official gazette.

To sum up, French labor legislation is obviously much more restrictive of the unions than similar legislation in the United States; conciliation and arbitration are clearly compulsory, the government wields considerable power over collective bargaining. Such legislation is both the cause and result of the sharpened class struggle of the postwar period.

On the other hand, the significance of the French labor-management antagonisms should also not be exaggerated. Much of the noise surrounding them at times is merely due to traditional politics that always permeates all issues, and also, in part, to the French temperament.

Wage and Labor Market Regulations

Wages have been much less effectively controlled than prices in France. Until 1950 all basic wage rates were fixed directly by the government, so that only supplementary premiums and fringe benefits were subject to local collective bargaining. Since then, however, the Ministry of Labor has been regulating wages mainly by means of periodic changes of the minimum wage, leaving above-minimum wages to national and local collective bargaining. Inasmuch as the Minister of Labor also possesses the right to prolong collective agreements by decree, he presumably can also impose a ceiling on wages at the rates specified in existing collective agreements. Actually, however, the government does not dare to use these particular powers. Any enforcement of wage ceilings obviously would be unpopular with the

---

[90] See *Journal Officiel*, no. 51, February 27-28, 1950, p. 2337.

voters. What the government resorts to instead is its indirect financial power over private enterprises: by withholding bank credits and permits for stock issue, for example, it produces pressure on the businessmen to refrain from wage increases.[91]

In this connection it is necessary to know that because of *extreme shortage of labor in the postwar period,* French businessmen have not only been more than usually willing to grant the unions' wage demands, but also quite frequently used various means of raising wages themselves so as to attract workers from their competitors. This is why the government's attempts to hold wages in line have for the most part been unsuccessful. In 1961 alone, for example, despite the Premier's repeated demands that wages not be increased more than 4 percent, they nevertheless went up 8 percent!

In France time wages are still the rule and piecework wages are the exception. Therefore, to develop the necessary incentives for the increases in productivity, French businessmen use all sorts of bonus systems and arrangements. Currently, combined bonuses calculated against various productivity indices supplement basic time wages by an average of 20 to 30 percent.[92] It is these bonuses as well as various fringe benefits that businessmen use to attract better and more labor. The labor unions only negotiate a wage rate that represents a minimum rate below which labor will not work. This rate cannot, of course, be below the national minimum wage imposed by the government. The actual wage rate and take-home pay is basically under the control of the management which often pays more than the rate set in the wage negotiation because of the labor shortage. This is then another reason why wage inflation in France is attributed to management, rather than to the unions.

The present government minimum-wage regulations were established by the law of February 11, 1950, and the decree of April 2, 1955. The law states that no employee may be paid less than the "minimum per-hour interoccupational guaranteed wage" (called the SMIG in the French abbreviation), which is fixed by decree upon recommendation of the Superior Collective Agreements Board of the Ministry of Labor. The SMIG is calculated on the basis of a minimum living-cost budget for an unmarried, unskilled laborer residing in the Paris area. In recent years the SMIG was as follows: September 1950—78 (old) francs; April 1956—126 (old) francs; Feb-

---

[91] For this and much of the following information the authors are grateful to M. F. Légéndre, member of the Economic and Social Council of France, conveyed in a private communication.

[92] *Encyclopédie française: L'Univers économique et social,* vol. IX (1960), p. 9-46-5. Of importance are also seniority bonuses and such fringe benefits as supplementary insurance, additional paid holidays, free transportation to and from work, low-priced lunches and dormitories, kindergartens and company housing projects, all paid for by the employers.

ruary 1959—156 (old) francs; June 1962—1.73 (new) francs.[93] The SMIG kept rising in this period almost every year, and sometimes more than once a year, to reflect rising living costs. Yet the 1962 SMIG only equaled 43 cents, compared to the U.S. legal minimum wage of $1.25.

Unlike the American, however, French minimum-wage laws cover almost all employees. Furthermore, the SMIG is also differentiated according to four territorial zones, though not according to professions. In order to induce transfer of labor, it is raised in certain zones by a maximum of 6 percent. In most other zones, however, it is lowered from 0.66 to 8 percent because living costs are lower than in the Paris area. The SMIG of the given region than becomes the point of departure in regional and industrial collective bargaining agreements. Every such agreement must list the exact coefficients, related to the SMIG, which are used in the calculation of wage rates of the given profession or skill covered by the agreement. Actual per-hour earnings in all French industries ranged on the average from 1.82 to 2.80 new francs in 1961 (one new franc is worth 20 cents).[94]

Most observers agree that the French government's wage control policies have been essentially pragmatic and not successful. The frequent changes of the SMIG by decree creates some difficulties and uncertainty for employers. On the other hand, the unions are not always happy about it either: some always seem to believe that the given increase is not large enough, others complain that increases in the SMIG benefit only the very lowest-paid workers. The number of workers paid as little as the basic SMIG rate does not exceed 500,000, compared to the total of some 13 million wage earners. Changes in the SMIG affect the whole pyramid of wage rates above the minimum indirectly but fairly promptly.

The French government also possesses important powers to supervise and control the labor market. Under the employment control ordinance of May 24, 1945, a manpower directorate was established in the Ministry of Labor. This organization is a national employment service with significant stand-by regulatory powers. The manpower directorate manages a network of regional labor and manpower inspectorates and local manpower services attached to the local governments. The latter act first of all as labor exchanges. (There are very few private employment agencies in France, especially for domestic help). The employers seeking laborers apply to the manpower services stating their wants and offers, and so do the workers seeking employment. All demands for labor not satisfied locally are then disseminated on the regional level, and finally on national level. The national manpower directorate publishes a weekly bulletin of advertisements

---

[93] This SMIG applies only to nonagricultural workers and employees. The agricultural minimum wage stood at 1.44 francs in 1962. All these data are taken from *Annuaire Statistique de la France 1962,* pp. 366 and 371.

[94] *Annuaire Statistique,* p. 367. New francs relate to old francs as 1:100.

for help wanted and offered. It can pay transportation costs for those work-ers who must resettle in order to find employment. If an employer's request cannot be met on the national level and through resettlement, the direc-torate permits him to apply to the National Office of Immigration for re-cruitment of foreign workers.

The manpower directorate operates several vocational training schools for youth as well as an occupational retraining program for the unem-ployed. The redistribution of labor on a national scale, combined with strong postwar demand for labor, has kept France's unemployment very low. The number of those who apply for work at the labor exchanges but do not find it amounted to 139,000 in 1959 and 112,000 in 1961; the number of those receiving unemployment insurance fluctuated between 20,000 and 40,000.[95] Presumably, this amounted to unemployment of less than 1.0 per-cent of the French labor force.[96] The French government does not compute unemployment statistics as a percentage of the labor force.

The French government's manpower services also possess the power to control the dismissals of employees. According to existing laws,[97] every em-ployer who wants to dismiss an employee for any reason whatever is re-quired to make a request, with reasons stated, to the manpower service of his area. If no reply reaches him within seven days (reduced to three days if the request alleges serious misconduct by the employee) the authorization is considered as granted. In case of refusal of authorization an appeal can be made to the regional manpower director, who gives a final decision after consulting a joint labor-management committee. If the employer neglects to request authorization or ignores a negative reply, he is subject to imprison-ment or a fine. The manpower services which receive requests to authorize dismissals act upon the instructions of the Ministry of Labor to take into account only probable economic repercussions on the general employment situation in the firm or in the area. Individual dismissals and dismissals without serious economic effects are therefore rarely opposed.

ACHIEVEMENTS OF THE SYSTEM

Not so long ago, France was called the sick man of Europe. The past *élan vital* of the French nation was supposed to have disappeared and many said that France was destined to decline to a third-rate power. It is never-theless a fact that since 1959 the French economy has enjoyed unprece-dented successes, rapid growth, and mounting prosperity. France is said to be wealthier now than Britain. Man for man, it is more productive. It is

[95] International Labour Office, *Year Book of Labour Statistics 1962*, p. 206.

[96] France's total labor force in 1964 exceeded 20 million. Excluding agricultural employment, the total was in the neighborhood of 12 million.

[97] See "Dismissal Procedures—France," *International Labour Review* (Geneva), vol. LXXIX, no. 6, June 1959, pp. 624-642.

growing much faster than most industrialized nations, including the United States. The key questions are: How has France done it? And can it keep up?

The keys to the recent French successes are several, and by no means the plan alone. Pierre Massé, head of the plan, says that French expansion "is due above all to the French people, to their work, their ingenuity, and the rejuvenation of the population. A second factor contributing to this success was the creation of the European Economic Community, which has provided French agriculture and industry with new outlets, but has at the same time exposed them to stimulating competition." And, thirdly, it was the successful financial recovery of 1959, ascribable to "political stability, devaluation carried out with technical efficiency, the influence of trade liberalization, and the emergence of the Common Market." Only after these factors does Massé list the plan. "The Plan has contributed to a better understanding of the realities of the economic situation. Moreover, it has encouraged industries to adopt within a coherent total environment higher targets than they would have chosen spontaneously." [98]

Other observers add sustained inflationary pressures,[99] rising personal incomes, optimism, and strong consumer demand [100] as factors in the recent French achievements.

That inflation contributed to French growth is strongly suggested by the following table:

Table 25.   Annual Rates of Growth of the Domestic GNP of France

Years	Percent growth	State of the economy
1949-1950	7.9	Inflation
1950-1951	6.4	Inflation
1951-1952	2.3	Devaluation and deflation
1952-1953	3.1	Relative price stability
1953-1954	5.4	Relative price stability
1954-1955	6.0	Inflation
1955-1956	5.2	Inflation
1956-1957	6.4	Inflation
1957-1958	1.8	Devaluation and deflation
1958-1959	2.5	Relative price stability
1959-1960	6.3	Relative price stability
1960-1961	5.0	Relative price stability
1961-1962	5.5	Slight inflation

SOURCE: *Annuaire Statistique de la France 1963.*

---

[98] *Looking Ahead*, pp. 3-4.
[99] See a report by John A. May in *The Christian Science Monitor*, January 5, 1963.
[100] The Chase Manhattan Bank, *Report on Western Europe*, no. 21, 1963.

Despite or because of financial maladjustments and inflation, the French economy has known little, if any, unemployment since the end of the war; it has often felt a shortage of labor. Real wages have been growing comparatively fast, although they still are about 50 percent of the American level (but some 20 to 25 percent higher than the Soviet). Between 1950 and 1961 consumption of food in France increased by 42.4 percent, of nonfood items, 83.1 percent, while total consumption measured in constant prices rose by 64.2 percent. Since the total population increased between 1950 and 1961 by 10.3 percent (the gainfully employed population was essentially the same size in both years) real consumption per capita rose by 48.9 percent, or by 3.6 percent per year, which is a very substantial rate of growth, indeed.[101]

The share of the income of the wage earners in the national income of France increased from 51.6 in 1938, to 52.7 in 1950, and 61.4 in 1960; the shares of the self-employed, farmers, and property owners decreased.[102] This redistribution of national income does not necessarily imply that the relative lot of the wage earners has been improving. Their share in the national income increased, first, because of the increase in their numbers and reduction in the number of farmers; and second, because of the increase in the number of hours worked. A rare but reliable study made in 1955, concluded that at that time the wage earners' share of the national income was *unchanged* compared to 1938.[103] Today, perhaps, this study is obsolete, but there is no other on which we can rely with confidence. One thing at least is probable, however, namely, that the real share of the French laboring classes in the national income has not been decreasing—even on a per capita basis.

Income inequalities in France are substantial, as Table 26 indicates, but when social welfare services are added to the incomes of low-income groups, these inequalities probably become smaller than, for example, in the United States. Data are not available that would indicate whether economic planning has accentuated or dampened the inequality of personal incomes.

French income tax rates are less progressive than those of the United States, but the level of the tax is somewhat lower than in the United States. In 1961, for example, maximum personal income tax rate actually withheld in France was 73 percent, compared to 91 percent in the United States. However, no personal income is exempt from income tax in France. Maxi-

---

[101] *Annuaire statistique de la France 1962,* pp. 401 and 404.

[102] SEEF, *Rapport sur les Comptes de la Nation de l'année 1960* (Paris, 1961), pp. 150-151.

[103] Claude Zarka, "Quelques conséquences de la redistribution horizontal des revenus," *Revue économique* (Paris), no. 2, March 1956, p. 253.

Table 26.   Percentage Distribution of Wages and Salaries in France, 1959

Annual salary after taxes (old francs)	Total salaried population (6,498,000)	Executives (269,000)	Technicians (535,000)	Office employees (1,214,000)	Workers (4,199,000)
Less than 200,000	3.2%	0.1%	0.9%	2.0%	3.8%
200,000-400,000	21.3	1.6	5.2	18.8	24.8
400,000-600,000	31.2	2.1	8.8	34.1	35.2
600,000-800,000	21.0	3.1	15.4	26.6	21.4
800,000-1,000,000	9.9	5.1	18.8	10.5	9.1
1,000,000-1,500,000	8.0	18.5	32.2	6.1	5.0
1,500,000-2,000,000	2.4	20.3	10.8	1.2	0.6
2,000,000-3,500,000	2.1	32.1	6.2	0.6	0.1
More than 3,500,000	0.9	17.1	1.7	0.1	—
Total	100	100	100	100	100

SOURCE: *Annuaire statistique de la France, 1961* (Paris, 1961), p. 419.

mum corporate income tax rates were higher in France, however; 62 percent, as compared to 52 percent in the United States.[104]

The social welfare system in France is one of the most advanced in the world today. Social security was established in 1928, and expanded in 1945-1946. Social insurance in France is compulsory and covers all employees and their families without exception, as well as more than half of the self-employed, including farmers; altogether more than 70 percent of the population is covered. The benefits include unemployment pensions, complete coverage of almost all medical bills, sickness wages, old-age pensions, etc. The costs of insurance are borne by the insured, their employers, and the state. The insured pay 6 percent of their wages, while 10 percent of their wages is paid by the employer. Some 27 percent of total social security costs are borne by the state. Social security and various welfare payments take some 12.8 percent of the French national income; they add more than 20 percent to the total wages and salaries received, and constitute 20.7 percent of the French personal disposable income (1960).[105]

Old-age pensions are paid at 65 for both men and women, but, on the average, they do not amount to more than 30 percent of the pensioner's wages earned when employed. Of special interest is the French system of family allowances. The government provides a wage supplement of 20 percent of basic salary for two children, 50 percent for three children, and 30

---

[104] First National City Bank of New York, *Monthly Letter,* January 1961, p. 7.

[105] P. Maurice, "Prestations sociales et comptabilité nationale française," *Revue économique* (Paris), no. 4, July 1962, p. 654.

percent more for every child after the third. (These allowances do not increase in direct proportion to salary level.) Families with only one breadwinner get more. Families with but one child get 20 percent for two years as an incentive to have more children. Newlyweds get a 10 percent wage supplement for two years as an incentive. Apart from this system, three other kinds of allowances are available: (1) a lump sum allowance for mothers during pregnancy, (2) similar maternity premiums for every child born alive, and (3) lodging allowances to newlyweds and large families to pay a part of the rent or debts incurred in buying a house. All these allowances have obviously been designed to increase the growth of France's population.

Health service is not nationalized in France, but most medical establishments are state- or municipal-owned anyway and most bills are paid by social insurance. Physicians are permitted to practice privately, however.

The educational system in France is highly centralized and government-controlled. Primary, secondary, and higher education is administered by the Ministry of Education. Higher education is chiefly supplied by state universities. Tuition is free and most other financial support of education is borne by the state. All students are insured under the social security system free of charge to them. State universities and colleges are supplemented by a few Catholic institutes, which are also free. Students are accepted by the higher schools only after keen competition, so that even a success in secondary training does not ensure entrance.

State subsidies are regularly extended also to almost all scientific and cultural establishments—the academies of arts and sciences, theaters, museums, and so forth. The French believe that the government should bear all such costs; culture is regarded as a national asset and therefore the entire nation is considered responsible for its maintenance and development. Considerable sums have been invested under the current national economic plan in cultural construction. France has a Ministry of Culture whose budget is relatively small, but sums are spent for cultural purposes by other ministries as well.

CONCLUSIONS

Who Decides What to Produce?

Consumers in France as in the United States can purchase whatever they please. Similarly, since French businessmen are free to respond to consumer demand, their output presumably reflects consumers' choices. As a matter of principle, government output plans are not applied to consumer products. Hence, basically it is consumers and producers who decide what consumer goods are produced in France.

The government does, however, directly influence the output of many nonconsumer goods. As a consequence, the output of some consumers goods is also affected, albeit indirectly. For example, the government partly determines the output of most basic industries both because some of these industries have been nationalized and by means of the different controls ..ready discussed. As a result, the supplies of such items as steel, aluminum, cement, chemicals, and petroleum are directly affected by the government; in turn, the prices of these things and of the consumer products into which they enter are also affected. Even more directly, the output of consumers goods might, in some cases, be limited by the available supplies of basic raw materials, which will partly reflect government policy and preferences concerning their allocation.

The French government exerts considerable influence over the output of basic industries and allows the output of consumers goods to be relatively free. More specifically, it decides what proportion of total output it would like in the form of producers goods and exerts considerable influence over the output of specific items; in the consumers goods sector, it allows resources to move relatively freely from item to item. Obviously Soviet controls are vastly more strict and detailed in both sectors.

Beyond the influence exerted by the government, output decisions in France are also affected by a large number of unofficial or quasi-official organizations. Included among them are trade associations and such uniquely French institutions as the *Patronat* and the *Conseil Économique et Social*. These organizations both participate in the formulation of plans and, outside the plans, affect the behavior of individual businessmen with regard to investments, prices, and product design.

In another respect, the allocation of resources in the French economy is more like that in the Soviet Union than that in the United States. This is in the sphere of "collective consumption" involving items like education, public health, scientific research, communal recreation, publishing, television, movie theatres, and cultural facilities generally. These are government-controlled and more or less centrally planned in France. French consumers have a free choice among these items, of course, but the volume of output and facilities in this sector are not guided by consumers' choices alone. Some decisions made by the ministers and planners are likely to run counter to the desires of most consumers. The French consider consumers' desires with respect to these matters to be insufficiently informed and "uneducated." They prefer to have decisions made on these matters by experts and civic leaders. Of course, consumers exercise considerable choice as to which elements of social consumption they will consume.

The facts are not always as important as what people believe the facts to be. In France the consumer has the feeling that he—rather than the government—decides what consumers goods are produced. French consumers decidedly do not have the impression that the government prevents the production of the things they wish to purchase.

There are three respects in which French consumers occupy a different position than do American consumers. First, the French consumer is offered a substantially different set of choices by businessmen than his American counterpart. Specifically, almost without respect to his preferences, the French consumer is offered individualized and distinctive merchandise rather than low-priced, mass-produced identical merchandise. (In recent years the supply of mass-produced, low quality, and inexpensive merchandise has been growing, but still represents a very small proportion of the goods available.) Second, the French consumer is not offered the option of patronizing low-cost, low-profit margin retail establishments. The supermarket and discount house and other forms of mass distributors are still curiosities in France, though their numbers are growing extremely fast. But in the case of individualistic merchandise and the low-margin retail businesses, it cannot be said for certain that the French consumers' wishes are being reflected in what is offered. It appears rather that the desire of merchants to avoid price competition mainly accounts for the limited number of low-margin retailers, and the skills and the flexible productive capacity of the small French manufacturers dictate the nature of merchandise that is produced. The third difference between the French and American consumers consists in the varying amount of sales pressure to which they are exposed. There is relatively little advertising in France, though it is far from absent. Indeed, as mentioned, the French government has stated clearly its determination to avoid any strong pressure on consumers from this source.

How Are Methods of Production Selected?

French businessmen are, perhaps, slightly less free than their American counterparts to use any production techniques they desire. Both groups are restrained by patent laws and availability of capital, as well as restrictions in the form of labor-safety legislation. In addition, labor unions, and labor committees, working through collective bargaining, affect production techniques to some degree.

However, the French government, primarily by its control of liquid capital for investment influences the amount of investment in new facilities. In this way it affects the methods of production employed in some industries. Furthermore, the modernization committees that function under the plan sponsor and press for improvements in production technique. Even outside the formal planning machinery, trade associations affect production methods. Most of them maintain cooperative technological research facilities and disseminate such knowledge among their members.

Competition among firms in France, as indicated earlier, is concentrated

primarily in the sphere of production technique. Whereas French businessmen may agree about price and allocate geographic markets among themselves, they strive constantly to lower production costs through improvements in technique and to gain an advantage over their competitors in this
way, though not to the extent of driving their competitors completely out of
business.

Who Decides Where to Employ Productive Agents?

As in the United States individuals are free to seek employment wherever
they wish, but in France they have access to more accurate information
about employment possibilities. French labor exchanges and employment
offices are highly developed and provide information on a nationwide scale.

The government influences the allocation of productive agents among
different employments indirectly. The vocational training of workers and
professionals is carried on largely at public expense in France, some, of
course, is carried out in plants at the expense of private or state-owned
enterprises. The government estimates requirements for different skills and
professions and provides training facilities on the basis of these forecasts.
Of course, individuals are free to ignore the government forecasts of labor
requirements and can decline to accept vocational training.

The French government also influences employment of resources in other
ways that are absent in the United States. Owners of property, of capital
and land, are often affected by the government's plans with respect to regional development. Capital investments are both supervised and influenced
in France by the government which is attempting to achieve balanced regional development. The initiative for new investment comes primarily
from the individual businessman rather than from the government, however. French businessmen are not required to make investments which they
do not wish to make, but sometimes are induced to change their minds.

Progressiveness of the French Economy

As indicated, the direct action committees engaged in planning, the modernization committees, have the power to recommend changes in productive
processes. In addition trade associations are engaged in technological research and actively disseminate their discoveries to all members of the
trade. In this way, technical advances are adopted relatively promptly.
Technical progress is one of the expressed goals of French planning. As
such, it receives considerable attention both within and outside the formal
planning arrangements, in the form of comparatively large grants. Government activity in this field probably is greater than the combined activities of
individuals and firms and their trade associations.

The French pride themselves on their inventiveness and imagination.
This vanity is no less among production engineers in France than among

those in any other nation. Many industrial establishments and farms are still technologically backward, but the newest facilities constructed in France are at least as efficient as those to be found elsewhere in the world.

How Is Personal Income Distributed?

The French government is committed, as a major goal of national policy, to increase the equality of personal incomes. The measures used to achieve this end are minimum wages, extensive social service, recognition of unions, progressive income taxation, and efforts to ensure that large income recipients pay their income tax obligations.

As in the United States, personal income is derived from many sources in France; also, many factors determine an individual's income. The most important of these are, as in the United States, productivity, personal property holding, social services, and personal and political influence.

GENERAL EVALUATION
OF THE FRENCH ECONOMIC SYSTEM

The French economic system obviously is neither a typical "price-and-profit" system as we know it in the United States, nor a "centrally-managed, one-firm" system of the Soviet type, but something in between. Yet it is also not a simple mixture of the two extremes, bur rather a blend of many elements, some of which are original. The French economy is the product of France's peculiar conditions and traditions: the comparatively noncompetitive attitudes of French businessmen; cartelized organizations composed still to some extent of family-sized firms in most industries and trades; a large nationalized sector of the economy; state control over the capital market and the price and wage system; workers', farmers', and other social groups' ability to bring their grievances to the floor of the parliament and make them the responsibility of the government. The French economy is similar to most West European economies in most of these respects; it differs in the nature of its planning arrangements and in the rather extreme centralization of control over social and economic affairs.

Under the conditions in France since World War II, the state could hardly avoid interfering with the economy. It had to be the arbiter among very politically conscious, contending socioeconomic classes; it had to be paternalistic, for Frenchmen traditionally have considered the government responsible for order and well-being in both social and economic affairs. Under such condititions, governments in power have felt responsible for the state of the French economy, and tried to guide and manage it. This "feeling" has been both the source and essence of French economic planning.

The economic system of modern France may be called a state-directed, welfare-oriented, nation-minded capitalism. The country which had coined the very term *laissez faire* decidedly has not followed a laissez-faire policy since the early thirties. Yet, economic planning is as appropriate for France as economic competition has been for the United States.

The French economy is neither governed by an automatically self-adjusting price-and-profit mechanism nor a system of compulsory centralized planning of all minute economic details. *In France economic conditions and actions are the result of continuous interaction among the market forces of supply and demand and state economic policies and planning.*

Concerted group action dominates and directs the French economy. Such action is only partly channeled through the market mechanism; it is largely channeled through socioeconomic and political institutions, including the government planning agencies, the *Patronat,* labor unions, and the parliament. Decisions made by these institutions affect the French economy as much as the buying and selling of individual firms in the market place. And yet, at the same time, these decisions are not wholly arbitrary and seldom are compulsory. They are, as a rule, democratic decisions and voluntary agreements; in most cases, they are carried out by means of economic incentives, appeal to civic duty, and the sense of collective responsibility for the common good. Of course, pressure groups and lobbies exist in France and their influence is likely to be neither equal nor to vary in proportion to their social-mindedness.

The ideal of common good, of the public interest, of some happy Golden Mean, which reconciles all the conflicting interests and satisfies everybody at least a little bit, lies at the heart of French planning. The French economy is a predominantly private capitalist economy, an economy of private firms and independent businessmen. And yet it is also fundamentally a government-planned economy, however paradoxical that may sound. French government plans are drawn for, and by, the businessmen themselves, in cooperation with the representatives of other groups of French society.

The economy of France is still mainly moved by private enterprise. Whatever economic plans the French state may design must be carried out largely by private business owners. Hence, if planning was to succeed, it had to be of a type that was acceptable to businessmen and would, at the same time, channel businessmen's activities in directions that served the common interests of all Frenchmen.

Perhaps the chief single idea underlying French planning is that it will overcome the conservatism of businessmen in their investment and output plans by providing them with information and with assurances of high levels of demand. French businessmen apparently were less likely than those in other nations to expand facilities simply on the basis of a general confidence in the future. But, all free enterprise economies suffer frequently from a type of unemployment and lost output that might be called the economic costs of underanticipations. These occur when businesses make conservative or pessimistic output and investment plans because of their fears that markets are weak. Having made such pessimistic plans, they will indeed face weak markets; if they had invested and produced more, the markets would have been far stronger and perhaps would have absorbed the added output.

The total demand for output thus depends upon the confidence of businessmen in a free enterprise and the way this is reflected in their investment and production decisions. By providing businessmen with information about future markets and reassuring them that the government would take *noncoercive* measures to achieve its optimistic output goals, those supporting French planning were able to win business support and to allay pessimism. Consequently, their decisions were less conservative and contributed to the strong markets needed to make their decisions valid. French businessmen developed confidence in both the strength of markets and in the validity of the plans drawn up during the period of high postwar demand. This growth of confidence—possibly for irrelevant reasons—has led to the widespread acceptance of the forecasts of demand that are prepared by the planners and has reinforced the validity of their plans. Should future developments shake that confidence, the basic underpinning of French planning might be damaged seriously.

The foregoing represents the chief *economic* rationale underlying French planning. It has also a political and almost a "spiritual" basis that must be understood. Most French businessmen now actively support economic planning. To say that is much like saying "man bites dog." French businessmen apparently favor economic planning largely because they dominate the planning process. In turn, they dominate the planning process primarily because they alone possess the information needed to make forecasts, to develop technical programs for expansion, and to direct efforts designed to speed technological change; in addition, highly informed, articulate, and intelligent labor union leaders that can "match" business representatives in debate are extremely few. And, of course, government technicians are careful to avoid giving offense to businessmen because of their control over vital information, the need for their cooperation, and their great political influence.

The "spiritual" basis of French planning consists in the belief in the benefits of getting the people together and the virtues of discussion. Some now describe France as a "Discussion Economy." [106] Belief in the value of discussion implies basic confidence in the similarity of economic interests—or a denial of "class conflict." Without discussing that issue directly, it appears that, to date, conflicting economic interests have been submerged at least

---

[106] Perroux, *Le IV Plan Française* (Paris, 1962), p. 16.

temporarily. But, to return to how and when French planners employ their powers: they use them sparingly and only after they make great efforts to persuade businessmen to conform to the plan without invoking their powers.

The "Spirit of the Plan" to which frequent allusion is made in France refers to more than faith in the virtues of discussion, and the benefits of exchanging information and viewpoints. It refers to the "lightness" of the planning structure—the small number of bureaucrats engaged in planning. In addition, the openness of the discussions associated with the preparation of plans contributes to this "Spirit." In both of these respects, France differs very greatly from the Soviet-type economies.

We have not, by any means, explained fully the rationale of the French economy. But we have stressed that it developed out of the fairly unique circumstances that prevailed in postwar France and is peculiarly adapted to a nation which places such a high value on the power of the intellect and human reason.

CHAPTER 5

GENERAL CONCLUSIONS

The foregoing description of three economies, which presented both basic rationale and details of structure and function, may have exaggerated some differences among them. They are indeed fundamentally different, however. Leibnitz once aptly observed that there have never been any two identical creatures in nature. Similarly, it is highly naïve to expect that organizations of human creatures—their economies, societies, political or cultural systems—can or must be one and the same all over the globe. The fact that all nations face the problem of scarcity does not imply that only one method can solve this problem in the best possible way. Even machines performing the same functions are frequently different. Yet, an economy is not a machine; it is a social, political, legal, and even cultural organization of production, distribution, and consumption carried on by people and for people. Hence, as people differ, so too, do their economic systems.

Not only do capitalist, Communist and middle-way economies differ; the Communist economic systems significantly differ from each other today, as do the capitalist and the middle-way systems. The systems of China and Yugoslavia, Poland and Cuba are quite dissimilar and unlike the Soviet system; and so are the systems of the United States and Japan, for example; and those of France, Sweden, Holland, and Great Britain.

However, the important similarities must not be overlooked. Points of similarity in economic systems that are very different indicate the economic devices that have been proved successful. What are the major points that the American, Soviet, and French economies have in common?

First, all three economies have these specific features in common: Money exchange is the rule in all. All resort to both direct and indirect taxes. Banks, exercising borrowing and lending functions, exist in all three. All rely heavily upon specialization and exchange. They employ roundabout methods of production involving high mechanization of production. All require that most of the population work under the direction of others.

Second, reliance on monetary incentives is common to all three systems.

240

Inequalities of personal income are substantial in all. However, all of them blunt monetary incentives by progressive taxes upon personal income. Moreover, each treats income from property differently—with disapproval or higher taxes—from payments for personal services. The three economies make considerable use of negative incentives. Punishments for not working according to one's employer's directions are strict. Penalties for producing or delivering unwanted goods and otherwise squandering resources are provided in all three systems.

Third, the economies of the United States, the Soviet Union, and France are also similar in that they rely upon free choice of occupations and of consumers goods. Although Soviet and French leaders do not shrink, at least in principle, from using direction or coercion when they think it would help matters substantially, actually they provide relatively free choice to workers and consumers. Freedom in these two matters presumably was found to be efficient in organizing economic activity as well as personally satisfying to the entire population.

Fourth, it appears that the price system, which is not "pure" or entirely "free" in any of the three systems, is still, though to a different extent, common to all. It seems that regulation of prices by government, business, and labor is on the increase in the United States. In France and the Soviet Union, on the other hand, price fixing seems to be in the process of gradual decentralization. With the passage of time all three economies seem to be slowly moving closer together in their use of the pricing mechanism as a device subordinate to the power and policies of either the government or big business and unions, or both.

Fifth, some degree of economic planning is also common to all three systems. There is an unmistakable similarity between the Soviet and the French economies in their use of long-range national economic plans, although the differences in their planning methods are very large. As time goes by, the similarity of Soviet and French planning seems to increase at least slightly, rather than to decrease. Similarly, in the United States big companies more and more plan their future growth, production, and sales. Also, although no national economic planning by the government occurs in the United States and very strong opposition exists to the very idea of such planning, the role of the U.S. government in the economy is obviously on the increase. By its fiscal and monetary policies, the U.S. government noticeably influences the state of business; moreover, a considerable amount of economic planning takes place in the country's defense sector and in many other budgetary expenditures.

Of course, even in the respects in which the three economies are similar, they considerably differ in degree. The most conspicuous differences are found in their use of the planning and price mechanisms. It is very easy to exaggerate the similarity of the economies of the United States, the Soviet

Union, and France. Certainly they are sufficiently different to warrant our considering them different types of economic systems—and that on real, rather than doctrinal, grounds. Had we compared the doctrinal "models" of these systems, they would have been different or similar by definition, that is, a priori. In our findings differences are not imaginary, they exist.

Apart from the satisfaction of personal curiosity about how other economic systems operate, what conclusions can an American draw from the foregoing discussion of the three economies? We must recognize at the outset that an overwhelming majority of Americans is opposed to socialism or communism, or to any other drastic change. Consequently, the question, Should we accept socialism or communism or some other system? is almost completely academic.

The greatest significance to the American of the foregoing discussion is its bearing on a central issue around which much popular discussion revolves: Should the government keep its hands off business? Foreign experience in meeting economic problems by employing government controls is definitely relevant to, although not conclusive in, the resolution of our own domestic economic issues. (This discussion makes no effort to point up what foreign readers might learn from us; it is written primarily for the American reader.)

No direct and reliable poll of Americans' views has been taken on this issue. Many unquestionably believe that government regulation is bad—no matter what is being regulated and no matter what the circumstances. They might be correct in holding this view, but before a convincing case can be made for it, one must study the effects of all government regulation. The foregoing discussion of the Soviet Union and France has shown that other major countries regulate, control, and directly operate far more economic processes than we do. As far as it is possible to judge, most people in those countries would not end their government's regulatory activities; many would extend them. These countries—and we ourselves in certain cases—have demonstrated that government regulation sometimes can greatly improve conditions.

A minority seems to hold a completely opposite view on the question of government control of business. They believe that almost all economic evils can be eliminated and almost anything can be improved simply by passing a law. Experiences in the Soviet Union and in France have shown that many economic processes—notably the choice of jobs and of consumers products—are best left free from regulation.

Clearly, all forms of government regulation cannot simply be assumed to be "bad" or "good." Some kinds of government control fall far short of achieving their goals and give rise to undesirable by-products. On the other hand, other kinds improve matters. One can only judge in actual cases whether a particular government regulation will make matters better or worse, or achieve results equal to those of free enterprise. The issue cannot be judged on the basis of general principle alone—that is clear. Only one principle has general validity in a democratic country: all measures, and only those measures, that contribute to general welfare should be adopted.

Clearly, we have not learned all there is to know about the way that economic systems behave. We learned little about the methods by which the performance of economic systems might be improved. Tomorrow we may find solutions to problems that we think are insoluble today. We rarely are offered tested and proved remedies. Every new regulation involves the risk of failure, but also might work out better than anticipated. Some risks are involved in any change. If we do not take the risks involved in change, however, we can be *certain* that conditions will not improve.

The fact that government control may have been effective in another country and in some industries in this country does not prove that more government regulation would be desirable in the United States. Successful government regulation requires a variety of circumstances that differ widely from country to country and from industry to industry within the same country. For example, big businesses are ordinarily easier to regulate and control than a large number of small ones. Nations with a well-trained civil service with high standards of public service have far better success with government regulation than nations in which government service is not highly regarded. The level of public morality also strongly influences the success with which government regulations achieve their goals. Assistance of the public at large in reporting violations and in assisting the authorities in various ways can spell the difference between government regulations that work well and that work badly. Each regulation that is proposed must be considered in the particular context in which it is to be applied.

For the average American, the foregoing discussion of different economic systems has another possible significance. It should increase his tolerance of economic systems that are different from his own. His own economy has been shown to have significant flaws. While other systems may have greater flaws, they still "do make some sense," and have recorded significant achievements in a relatively short time. Accordingly, study of other economies should make the American more sympathetic toward and interested in nations that are trying out other types of economic system. In addition, it should indicate that differences in needs, desires, and circumstances from country to country are substantial. No one system is likely to be the best for all nations in the foreseeable future.

Different systems compete, however, both in the world markets and for the minds of the people. This competition spurs the leaders of different nations to excel in efficiency and to satisfy the needs of their people as much as possible. To the extent that this competition does not lead to war, it must be welcomed as healthy and beneficial to all. The outcome of this competition, although a very distant one, may show at the end which economic system was the best for humanity—if indeed any one could at all be truly superior for all nations.

AUTHOR INDEX

SUBJECT INDEX